Apple Training Series

Mac OS X Directory Services v10.5

Arek Dreyer

Apple
Certified

Apple Training Series: Mac OS X Directory Services v10.5
Arek Dreyer

Published by Peachpit Press. For information on Peachpit Press books, contact:
Peachpit Press
1249 Eighth Street
Berkeley, CA 94710
510/524-2178
510/524-2221 (fax)

Find us on the Web at: http://www.peachpit.com
To report errors, please send a note to errata@peachpit.com
Peachpit Press is a division of Pearson Education

Project Editors: Rebecca Freed, Kim Saccio-Kent
Editor: Linda Laflamme
Production Editor: Danielle Foster
Copyeditor: Kim Saccio-Kent
Tech Editors: Steve Brokaw, John Signa, Joel Rennich
Contributors: Andre LaBranche, David Colville
Proofreader: Emily K. Wolman
Compositor: Danielle Foster
Indexer: Karin Arrigoni
Cover design: Mimi Heft

ISBN 13: 978-0-321-50973-4
ISBN 10: 0-321-50973-0

9 8 7 6 5 4 3 2 1

Printed and bound in the United States of America

Acknowledgments

I want to thank my wife and love of my life, Heather Jagman, who supported me while I spent most of my waking hours working on, or thinking about, this project.

This book is just part of a bigger project of producing instructional materials for the four-day Directory Services class. Thanks to Steve Brokaw for putting together the outline for the class so all I had to do was fill in the details. Thanks to John Signa for stepping in for Brokaw and helping finish the project. Thanks to LeRoy Dennison for trusting me to work on the project.

Thanks to Rebecca Freed and Kim Saccio-Kent for managing the project despite my best efforts to stretch the deadlines out into the infinite future. Thanks to Linda Laflamme for providing excellent corrections and feedback that helped me throughout the entire process.

Thanks to Andre LaBranche for writing the exercises in the classroom workbook; John Welch for composing and editing Keynote slides and instructor notes; and Tycho Sjögren and David Colville for reviewing materials.

Thanks to Joel Rennich for providing technical review and corrections. Thanks to Nicole Jacque, Randy Saeks, Michael Dhaliwal, Timo Perfitt, Nigel Kersten, Ben Griesler, Adam Karneboge, Kevin White, and Paul Suh for their technical help and encouragement.

Thanks to Schoun Regan for helping me get involved with this project, and for trying to warn me how consuming it would be.

Contents

Getting Started

Mac OS X Directory Services v10.5 is based on the same criteria used for Apple's official training course, Mac OS X Directory Services v10.5, an in-depth exploration of the technical architecture of directory services for Mac OS X and Mac OS X Server. This reference guide serves as a self-paced tour of directory services in Mac OS X and Mac OS X Server. It begins at the basic level of accessing user accounts stored in a stand-alone Mac OS X computer, moves on to using the directory services of an Open Directory master or replica hosted by Mac OS X Server, and then finishes up with third-party directory services, with an emphasis on Microsoft's Active Directory.

The book's primary goal is to prepare system administrators and IT professionals to run a robust, scalable directory system using Apple's Open Directory services. Along the way, you will learn how to enable users to log in with a network user account and access a network home folder, whether the user account is defined in a standalone Mac OS X computer, an Open Directory master or replica hosted by Mac OS X Server, a standard LDAP server, or Microsoft's Active Directory. You will also gain the ability to augment an existing directory service infrastructure with information to be used by Mac OS X.

Whether you are an experienced system administrator or just want to dig deeper into Mac OS X and Mac OS X Server, you'll learn in-depth technical information and procedures used by Apple Certified System Administrators to access and run a robust, scalable directory system using Apple's Open Directory services.

Before getting started, however, you should have experience in the following areas:

▶ Apple Certified Technical Coordinator 10.5 (ACTC) certification or equivalent knowledge

▶ An understanding of basic IP networking, including IP addresses, subnet masks, ports, and protocols

▶ A working familiarity with the command-line interface and the Secure Shell protocol (SSH)

   NOTE ▶ Unless otherwise specified, all references to Mac OS X and Mac OS X Server refer to Mac OS X version 10.5.3, which was the most current version available at the time of writing. Due to subsequent upgrades, some dialogs, features, and procedures may be slightly different from those presented in these pages.

Learning Methodology

This book is based on lectures and exercises provided to students attending the four-day, hands-on Mac OS X Directory Services v10.5 course. For consistency, the book follows the basic structure of the course material, but you may work through it at your own pace.

Each chapter is designed to help experienced system administrators become user-support experts by:

▶ Providing *knowledge* of how directory services work in Mac OS X

▶ Showing how to use diagnostic and repair *tools*

▶ Explaining troubleshooting and resolution *procedures*

For example, in Chapter 6, "Configuring Open Directory Replicas," you'll learn why it is important to have an Open Directory replica and what processes carry out the tasks of replication (knowledge); you'll acquire configuration techniques using Server Admin and command-line tools; and you'll explore methods for troubleshooting replication issues (procedures). In addition, most chapters include troubleshooting techniques for dealing with common issues related to the topic under consideration.

Each chapter focuses on a different aspect of directory services, with the first four focusing on Mac OS X and the final four on Mac OS X Server. Specifically, the key topics covered in each chapter are as follows:

▶ Chapter 1, "Accessing the Local Directory Service"—Creating and editing local user records; creating and editing local group records; troubleshooting login issues.

▶ Chapter 2, "Accessing an Open Directory Server"—Configuring a Mac OS X computer to bind to an Open Directory server; configuring directory service search paths; troubleshooting binding issues; troubleshooting login issues.

▶ Chapter 3, "Accessing a Third-Party LDAP Service"—Populating an LDAP server with information required by Mac OS X for network login; configuring a Mac OS X client computer to log in using a standard LDAP server; troubleshooting login issues.

▶ Chapter 4, "Accessing an Active Directory Service"—Configuring a Mac OS X client computer to log in using an Active Directory system; troubleshooting binding issues; troubleshooting login issues.

▶ Chapter 5, "Configuring Open Directory Server"—Configuring Mac OS X Server as an Open Directory master; configuring a computer running Mac OS X Server as a Primary Domain Controller; managing data stored in an Open Directory master; troubleshooting issues promoting Mac OS X Server to an Open Directory master.

▶ Chapter 6, "Configuring Open Directory Replicas"—Configuring Mac OS X Server as an Open Directory replica; troubleshooting Open Directory replication.

▶ Chapter 7, "Connecting Mac OS X Server to Open Directory"—Configuring a computer running Mac OS X Server to connect to an existing Open Directory server; configuring a service to use an Open Directory network user or group; troubleshooting binding issues; troubleshooting authentication issues.

▶ Chapter 8, "Integrating Mac OS X Server with Other Systems"—Configuring Mac OS X Server to supplement directory data provided by a third-party server; configuring Mac OS X Server services to authenticate in a third-party Kerberos realm; configuring a third-party server to authenticate using an Open Directory Kerberos Key Distribution Center (KDC).

In addition, two appendices lay out the general steps necessary to extend the schema of your Novell or your Active Directory server so that you can store Apple-specific data in your third-party directory. A third appendix discusses the Local KDC, a feature new in Mac OS X v10.5 and Mac OS X Server v10.5 that facilitates single sign-on for file and screen sharing.

Chapter Structure

Each chapter begins with a list of the learning goals for the chapter and an estimate of the time needed to complete it. The explanatory material is augmented with hands-on exercises essential to developing your skills. Each chapter closes with a short "What You've Learned" section that recaps the key material covered, provides a list of references, and presents a series of questions for your review.

To perform some of the exercises you will need specific equipment, as listed here:

▶ Chapter 1—A Macintosh computer running Mac OS X v10.5 or later.

▶ Chapters 2 and 3—A Mac OS X Server or any other DNS server; a Macintosh computer running Mac OS X Server v10.5 or later.

▶ Chapter 4—A Mac OS X Server or any other DNS server; a Macintosh computer running Mac OS X v10.5 or later; an Active Directory server. The exercises will work with Microsoft Windows 2000 Server, Windows Server 2003, or Windows Server 2008.

▶ Chapter 5—A Mac OS X Server or any other DNS server; a Macintosh computer running Mac OS X v10.5 or later; a Macintosh computer running Mac OS X Server v10.5 or later. There are two user import files that you can optionally download from http://www.peachpit.com/asca.directory-services/.

▶ Chapter 6—A Mac OS X Server or any other DNS server; a Macintosh computer running Mac OS X v10.5 or later; a Macintosh computer running Mac OS X Server v10.5 or later; a second Mac OS X Server to become a replica; a third Mac OS X Server to configure a replica of a replica.

▶ Chapter 7—A Mac OS X Server or any other DNS server; a Macintosh computer running Mac OS X v10.5 or later; a Macintosh computer running Mac OS X Server v10.5 or later; an additional Macintosh computer running Mac OS X Server v10.5 (you can change the role of one of your replicas).

▶ Chapter 8—A Mac OS X Server or any other DNS server; a Macintosh computer running Mac OS X v10.5 or later; a Macintosh computer running Mac OS X Server v10.5 or later; an Active Directory server. The exercises will work with Windows 2000 Server, Windows Server 2003, or Windows Server 2008.

If you lack the equipment necessary to complete a given exercise, you are still encouraged to read the step-by-step instructions and examine the screen shots to understand the procedures demonstrated.

> **NOTE ▶** Some of these exercises can be disruptive—for example, they may turn off network services temporarily—and some exercises, if performed incorrectly, could result in data loss or damage to system files. It's recommended that you perform these exercises on computers that are not critical to your daily productivity. Apple Computer, Inc., and Peachpit Press are not responsible for data loss or equipment damage that may occur as a direct or indirect result of following the procedures described in this book.

This book refers to Apple Knowledge Base documents throughout the chapters, and each chapter closes with a list of documents, books, and websites related to the topic of the chapter. These references are merely for your edification and are not considered essential for the coursework or certification.

The Apple Knowledge Base is a free online resource (http://www.apple.com/support) containing the latest technical information on all Apple's hardware and software products.

Apple Certifications

After reading this book, you may wish to take the Mac OS X Directory Services v10.5 exam, which is one step towards earning the Apple Certified System Administrator 10.5 (ACSA) certification, the highest level of Apple's certification programs for Mac OS X professionals.

The ACSA certification verifies an in-depth knowledge of Apple technical architecture and an ability to install and configure machines; architect and maintain networks; enable, customize, tune, and troubleshoot a wide range of services; and integrate Mac OS X, Mac OS X Server, and other Apple technologies within a multiplatform networked environment. This certification is intended for full-time professional system administrators and engineers who manage medium to large networks of systems in complex multiplatform deployments. You need to pass the Mac OS X Server Essentials v10.5, Directory Services v10.5, Deployment v10.5, and Advanced Administration v10.5 exams in order to obtain ACSA certification.

> **NOTE ▶** Although all the questions in the Mac OS X Directory Services v10.5 exam are based on material in this book, simply reading this book will not adequately prepare you for all the issues that the exam addresses. Apple recommends that before taking the exam, you spend time setting up, configuring, and troubleshooting Mac OS X. You should also download and review the Skills Assessment Guide, which lists the exam objectives, the total number of items, the number of items per section, the required score to pass, and how to register. To download the skills assessment guide, visit http://training.apple.com/pdf/server-essentials-sag-v10.5.pdf.

Other Apple certifications for Mac OS X professionals include:

▶ Apple Certified Support Professional 10.5 (ACSP)—This is ideal for help desk personnel, service technicians, technical coordinators, and others who support Mac OS X customers over the phone or who perform Mac OS X troubleshooting and support in schools and businesses. The ACSP certification verifies an understanding of Mac OS X core functionality and an ability to configure key services, perform basic troubleshooting, and assist users with essential Mac OS X capabilities. To receive this certification, you must pass the Mac OS X Support Essentials v10.5 exam.

▶ Apple Certified Technical Coordinator 10.5 (ACTC)—This certification is intended for Mac OS X technical coordinators and entry-level system administrators who are tasked with maintaining a modest network of computers using Mac OS X Server. Since the ACTC certification addresses both the support of Mac OS X clients and the core functionality and use of Mac OS X Server, the learning curve is correspondingly longer and more intensive than that for the ACSP certification, which addresses Mac OS X client support only. This certification is not intended for high-end system administrators or engineers, but may be an excellent step to take on an intended career path to system administration. You must pass both the Mac OS X Support Essentials v10.5 and Mac OS X Server Essentials v10.5 exam to receive this certification.

This book is intended to provide you with the knowledge and skills to pass the Mac OS X Support Essentials v10.5 exam.

Achieving any of the Mac OS X certifications qualifies you for free membership in the Mac OS X Certification, an organization that recognizes and supports the thousands of Mac OS X experts worldwide. For more information, visit http://training.apple.com/certification/macosx.

About the Apple Training Series

Mac OS X Directory Services v10.5 is part of the official training series for Apple products developed by experts in the field and certified by Apple. The chapters are designed to let you learn at your own pace. You can progress through the book from beginning to end, or dive right into the chapters that interest you most.

For those who prefer to learn in an instructor-led setting, Apple offers training courses at Apple Authorized Training Centers worldwide. These courses are taught by Apple-certified trainers, and they balance concepts and lectures with hands-on labs and exercises. Apple Authorized Training Centers have been carefully selected to meet Apple's highest standards in all areas, including facilities, instructors, course delivery, and infrastructure. The goal of the program is to offer Apple customers, from beginners to the most seasoned professionals, the highest-quality training experience.

To find an Authorized Training Center near you, please visit http://training.apple.com.

1

Time   This chapter takes approximately 3 hours to complete.

Goals   Create and edit local user records

              Create and edit group records

              Troubleshoot login issues

Chapter 1

Accessing the Local Directory Service

In this first chapter, you will learn the benefits and features of directory services in Mac OS X version 10.5. This chapter begins with a quick review of definitions. It then introduces more advanced directory services concepts, including how applications and operating systems use standardized requests for identification and authentication to the DirectoryService daemon (which uses plug-ins that you configure) to provide access to multiple sources of directory data, including Microsoft's Active Directory. You will also learn how to use dscl (the directory services command-line tool) to explore and troubleshoot issues.

This chapter focuses on users and groups that are local to your Mac OS X computer. You will learn where Mac OS X stores its local directory services information, and then practice using several tools to edit and create local user accounts as well as local groups. Finally, you will learn how to enable and inspect detailed debugging of local directory services. The directory services infrastructure is the same whether you are using Mac OS X or Mac OS X Server. The knowledge and tools that you master in this lesson will help you to understand and troubleshoot Mac OS X Server as well.

Exploring Directory Services

The Mac OS X Server Essentials course contains a general introduction to directory services, which you can find on page 184 of *Mac OS X Server Essentials, Second Edition*. Directory services provide a central repository for information about the computers, applications, and users in an organization. Directory services can be defined as the processes, protocols, and data stores that provide a method for requesting data and receiving that data in a scalable, centralized, and distributable manner. In this context, the following definitions apply:

▶   Process—An executable that handles client requests and retrieves data.

▶   Protocol—A common set of rules for requesting and receiving data on a network.

▶   Directory—A database that follows a particular method of organizing data for a directory service.

▶   Data store—A specialized read-optimized database.

▶   Requestor—An application or operating system function that makes requests of the directory service.

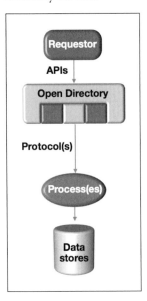

The terms *directory node, directory domain, node, domain,* and *directory* are interchangeable: They all refer to a directory within directory services.

Apple's extensible directory services architecture, called Open Directory, is built into Mac OS X and Mac OS X Server. The main process that provides directory services is called DirectoryService.

The fundamental nature of a directory service is to abstract the means of accessing data from the means of storing data. In Mac OS X and Mac OS X Server, this abstraction is achieved in the form of a set of standardized tools and APIs (application programming interfaces, used by software developers) for editing directory services data that interact with the DirectoryService daemon. The DirectoryService daemon has a plug-in architecture that allows it to work with a variety of data stores, such as flat files, XML-based property list files, or Berkeley DB files. The following figure illustrates how requestors, such as applications and command-line tools, make standard calls to the DirectoryService daemon, which uses its plug-ins to retrieve data from various data stores.

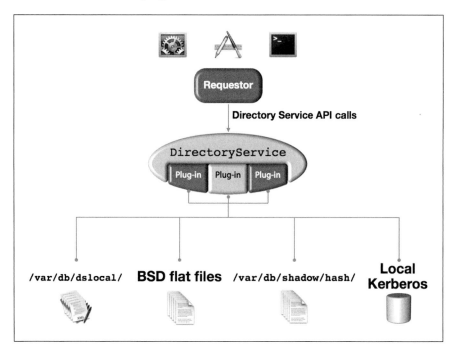

Before directory services, operating systems stored resources in flat files, such as /etc/hosts and /etc/master.passwd, and you needed to update the operating system and applications if the location or format of the resource files changed. (As you'll learn later in the chapter, Mac OS X v10.5 still supports some of these BSD flat files for compatibility.)

Software can use APIs to interact with Open Directory, which means that the underlying data structures and protocols can change and the APIs will continue to work. For example, previous versions of Mac OS used NetInfo as a data store, but Mac OS X v10.5 no longer uses NetInfo. Applications that you used with Mac OS X v10.4 that use the Open Directory APIs don't need to be changed; they work fine with Mac OS X v10.5.

As long as a tool uses directory services, you can use it to access and edit data in any supported directory node, regardless of the back-end storage mechanism. This architecture ensures that the means of interacting with directory services data need not change when a new back-end format is adopted, as with the transition from NetInfo to local plist files.

> **NOTE ▶** If you are familiar with earlier versions of Mac OS X, you may be familiar with NetInfo. As of Mac OS X v10.5, the NetInfo database and related tools, such as NetInfo Manager and /var/db/netinfo/, no longer exist. The NetInfo command-line interface tools that start with ni-, such as nicl and niutil, are gone, and administrators have been encouraged to start replacing these commands in scripts with the dscl command and the other ds* commands.

The man page for DirectoryService brings this all together: "Apple's Open Directory architecture includes source code for both directory client access and directory servers. Open Directory forms the foundation of how Mac OS X accesses all authoritative configuration information (users, groups, mounts, managed desktop data, etc.). Mac OS X obtains this information via abstraction APIs, enabling use of virtually any directory system."

A *local* directory service is accessible only to the computer on which it is stored. Mac OS X and Mac OS X Server each provide two local directory nodes. The /Local/Default node is new in Mac OS X v10.5 and replaces NetInfo. Unlike NetInfo, which used a binary and proprietary file format to store directory data, the new DSLocal node stores directory data in human-readable XML property lists. Another local directory node, /BSD/local, is present on all Mac OS X and Mac OS X Server systems, but by default is not used for user and group information. Data in the /BSD/local node is stored in a more traditional flat-file format, as on various other UNIX operating systems. The following figure shows how `DirectoryService` uses local plug-ins to retrieve data from local data stores.

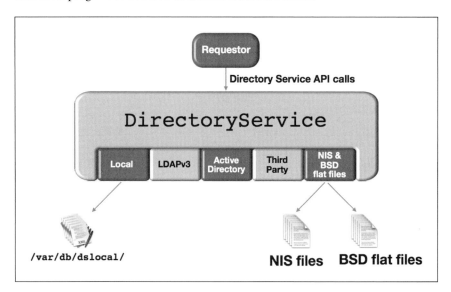

In Chapter 2 you will learn how to access a remote directory using the common LDAP. In this lesson you will learn how to access, create, and edit directory services data in the /Local/ Default and /BSD/local nodes using a variety of command-line and graphical tools. You will use these tools in later chapters to access and edit data stored in remote directory services.

Directory Services Definitions

Here is a review of the definitions from the previous section:

▶ Directory services—Processes, protocols, and data stores that provide a method for requesting data and receiving that data in a scalable, centralized, and distributable manner

▶ Process—An executable that handles client requests and retrieves data

▶ Protocol—A common set of rules for sending and receiving data on a network

▶ LDAP—A common protocol for directory access

   NOTE ▶ Mac OS X and Mac OS X Server use OpenLDAP, an open-source implementation.

▶   Directory—A database that follows a particular method of organizing data for a directory service

>   **NOTE ▶** A Berkeley DB database, which is structured to be accessed via LDAP, is an LDAP directory.

▶   Data store—A specialized read-optimized database

▶   Open Directory—Apple's architecture for directory services for Mac OS X and Mac OS X Server

▶   `DirectoryService`—The process on Mac OS X and Mac OS X Server that handles directory services requests

▶   API—Code made available to software developers to handle various tasks in a simplified and standardized way

▶   Node, domain, directory node, directory domain, directory—Interchangeable terms for a directory within directory services

Understanding the BSD/local Node and BSD Flat Files

The /BSD/local node is always active. The files used to store the /BSD/local data are in the same format and file system locations that many other UNIX systems use.

The files in the /BSD/local node are called *flat files* because they are typically line-oriented. Each line of the file is treated as a separate record; an end-of-line character marks the end of a record. A list of record attributes must be specified in a certain defined order, and the attributes must be separated be a certain delimited character, usually a colon. The comma character typically separates multivalue attributes. There is generally no support in flat files for more advanced data structures such as dictionaries or binary data. XML files such as those used by the Local Default node have much more flexibility than flat files.

The entries in /etc/hosts are used for host name–to-IP resolution and must be formatted with an IP address first, followed by a host name. /etc/passwd contains user records, and this file is readable by all local users. /etc/master.passwd contains the same user records, but because it may contain encrypted passwords, it is readable only with root privileges. /etc/groups contains group information.

>   **MORE INFO ▶** For a complete list of BSD flat files and what they are used for, see *Mac OS X Server Open Directory Administration for Version 10.5 Leopard, Second Edition.*

It is important to note that /BSD/local is a discrete directory node. It is in no way synchronized with or linked to the /Default/Local node. Additionally, as is discussed in the next section, Open Directory will not use any of the users or groups found in the /BSD/local node unless you specifically enable it with Directory Utility.

Directory services tools may access /BSD/local node data, but it can be changed only by operating directly on the flat files themselves. This is a distinct difference from the /Local/Default node, in which it is preferable to make changes using directory services tools.

Examining DNS Information

Before delving into user records, take a look at how Open Directory handles DNS record information.

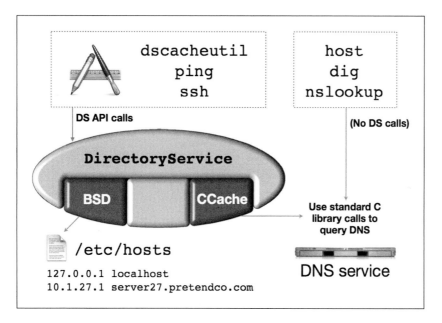

Tools such as ping and ssh, as well as Safari, Mail, and other applications, query Open Directory for host name–to-IP address information. Open Directory uses its various plug-ins to find DNS resolution. One of the plug-ins is BSD, which DirectoryService uses to query the /etc/hosts file before querying DNS resolvers. You can edit the /etc/hosts file (with root privileges) to add entries, and these new entries should be available right away to the BSD plug-in of Open Directory. If the BSD plug-in does not find the information, DirectoryService uses its CCache plug-in (which you will not edit or configure) to use standard C library calls to query your DNS servers. DNS resolution tools, such as dig, nslookup, and host, do not use DirectoryService calls and do not consult /etc/hosts; they use standard C library calls to query DNS servers, just like the CCache plug-in does. The BSD plug-in is always active, however; Mac OS X is configured by default to ignore user and group information stored in the /BSD/local/node.

> **NOTE** ▶ In previous versions of Mac OS X and Mac OS X server, the lookupd daemon and its plug-ins complicated the task of getting information, including DNS resolution. lookupd has gone the way of NetInfo and is not part of Mac OS X v10.5.

The following example shows the contents of /etc/hosts, with an extra definition for bsdhost. pretendco.com at the IP address 10.20.1.100, and then looks for the entry with the host command, which fails. Next it looks for information with the ping command, which succeeds.

```
client17:~ cadmin$ cat /etc/hosts
##
# Host Database
#
# localhost is used to configure the loopback interface
# when the system is booting. Do not change this entry.S
##
127.0.0.1               localhost
255.255.255.255         broadcasthost
::1                     localhost
fe80::1%lo0             localhost
10.20.1.100             bsdhost.pretendco.com
```

> **NOTE** ▶ The ::1 and fe80::1%lo0 are IPv6 entries.

The host command uses standard C library calls to contact the DNS resolvers directory; it does not use DirectoryService. In the following example, the host command does not find the record:

```
client17:~ cadmin$ host bsdhost.pretendco.com
Host bsdhost.pretendco.com not found: 3(NXDOMAIN)
```

Using dscl, however, you can successfully see the record:

```
client17:~ cadmin$ dscl /Search -read /hosts/bsdhost.pretendco.com
AppleMetaNodeLocation: /BSD/local
IPAddress: 10.20.1.100
RecordName: bsdhost.pretendco.com
```

Finally, the ping command will successfully find the IP address of the name you specified in /etc/hosts, even though there is no response at that IP address. The example uses -c1 to set a count of only one instead of five packets and -t1 to set the timeout to just 1 second (so you do not have to wait long for this command to fail):

```
client17:~ cadmin$ ping -c1 -t1 bsdhost.pretendco.com
PING bsdhost.pretendco.com (10.20.1.101): 56 data bytes
--- bsdhost.pretendco.com ping statistics ---
1 packets transmitted, 0 packets received, 100% packet loss
```

Software such as Safari, Mail, and most command-line utilities (ftp and ssh, for example) use the entries in /etc/hosts because they use DirectoryService for DNS resolution.

> **NOTE ▶** If you add multiple entries to /etc/hosts, you might notice that dscl displays your hosts in alphabetical order. If you have multiple IP addresses for the same host name, the IPAddress variable can have multiple values depending on the order they appear in /etc/hosts.

You can also use dscl to look at the new record:

```
client17:~ cadmin$ dscl /Search read /hosts/bsdhost.pretendco.com
AppleMetaNodeLocation: /BSD/local
IPAddress: 10.20.1.100
RecordName: bsdhost.pretendco.com
```

Open Directory's BSD plug-in is always active, as the example demonstrated earlier by showing that new entries to the BSD file /etc/hosts are immediately available.

Defining User Records

Before you start creating local users and groups, it is helpful to understand the kind of information that you need to define for these objects. In the context of directory services, the following definitions can help you understand how Open Directory treats user objects:

▶ Record—An individual entry or entity stored in a directory; a collection of record attributes and the values or data stored therein

▶ Attribute or record attribute—A named data item, which can contain a specific type of information

> NOTE ▶ Some record attributes can contain only one value, such as short name. Other record attributes, such as Keywords, can contain zero, one, or many values.

▶ Value—The data stored in the record attribute

▶ Object class—A set of rules that define similar objects in a directory domain by specifying attributes that each object *must* have and other attributes that each object *may* have

▶ Schema—The collection of files that define the types of object classes, records, and attributes contained in a directory

To get a feel for which attributes must (and which attributes may) be part of a user record, look at the `apple-user` object class in the file /etc/openldap/schema/apple.schema. The file contains definitions in snippets of code; each definition is for either an `attributetype` (for example, `apple-mcxflags` and `apple-user-picture`) or an `objectclass` (for example, `apple-user`).

Each user record must have a short name; the short name is stored in the record's `RecordName` attribute. The data stored in the record, which might be something like "cadmin," is the *value* of the attribute.

Take a look at a sample user created with the Setup Assistant as shown in Table 1.1. In the Accounts pane of System Preferences, Control-click an account and choose Advanced Options from the context menu. You can view the attributes and edit or view the values. Do not edit these values right now; just take a look.

Table 1.1   Sample User Record Attributes and Values

Accounts Pane Attribute Name	Value
User ID	501
Group ID	20
Short Name	cadmin
Login Shell	/bin/bash
Home Directory	/Users/cadmin
UUID	8D44CF02-A3BC-475B-A7C3-1785343C3940
Aliases	[no value]

NOTE ▶ You may be tempted to change the values, but this may cause unforeseen consequences, such as the user being unable to access resources.

Distinguishing Between Standard and Native Attributes

Although the attributes appear with familiar names such as short name, the actual attributes in a particular directory node may be stored with a different attribute name. Open Directory attributes have the prefix dsAttrTypeStandard. Attributes with the prefix dsAttrTypeNative refer to attribute names as they are actually stored in the directory node.

Throughout this book you will see that various directory nodes store attributes with different Native attribute names, which can be confusing. Part of the challenge of managing directory services is understanding which Open Directory attribute you want to create or modify, and understanding which Native attribute for a given directory node matches the Standard Open Directory attribute.

Table 1.2 shows that System Preferences, Open Directory, and the data store all refer to the same piece of data with different attribute names. The first entry contains the value 501. System Preferences labels this attribute as User ID, but the value is stored on disk with the attribute name uid, and Open Directory refers to this attribute as UniqueID.

Table 1.2   Standard and Native Attributes for a Sample User Record

System Preferences Attribute	Open Directory Attribute (dsAttrTypeStandard)	Attribute Stored in Local Default Node plist	Value
User ID	UniqueID	uid	501
Group ID	PrimaryGroupID	gid	20
Short Name	RecordName	name	cadmin
Login Shell	UserShell	shell	/bin/bash
Home Directory	NFSHomeDirectory	home	/Users/cadmin
UUID	GeneratedUID	generateduid	8D44CF02-A3BC-475B-A7C3-1785343C3940

Table 1.3 provides a closer look at the attribute for the user's home directory.

Table 1.3   Home Directory Attribute

Attribute Type	Attribute Name
dsAttrTypeStandard	NFSHomeDirectory
dsAttrTypeNative	home

Using dscl to Examine the Local Default Node

The DirectoryService command-line tool, dscl, is a very capable editing and troubleshooting resource. It can use either Standard (Open Directory) or Native (native to the directory where the record is stored) attribute names. In this section you will learn how to use dscl to view directory services data in Mac OS X. You will see how directory nodes, records, record attributes, and attribute values are presented in the interactive dscl interface.

According to the man page for dscl, the format of the command is

```
dscl [options] [datasource [command]]
```

A useful `dscl` option is `-raw`, which displays all attribute names without stripping the prefix. By default, `dscl` strips `dsAttrTypeStandard` from Standard attribute names. Another option is `-f` *filepath*, which allows you to operate on a node located at the file path you specify. This is useful for editing a node located on a disk image or on a Mac OS X computer that is booted into FireWire target disk mode.

You specify the node you want to use with the `datasource` option. In this lesson you will use `localhost` or simply a dot (.) to specify the local node.

If you do not specify any arguments to `dscl`, you will get an interactive `dscl` shell.

There are a number of commands to use with `dscl`. For example, `read` displays data contained in a node. Later you will use other commands such as `create` and `append`.

Directory services data is organized in a hierarchy that contains node types at the top level, followed by instances of that node type, followed by record types, and finally the records themselves. Traversing this hierarchy with `dscl` is similar to traversing a file system hierarchy using a UNIX command line. You can construct paths from labels separated by a forward slash; you can change the current location using the `cd` command; and you can list items using the `ls` command.

Use the following steps to open an interactive session with `dscl`:

1   Open Terminal, located in the /Applications/Utilities folder.

2   Run `dscl` in interactive mode.

```
client17:~ cadmin$ dscl

Entering interactive mode... (type "help" for commands)
```

3   At the prompt, type `ls` to show the nodes.

```
> ls

BSD

Local

Search

Contact
```

4   At the prompt, use `cd` to move down the hierarchy into the Local node. Note that the prompt changes.

```
> cd Local

/Local >
```

5   Move into the `/Local/Default` node.

```
/Local > cd Default

/Local/Default >
```

6   List the record types in `/Local/Default`.

```
/Local/Default > ls
```

7   Move into Users and list the user records.

```
/Local/Default > cd Users

/Local/Default/Users > ls
```

8   Read cadmin's user record.

```
/Local/Default/Users > read cadmin
```

9   Skim through the information for cadmin's user record, and note that some attributes are prefixed with `dsAttrTypeNative` and the Standard attribute names have no prefix.

10   Display the root user record and note that this record is much shorter; for instance, it does not have anything defined for the attribute `JPEGPhoto`.

```
/Local/Default/Users > read root
```

11   Navigate to the listing of group records in /Local/Default and display the list. You will see a record for each group in /Local/Default.

```
/Local/Default/Users > cd ../Groups

/Local/Default/Groups > ls
```

12 Display the contents of the admin group record. Note that the Standard attribute GroupMembership contains the short names of users that are members of the group, root and cadmin.

```
/Local/Default/Groups > read admin
```

13 Quit dscl.

```
/Local/Default/Groups > quit
```

The next example uses dscl to search for the home directory attribute, first using the Open Directory Standard attribute name NFSHomeDirectory, and then using the Native attribute name as it is stored in the data store, home.

```
client17:~ cadmin$ dscl . read /Users/cadmin NFSHomeDirecory
NFSHomeDirectory: /Users/cadmin
client17:~ cadmin$ dscl . read /Users/cadmin home
dsAttrTypeNative:home: /Users/cadmin
```

Using the File System to Examine the Local Default Node

In a fresh installation of Mac OS X v10.5, any user can navigate to /var/db/dslocal/.

> **NOTE ▶** For simplicity, this book refers to the directory /var, even though /var is a symbolic link to /private/var.

There are three stock directories: dsmappings, indices, and nodes. Take a look at each of these three subdirectories:

```
client17:~ cadmin$ cd /var/db/dslocal
client17:dslocal cadmin$ ls
dsmappings   indices  nodes
```

The dsmappings directory contains two plists: one for records and one for attributes. These files contain information about how Standard Open Directory records and attributes map to Native records and attributes stored in the Local Default plists. The /var/db/dslocal/dsmappings/AttributeMappings.plist file contains entries with a prefix of dsAttrTypeStandard and corresponding Native attributes that are stored in the Local Default node plists:

```
client17:dslocal cadmin$ ls dsmappings/
AttributeMappings.plist      RecordMappings.plist
```

Below are the first few lines of the `AttributeMappings.plist` file. The Standard attribute `RecordName` maps to the Native attribute `name`; Standard `RealName` maps to Native `realname`; Standard `Password` maps to Native `passwd`. Again, the Native attributes in this context are the names of the attributes as they are stored in the Local Default node plists, which you will examine shortly.

```
client17:dsmappings: cadmin$ head AttributeMappings.plist
<?xml version="1.0" encoding="UTF-8"?>
<!DOCTYPE plist PUBLIC "-//Apple Computer//DTD PLIST 1.0//EN" "http://www.apple.com/
DTDs/PropertyList-1.0.dtd">
<plist version="1.0">
<dict>
    <key>dsAttrTypeStandard:RecordName</key>
    <string>name</string>
    <key>dsAttrTypeStandard:RealName</key>
    <string>realname</string>
    <key>dsAttrTypeStandard:Password</key>
    <string>passwd</string>
```

`/var/db/dslocal/indices/Default/` contains an index file used for SQLite, which helps to provide faster search results for commonly requested attributes:

```
client17:dslocal cadmin$ ls indices/Default/
index
```

`/var/db/dslocal/nodes/` contains the Default directory:

```
client17:dslocal cadmin$ ls nodes/
Default
```

`/var/db/dslocal/nodes/Default` contains one directory for each of several (Native) record types, such as `users`. You can view these files only after authenticating as the System Administrator or with `sudo`:

```
client17:dslocal cadmin$ ls nodes/Default/
ls: Default: Permission denied
```

```
client17:dslocal cadmin$ sudo ls nodes/Default/
aliases      groups       networks
config       machines     users
```

Instead of running the rest of these commands preceded by the `sudo` command, use `sudo -s` to get a shell as the root user. Provide the password for the currently logged-in user:

```
client17:dslocal cadmin$ sudo -s
Password: [type the password of the currently logged-in user]
bash-3.2#
```

The `Users` directory contains all the users defined in the Local Default node. There are several predefined users, preceded by an underscore (as in `_ard.plist`), for use by various system processes and daemons; do not edit these. The cadmin.plist file is visible in the listing below:

```
bash-3.2# ls /var/db/dslocal/nodes/Default/users
_amavisd.plist       _mailman.plist        _teamsserver.plist
_appowner.plist      _mcxalr.plist         _tokend.plist
_appserver.plist     _mdnsresponder.plist  _unknown.plist
_ard.plist           _mysql.plist          _update_sharing.plist
_atsserver.plist     _pcastagent.plist     _uucp.plist
_calendar.plist      _pcastserver.plist    _windowserver.plist
_clamav.plist        _postfix.plist        _www.plist
_cvs.plist           _qtss.plist           _xgridagent.plist
_cyrus.plist         _sandbox.plist        _xgridcontroller.plist
_devdocs.plist       _securityagent.plist  cadmin.plist
_eppc.plist          _serialnumberd.plist  daemon.plist
_installer.plist     _spotlight.plist      nobody.plist
_jabber.plist        _sshd.plist           root.plist
_lp.plist            _svn.plist
```

Creating and Editing Local Users

When you first turn on a fresh, out-of-the-box, Mac OS X computer, the Setup Assistant walks you through the steps of creating the first user account. You should be familiar with the Accounts Preferences pane, where you can add, delete, and edit users. With a little knowledge, you can do much more. For instance, local user accounts are stored in

/var/db/dslocal/nodes/Default/users as clear text plist files. You can edit and even move these files around if you have the right tools. This section first examines a sample record, and then discusses the various tools you need to create and edit your own local user records.

Understanding the Structure of User Records

To begin, consider the System Administrator record in the Local Default node. Each Native attribute is surrounded by the tags <key> and </key>, and its value is defined afterwards. In this example, all the values are of type string, but you may see other attributes with different data types—for example, <data> for the Native attribute jpegphoto, an attribute not defined for the System Administrator record. In the record below, note that the following Native attributes are present: gid, home, name, passwd, realname, shell, uid, and generateduid.

```
bash-3.2# cat /var/db/dslocal/nodes/Default/users/root.plist
<?xml version="1.0" encoding="UTF-8"?>
<!DOCTYPE plist PUBLIC "-//Apple Computer//DTD PLIST 1.0//EN" "http://www.apple.com/
DTDs/PropertyList-1.0.dtd">
<plist version="1.0">
<dict>
    <key>gid</key>
    <array>
            <string>0</string>
    </array>
    <key>home</key>
    <array>
            <string>/var/root</string>
    </array>
    <key>name</key>
    <array>
            <string>root</string>
    </array>
    <key>passwd</key>
    <array>
            <string>*</string>
    </array>
    <key>realname</key>
```

```
		<array>
				<string>System Administrator</string>
		</array>
		<key>shell</key>
		<array>
				<string>/bin/sh</string>
		</array>
		<key>uid</key>
		<array>
				<string>0</string>
		</array>
		<key>generateduid</key>
		<array>
				<string>FFFFEEEE-DDDD-CCCC-BBBB-AAAA00000000</string>
		</array>
	</dict>
	</plist>
```

The generateduid is supposed to be unique; no two users on any two systems should ever have the same generateduid. However, the generateduid for some system users, such as the System Administrator (root), is the same across all Mac OS X v10.5 and Mac OS X Server v10.5 systems. The users daemon and nobody do not have a generateduid.

> **NOTE** ▶ If you restore an imaged system, the users will have the same generateduid as on the image source.

The passwd attribute is *, which is a special case. The password has not yet been set for the System Administrator account.

> **NOTE** ▶ Even though the root password is not yet set, an administrator can still use sudo and supply his or her own login password to run a command as the System Administrator.

A passwd attribute consisting of a series of asterisks indicates that the password is not stored in the user record; it is a shadow password, stored in a more secure location (/var/db/shadow/hash/, which is readable only by root).

When you need to search and edit the XML files for user records, traditional UNIX tools such as grep, sed, and awk may not be immediately useful, but dscl is. Note how the lowercase attribute name (generateduid) is native to the Local Default node, and the attribute name with uppercase characters (GeneratedUID) is Standard to Open Directory. dscl automatically uses the prefix dsAttrTypeNative: with the results from the Native attribute.

```
bash-3.2# dscl . read /Users/root generateduid
dsAttrTypeNative:generateduid: FFFFEEEE-DDDD-CCCC-BBBB-AAAA00000000
bash-3.2# dscl . read /Users/root GeneratedUID
GeneratedUID: FFFFEEEE-DDDD-CCCC-BBBB-AAAA00000000
```

You could use grep to search the BSD file /etc/master.passwd for any user with a particular uid, but because XML is multiline, grep will not help with this type of search in the Local Default node. For example, the search results below reveal that the file cadmin.plist contains the string 501, but the results do not show which attribute that value is for:

```
bash-3.2# cd /var/db/dslocal/nodes/Default/users
bash-3.2# grep 501 *
cadmin.plist:        <string>501</string>
```

Instead, use the dscl search command. The following example searches for any users with the uid of 501. The formatting is a little choppy, but the results return the record name (cadmin), the attribute (dsAttrTypeNative:uid), and the value (501):

```
bash-3.2# dscl . search /Users uid 501
cadmin        dsAttrTypeNative:uid = (
    501
)
```

The dscl search command works with multiple records as well. The following search for the home attribute of /var/empty returns many results, as several of the predefined system users have their home directory set to /var/empty. The example pipes the output to the head command to show only the first few lines of the results (in this case, the users _appowner, _appserver, _ard, and _atsserver):

```
bash-3.2# dscl . search /Users home /var/empty | head
_appowner              dsAttrTypeNative:home = (
  "/var/empty"
)
_appserver             dsAttrTypeNative:home = (
  "/var/empty"
)
_ard          dsAttrTypeNative:home = (
  "/var/empty"
)
_atsserver             dsAttrTypeNative:home = (
```

Now that you understand the structure of user records, take a look at some of the tools available for creating and editing them.

Creating and Editing User Records with Workgroup Manager

Workgroup Manager is more than a directory editor. Just as you use Workgroup Manager to edit shared directories on Mac OS X Server, you can also use it to edit and inspect the Local Default node. Be aware, however, that Workgroup Manager exposes some operations that are not appropriate for the Local Default node or not compatible with that node.

Because server administration tools are not included with Mac OS X, you will need to install them if you are not using Mac OS X Server. You can download the Server Admin tools from Apple's website, and they are also included in the Mac OS X Server installation media; look in the folder named Other Installs and use the package ServerAdministrationSoftware.mpkg.

TIP ▶ To quickly find the Server Admin Tools installer, search for Download ID sd15816 from www.apple.com/support.

MORE INFO ▶ Although this chapter addresses Mac OS X only (not Mac OS X Server), see Apple Knowledge Base article # 301590 "Admin tools compatibility information" for information about using Mac OS X Server v10.5 tools with earlier versions of Mac OS X Server.

To use Workgroup Manager to create and edit accounts follow these steps:

1   Launch Workgroup Manager (in /Applications/Utilities), but don't click anything or type in the default authentication window.

2   From the Server menu, select View Directories.

3   Choose OK if you see a warning that starts with "You are working in the local configuration database."

4   Ensure that you are looking at the Local Default directory. The globe in the upper-left corner of Workgroup Manager, just below the toolbar, should indicate "Viewing local directory: /Local/Default. Not authenticated." If this is not the case, click the globe and choose Local.

5   Click the lock in the upper-right corner of Workgroup Manager, just below the toolbar, and authenticate with a local administrator account. If you select "Remember this password in my keychain," you will not need to authenticate the next time you launch Workgroup Manager.

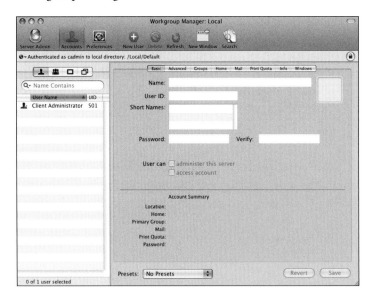

6   Click the New User button in the toolbar, fill in the fields, and then click the Save button.

You have just successfully created a new user.

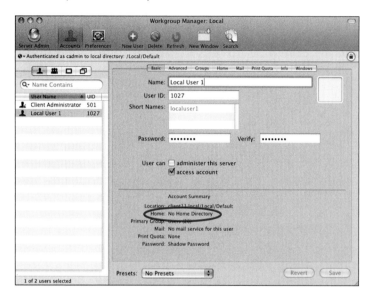

This procedure is similar to creating a new user with the Accounts pane in System Preferences. Note that in Workgroup Manager, by default you do not have the ability to view the GeneratedUID, and you have to manually set the Home attribute.

When you use Workgroup Manager in the Local Default directory to edit a user and specify a password, the user's shadow password hash file is automatically created and populated with the default hashes. This also happens with the Accounts pane in System Preferences.

You need to manually specify a home directory with Workgroup Manager, which sets the attribute to None by default. The other choices available, however, might not be appropriate. If you haven't created any other users with the Accounts pane in System Preferences, your only choice for home is the Public folder of the user already created (/Users/cadmin/Public). If a choice of /Users is not available, click the Add button (+). You will see three fields that are more appropriate for network user records; for a record in the Local Default node, enter the full path in the Full Path field, /Users/*shortname* (replace *shortname* with the short name of the user), then click OK.

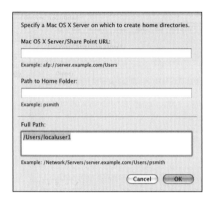

Now the /Users option will be available to select for this and all subsequently created users. Note that the full path will be correctly displayed above the list of selections as /Users/*shortname*.

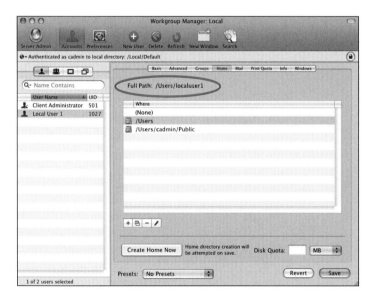

Click the Save button to save this new home folder setting.

NOTE ▶ At the time this writing, clicking the Save button results in an error message, which you can ignore.

Use the command-line tool `createhomedir` to create the home directory and populate it with the default files:

```
client17:~ cadmin$ sudo createhomedir -c
creating home directories for (client17.local)
created (/Users/localuser1)
```

NOTES ▶ The -c option creates home directories for local home paths only.

The home directory will be created the first time the user logs in if you haven't already created it manually.

Both the Accounts pane in System Preferences and the default settings for Workgroup Manager display only a select few attributes for a user record. Workgroup Manager, however, enables you to display all the attributes of a user record. In Workgroup Manager preferences, select the checkbox labeled "Show 'All Records' tab and inspector." Be aware, however, that you can now cause data loss or otherwise make your system inoperable by incorrectly editing raw data. Click OK at the warning message to this effect. Workgroup Manager now gives you an All Records button (which looks like a bull's-eye or target) next to the Users, Groups, Computer, and Computer Group buttons.

If you click the All Records button, the default pop-up button's menu selection is Users, and you see a list of the previously hidden system users. When you click one of these users, the Inspector pane on the right displays the user record's attributes and their corresponding values. Note that each attribute is listed with its Open Directory Standard attribute name, not the Native attribute name that is stored in the plist file.

To edit an attribute, select it and click the Edit button.

To delete an attribute, select it and press the Delete key. Do not click the Delete button in the toolbar: This will delete the entire user account, not just the highlighted attribute.

You can click the New Value button to add another value entry for most attributes, but that attribute might not allow multiple data values. Just because the button is available, that doesn't mean that using it is always a good idea.

Similarly, you could click the New Attribute button to add a new attribute to the user record. <Native> is the default option, with a blank text field in which you can type in the new Native attribute name. You might be better off clicking the drop-down menu and selecting the Standard (Open Directory) attribute name, however, to avoid making a typing error.

When you create a new attribute, it is stored in the plist file with the Native attribute name, but Workgroup Manager displays the Standard attribute name. The Options button in the Inspector pane for a user record lets you change how the attribute names are displayed and which types of attributes to display. By default, Workgroup Manager displays all the Standard and Native attributes, but only prefixes the Native attribute names.

If you prefer, you can select all the checkboxes above: Workgroup Manager will display all possible attributes with the Standard attribute name, and display any extra attributes with the Native attribute prefix and name. If you do not select Show Standard Attributes, it may appear that the user record has no attributes; this simply means that all of the Native attributes can be mapped to Standard attributes. In the figure below, Workgroup Manager displays a user record with both Standard and Native prefixes, and both Standard and Native attributes.

You can get a similar view in Workgroup Manager by clicking the Users button, selecting a user, and then clicking the Inspector button in the upper-right corner. The figure below shows that you can select a user and click the Inspector tab for that user.

Workgroup Manager may not be the best tool to use for creating user records in the Local Default node, because of limitations with creating the user's actual home directory, but it is excellent for inspecting user record attributes and their values.

Creating a Local User Record with dsimport

Like Workgroup Manager, dsimport works through DirectoryService, which then makes changes to the underlying data structures. You can use dsimport to create user and group records in the local directory node. See the man page for dsimport, dsimport -h, or *Mac OS X Server Command-Line Administration for Version 10.5 Leopard* for more information on dsimport. The structure of the command is:

```
dsimport <-g|-s|-p|-x> filepath DSnodePath <O|M|A|I|N> -u username [<options>]
```

NOTES ▶ The -g option specifies a character-delimited file, as opposed to an XML file exported from earlier versions of Mac OS X Server or from AppleShare IP.

For the Local Default node, DSnodePath should be /Local/Default.

The I option ignores a potential new record if it would duplicate an existing record.

You can't just give a random list of information to dsimport; you have to include a record description that specifies the type of record you are creating, as well as the list of attributes for which you are providing data. There are a few ways to specify this information:

▶   Include a record description line at the beginning of the import file.

▶   Use the -recordFormat option and include the record description in the dsimport command itself.

▶   Use the -T xDSStandardUser or -T xDSStandardGroup option.

Specifying the Record Description in the Input File

If you choose to include a record description at the beginning of the import file, the first line of the input file must specify the following elements in this order, each separated by a space character:

1.   The character used for end of record (in hex notation)

2.   The escape character (in hex notation)

3.   The character used to separate fields (in hex notation)

4.   The character used to separate values (in hex notation)

5.   The type of record that you are creating

6.   The number of attributes in each record

7.   A list of the attributes themselves

Here's a sample record description:

```
0x0A 0x5C 0x3A 0x2C dsRecTypeStandard:Users 8 dsAttrTypeStandard:RecordName
dsAttrTypeStandard:AuthMethod dsAttrTypeStandard:Password dsAttrTypeStandard:UniqueID
dsAttrTypeStandard:PrimaryGroupID dsAttrTypeStandard:Comment
dsAttrTypeStandard:RealName dsAttrTypeStandard:UserShell
```

If an attribute is type dsAttrTypeStandard, you can omit the prefix—but you cannot omit the record-type prefix. Here's the same record description, simplified:

```
0x0A 0x5C 0x3A 0x2C dsRecTypeStandard:Users 8 RecordName AuthMethod Password UniqueID
PrimaryGroupID Comment RealName UserShell
```

Here is a sample record for this description:

```
imp1:dsAuthMethodStandard\:dsAuthClearText:spoon53snow:8001:20:This is a
comment:Imported User 1:/bin/bash
```

NOTE ▶ The colon is usually used as a field separator, so the colon in `dsAuthMethodStandard:dsAuthClearText` needs to be "escaped" to keep it from being used as a field separator. You can specify any character you like for the special characters, but it makes sense to stick with commonly used special characters. In the example above, the escape character is the backslash.

TIP ▶ If you periodically import users from a data source, you can keep your standard record description in a file by itself, then concatenate the file containing the record description with a file containing the new records, resulting in a new import file ready for `dsimport`.

The transcript below displays the contents of an import file, imports the file, confirms that the account got imported, and then confirms the password with `dirt` (a directory tool for testing authentication with `DirectoryService`). The short name is `imp1`, and the password is `spoon53snow`.

```
client17:~ cadmin$ cat import1.txt
0x0A 0x5C 0x3A 0x2C dsRecTypeStandard:Users 8 RecordName AuthMethod Password UniqueID
PrimaryGroupID Comment RealName UserShell
imp1:dsAuthMethodStandard\:dsAuthClearText:spoon53snow:8001:20:This is a
comment:Imported User 1:/bin/bash
client17:~ cadmin$ dsimport -g import1.txt /Local/Default I -u cadmin
cadmin's password: [typed "apple" but this is hidden]
Total Bytes =237
client17:~ cadmin$ id imp1
uid=8001(imp1) gid=20(staff) groups=20(staff),101(com.apple.sharepoint.
group.1),102(com.apple.sharepoint.group.2)
client17:~ cadmin$ dirt -u imp1
User password: [typed "spoon53snow" but this is hidden]
2008-03-05 09:32:46.429 dirt[26776:10b] password is : spoon53snow
```

```
Call to dsGetRecordList returned count = 1 with Status : eDSNoErr : (0)
Username: imp1
Password: spoon53snow
Success
```

NOTE ▶ Be careful with the `dirt` command. The password that you test is not only displayed in clear text in the output of `dirt`, but it is also logged in /var/log/system.log:

```
Mar 5 11:31:53 client17 dirt[27036]: password is : spoon53snow
```

Specifying the Record Description as an Option to the dsimport Command

An alternative to specifying the record description in the import file is to specify it in the command itself with the `-recordFormat` option:

```
client17:~ cadmin$ dsimport -g import2.txt /Local/Default I -u cadmin -recordFormat
"0x0A 0x5C 0x3A 0x2C dsRecTypeStandard:Users 8 RecordName AuthMethod Password
UniqueID PrimaryGroupID Comment RealName UserShell"
```

The import file `import2.txt` could then look like this, with attributes that are specified in the above command:

```
imp2:dsAuthMethodStandard\:dsAuthClearText:pear62coup:8002:20:Comment:Imported User
2:/bin/bash
```

Using the Standard User Record Option

Using the `-T <xDSStandardUser>` option lets you avoid needing to specify the record description. With this option, your import file must contain the fields in the following order:

1. `RecordName`

2. `Password`

3. `UniqueID`

4. `PrimaryGroupID`

5. `DistinguishedName`

6. `NFSHomeDirectory`

7. `UserShell`

Here's an example import file and the command syntax to use it:

```
client17:~ cadmin$ cat import3.txt
imp3:pass:8003:20:Imported User 3:/Users/imp3:/bin/bash
client17:~ cadmin$ dsimport -g import3.txt /Local/Default I -u cadmin -T
xDSStandardUser
cadmin's password: [hidden]
Total Bytes =55
client17:~ cadmin: id imp3
uid=603(imp3) gid=20(staff) groups=20(staff),101(com.apple.sharepoint.
group.1),102(com.apple.sharepoint.group.2)
```

The `-T xDSStandardUser` method used above does not specify the `dsAuthMethodStandard:` `dsAuthClearText` attribute, which means that `dsimport` does not set up the user's shadow password hash file, nor does it convert the clear text contents of the password field to an encrypted password. It stores the clear text password as if it were already encrypted.

> **TIP** You can use the `slappasswd` command to encrypt a string of characters suitable for importing in a user record.

The example below shows that the new user record has no `AuthenticationAuthority` and dirt fails to check the password (the imported password was "pass").

```
client17:~ cadmin$ dscl . read /Users/imp3 passwd
dsAttrTypeNative:passwd: pass
client17:~ cadmin$ dscl . read /Users/imp3 AuthenticationAuthority
No such key: AuthenticationAuthority
client17:~ cadmin$ dirt -l -u imp3
User password: ["pass" typed in but hidden]
2008-03-04 20:07:52.817 dirt[25642:10b] password is : pass
Call to dsGetRecordList returned count = 1 with Status : eDSNoErr : (0)
Username: imp3
Password: pass
Error : eDSAuthFailed : (-14090)
```

NOTE ▶ You cannot store a clear text password in the user record and have it be used for authentication.

Once you change the password with `sudo passwd`, the user's password type is converted from crypt to shadow: The user gets a shadow password hash file and an entry in the local Kerberos Key Distribution Center (LKDC).

```
client17:~ cadmin$ sudo passwd imp3
Password: [typed in cadmin's password but hidden]
Changing password for imp3.
New password: [typed in "new" but hidden]
Retype new password: [typed in "new" but hidden]
client17:~ cadmin$ dirt -u imp3
User password: [typed in "new" but hidden]
2008-03-04 20:14:30.085 dirt[25673:10b] password is : new
Call to dsGetRecordList returned count = 1 with Status : eDSNoErr : (0)
Username: imp3
Password: new
Success
client17:~ cadmin$ dscl . read /Users/imp3 AuthenticationAuthority
AuthenticationAuthority: ;ShadowHash; ;Kerberosv5;;imp3@LKDC:SHA1.07E6D260A31AA81B57C
B6F7528D5E1A0AF160BF9;LKDC:SHA1.07E6D260A31AA81B57CB6F7528D5E1A0AF160BF9;
```

When you use `dslocal` to import users into the Local Default node, remember that the record description is quite important, but cumbersome. There are three ways of specifying this:

▶ Including it as the first line in your import file

▶ Including it as an option in the `dsimport` command

▶ Using the `-T <xDSStandardUser>` option and including the standard seven attributes, and then using `passwd` to set up the `AuthenticationAuthority` attribute values

Creating a Local User Record by Copying a Record File

Workgroup Manager and `dsimport` are great tools, but they call upon `DirectoryService` to make changes. What do you do if you need to make changes when `DirectoryService` is not running, perhaps when you're in single-user mode?

> **NOTE** ▶ Previous versions of Mac OS X used NetInfo, which many considered unpleasant to work with in single-user mode.

Circumventing DirectoryService by directly creating, removing, or editing the files that contain user records is not supported while DirectoryService is running. You can, however, create a user record from an existing record file:

1 Create a new user record in XML format, perhaps using an existing user record as a template.

> **NOTE** ▶ You will need root privileges to do steps 2 through 4.

2 Copy the user record file to /var/db/dslocal/nodes/Default/users.

3 Copy the shadow password hash file to /var/db/shadow/hash, or set up the password and Kerberos principal with sudo passwd <newusername>.

4 Use sudo killall DirectoryService to stop and restart DirectoryService so it knows about the changes you just made.

> **NOTE** ▶ The killall command searches for a process by name; the kill command requires a process ID. Both commands send a signal to a process or processes. If you don't specify which signal to send, the default signal is TERM, which is a signal to terminate. Once the currently running DirectoryService process terminates, launchd immediately launches a new instance of DirectoryService as needed. It is not sufficient to send a HUP (hang up) signal for DirectoryService to notice these changes.

Modifying a Local User Record with a Text Editor

Although you cannot create, remove, or edit directory services data while DirectoryService is running, you can change a user's attributes by editing the user record with a text editor. You must choose your editor carefully: If you use a graphical tool such as TextEdit or Property List Editor, you will not be able to navigate to /var/db/dslocal/nodes/Default/users unless you enable root and log in as root, which is not recommended.

TIP A workaround is to copy the user record to a temporary location (such as your desktop) with sudo, edit it as a non-root user, then copy it back with sudo to /var/db/dslocal/nodes/Default/users/.

You can use the vi editor to edit the plist, but you should edit the attribute data only; do not change the attribute name. For example, if you wanted to edit imp1's home directory from its default location to another location, edit the attribute value (/Users/imp1) in the following snippet of the user record:

```
<key>home</key>
    <array>
<string>/Users/imp1</string
    </array>
```

With the following two commands, you can edit the user record, then restart DirectoryService to alert it to any changes:

```
client17:~ cadmin$ sudo vi /var/db/dslocal/nodes/Default/users/imp1.plist
client17:~ cadmin$ sudo killall DirectoryService
```

TIP If you want access to a user account for testing purposes, but don't know the user's password and don't want to irreversibly change the user's password, you can temporarily make the user record's AuthenticationAuthority point to a different shadow password hash file, perhaps your own. Be sure to switch it back, otherwise the user won't be able to authenticate.

Modifying a Local User Record with dscl

Because it makes calls to DirectoryService, dscl is the preferred command-line tool for creating and modifying directory services records such as user records. The man page for dscl refers to keys and values. The *key* is the attribute name, and the *value* is the value stored for that attribute.

The man entry for dscl starts out with this synopsis:

```
dscl [options] [datasource [command]]
```

The man entry for the change command in dscl includes:

```
change record_path key old_val new_val
```

To change the NFSHomeDirectory attribute for the user imp1, the data source is the Local Default node, or a period; the command is change; the record_path is /Users/imp1; the key is the attribute you want to change, NFSHomeDirectory; the old_val is the old value, /Users/imp1; and the new_val is what you want to change it to. So the following example inspects the NFSHomeDirectory attribute, changes it with the change command of dscl, and confirms that it has been changed:

```
client17:~ cadmin$ dscl . read /Users/imp1 NFSHomeDirectory
NFSHomeDirectory: /Users/imp1
client17:~ cadmin$ sudo dscl . change /Users/imp1 NFSHomeDirectory /Users/imp1
/OtherHomes/imp1
client17:~ cadmin$ dscl . read /Users/imp1 NFSHomeDirectory
NFSHomeDirectory: /OtherHomes/imp1
```

> **NOTE ►** The above example does not ensure that the new home directory exists, nor does it move the files from the old home directory to the new home directory. It simply uses dscl to change the value of an attribute.

You may need to populate an attribute with multiple values, which you can do with the append command of dscl. The append command creates a key if one does not already exist; it does not overwrite any existing values. The man page for dscl lists:

```
append record_path key val ...
```

For example, you could use dscl's append command twice to append data to the Keywords attribute.

> **NOTE ►** The Keywords attribute isn't used for local users, but it is a good example because it is an attribute that can handle multiple values.

```
client17:~ cadmin$ dscl . read /Users/imp1 Keywords
No such key: Keywords
client17:~ cadmin$ sudo dscl . append /Users/imp1 Keywords foo
client17:~ cadmin$ dscl . read /Users/imp1 Keywords
```

```
Keywords: foo
client17:~ cadmin$ sudo dscl . append /Users/imp1 Keywords baz
client17:~ cadmin$ dscl . read /Users/imp1 Keywords
Keywords: foo baz
```

You can clean up that example a bit by using the delete command to remove an attribute:

```
client17:~ cadmin$ sudo dscl . delete /Users/imp1 Keywords
client17:~ cadmin$ dscl . read /Users/imp1 Keywords
No such key: Keywords
```

You can use the create command of dscl to create a user record. Because dscl makes calls to DirectoryService, the new user record's GeneratedUID attribute gets populated automatically. However, you still must populate other attributes, such as UniqueID, RealName, NFSHomeDirectory, PrimaryGroupID, and UserShell, and set the user's password with passwd. Similarly, if you use the delete command to remove a user record, DirectoryService not only removes the user record, but it also removes the user's shadow hash entry and local KDC principal.

Creating and Modifying a Local User Record in the /BSD/local Node with a Text Editor

User and group records in the/BSD/local node are special cases. Recall that the BSD plug-in for Open Directory is always active. However, the users and groups defined in the /BSD/local node are not used, by default. This is because the file DSRecordTypeRestrictions.plist in the directory /Library/Preferences/DirectoryService specifies to use neither Users nor Groups record types. Take a quick look at the default file before you enable /BSD/local users and groups via Directory Utility:

```
bash-3.2# cd /Library/Preferences/DirectoryService/
bash-3.2# cat DSRecordTypeRestrictions.plist
<?xml version="1.0" encoding="UTF-8"?>
<!DOCTYPE plist PUBLIC "-//Apple//DTD PLIST 1.0//EN" "http://www.apple.com/DTDs/
PropertyList-1.0.dtd">
<plist version="1.0">
<dict>
    <key>BSD</key>
    <dict>
        <key>/BSD/local</key>
```

```
        <dict>
                <key>Deny Record Types</key>
                <array>
                        <string>dsRecTypeStandard:Users</string>
                        <string>dsRecTypeStandard:Groups</string>
                </array>
        </dict>
    </dict>
    <key>Version</key>
    <string>1.0</string>
</dict>
</plist>
```

To enable the users and groups in the/BSD/local node:

1   Open Directory Utility and, if necessary, click Show Advanced Settings.

2   Click the Services button.

3   Select the BSD Flat File and NIS service.

4   Click the Edit button (a pencil in the lower-left corner).

5   Enable the checkbox labeled "Use User and Group records in BSD Local node" and click OK to dismiss the pane.

6   If the Apply button is active, click Apply.

7 Quit Directory Utility.

See how the DSRecordTypeRestrictions.plist file changed; there are no longer any restrictions listed:

```
bash-3.2# cat DSRecordTypeRestrictions.plist
<?xml version="1.0" encoding="UTF-8"?>
<!DOCTYPE plist PUBLIC "-//Apple//DTD PLIST 1.0//EN" "http://www.apple.com/DTDs/
PropertyList-1.0.dtd">
<plist version="1.0">
<dict>
    <key>Version</key>
    <string>1.0</string>
</dict>
</plist>
```

Rather than using dscl, you should use the legacy tools like vipw to edit user information. It is not advisable to edit the traditional files directly because vipw checks the integrity of the internal data structure of the password file and takes care of file locking. vipw launches a command-line editor and allows you to edit a temporary copy of the /etc/master.passwd file. Once you quit the editor, vipw runs sanity checks on your changes; if your edits are valid, vipw updates /etc/passwd and /etc/master.passwd, and then finally runs pwd_mkdb to update the user database. You must run vipw with root privileges.

> **NOTE ▶** vipw uses the EDITOR environment variable if it exists; otherwise it uses the vi text editor.

> **TIP ▶** If your shell is the default (/bin/bash), you can change your EDITOR environment variable to the nano text editor with the following commands:
>
> EDITOR=/usr/bin/nano; export EDITOR
>
> If your shell is a C shell (like /bin/csh), you can change your EDITOR environment variable to the nano text editor with the following commands:
>
> setenv EDITOR /usr/bin/nano

> **NOTE ▶** The EDITOR and setenv commands set the environment variable for that session only; you can make more permanent changes with your ~/.cshrc or ~/.bashrc files, which is outside the scope of this book.

When you edit the temporary `passwd` file, follow the example of the existing users in the file. The colon character separates the attributes, or fields. The `man` page entry for `master.passwd` lists a user record's attributes in this order:

▶ name

▶ password

▶ uid

▶ gid

▶ class

▶ change

▶ expire

▶ gecos

▶ home_dir

▶ shell

> **TIP** ▶ Some of the fields above are optional.

Specify the encrypted version of the user password, or set it as an asterisk for the time being. If you leave the password field blank, this creates a blank password—not a good practice.

Following are two entries that you could add with `vipw`. The text `OpnSC65.QhkYc` is the encrypted form of the string `helloworld`. You'll learn to set the second user's password later.

```
bsduser1:OpnSC65.QhkYc:5000:20::0:0:BSD User 1:/Users/bsduser1:/bin/bash
bsduser2:*:5001:20::0:0:BSD User 2:/Users/bsduser2:/bin/bash
```

With the `id` command, you can verify that `DirectoryService` is aware of the user:

```
client17:~ cadmin$ id bsduser1
uid=5000(bsduser1) gid=20(staff) groups=20(staff),101(com.apple.sharepoint.
group.1),102(com.apple.sharepoint.group.2)
```

With the `dirt` command, confirm that you can authenticate with the password:

```
client17:~ cadmin$ dirt -u bsduser1 -p helloworld
2008-03-11 14:29:39.068 dirt[40548:10b] password is : helloworld
```

```
Call to dsGetRecordList returned count = 1 with Status : eDSNoErr : (0)
Call to checkpw(): Success
path: /BSD/local
Username: bsduser1
Password: helloworld
Success
```

You cannot use chpass to change a user in the BSD Local node, but you can use the passwd command for a user in the BSD Local node if you specify the option -i file. The following example sets a new password for bsduser2. First it tries just a few characters, 123, but then it gets an error message because passwd requires at least five characters. Finally, entering a password that meets the requirements means the change in password succeeds, and the command prompt returns.

```
client17:~ cadmin$ sudo passwd -i file bsduser2
Changing password for bsduser2.
New password: [typed 123 but this is hidden]
Password must be at least 5 characters long.
New password: [typed chair65water but this is hidden]
Retype new password: [typed chair65water again but this is hidden]
client17:~ cadmin$
```

Creating and Editing Local Groups

Many of the techniques for creating user records are applicable to group records as well. You should be familiar with the ability to create groups with Accounts Preferences, even though it is a new feature in Mac OS X v10.5. In this section you will learn which attributes are contained in local group records, and how to use various graphical and command-line tools to create and edit local groups.

> **NOTE** ▶ In Mac OS X v10.4, when you created a user with Accounts Preferences, DirectoryService would also create a group with the same short name as the short name of the user. In Mac OS X v10.5 this does not happen; the default group for new users is the group with dsAttrTypeStandard:RealName Users and dsAttrTYpeStandard:RecordName staff. The name staff is legacy.

Understanding the Attributes of Group Records

As with local user records, each group attribute may have a differently named attribute for `dsAttrTypeStandard` and `dsAttrTypeNative`. The attribute names that you see depend on how you look at the data. If you are using `dscl` or another tool that is mediated by `DirectoryService`, you will see the `dsAttrTypeStandard` attribute names. However, if you look at the straight text files in /var/db/dslocal/nodes/Default/, you will see the `dsAttrTypeNative` attribute names. Table 1.4 lists some of the key attributes that define a group record, their names, and a brief explanation of how each is used. Note that the different attributes `GroupMembership` and `GroupMembers` have very similar names.

Table 1.4 Attributes of a Local Group Record

dsAttrTypeStandard	dsAttrTypeNative for /Default/Local	Explanation
RecordName	name	Short name for the group (for example, `admin`)
RealName	realname	Long name for the group (for example, `Administrators`)
PrimaryGroupID	gid	Numerical ID to identify the group (for example, `80`)
GroupMembership	members	Short names of users that are members of the group
GeneratedUID	generateduid	128-bit value guaranteed unique across space and time
SMBSID	smb-sid	SMB Primary Group Security ID
Password	passwd	Usually an asterisk
GroupMembers	groupmembers	GUIDs of users that are members of the group
NestedGroups	nestedgroups	GUIDs of groups that are members of the group

NOTE ▶ Like some standard system user records, some standard system groups have the same 128-bit GeneratedUID across all Mac OS X systems.

MORE INFO ▶ For more information about the Security ID (SID), see Apple Knowledge Base article # 243330, "Well-known security identifiers in Windows operating systems."

Take a look at the text file that defines the admin group record. This contains the dsAttrTypeNative attribute names such as generateduid, gid, name, passwd, realname, smb_sid, and users:

```
bash-3.2# cat /var/db/dslocal/nodes/Default/groups/admin.plist
<?xml version="1.0" encoding="UTF-8"?>
<!DOCTYPE plist PUBLIC "-//Apple//DTD PLIST 1.0//EN" "http://www.apple.com/DTDs/
PropertyList-1.0.dtd">
<plist version="1.0">
<dict>
    <key>generateduid</key>
    <array>
            <string>ABCDEFAB-CDEF-ABCD-EFAB-CDEF00000050</string>
    </array>
    <key>gid</key>
    <array>
            <string>80</string>
    </array>
    <key>name</key>
    <array>
            <string>admin</string>
    </array>
    <key>passwd</key>
    <array>
            <string>*</string>
    </array>
    <key>realname</key>
    <array>
            <string>Administrators</string>
    </array>
```

```
        <key>smb_sid</key>
        <array>
                <string>S-1-5-32-544</string>
        </array>
        <key>users</key>
        <array>
                <string>root</string>
                <string>cadmin</string>
        </array>
    </dict>
    </plist>
```

A group's membership is not limited to members listed in the group record; a user's primary group ID (`dsAttrTypeStandard:PrimaryGroupID`) also comes into play. There are several ways in which a user may belong to a group. A user belongs to a local group if the:

▸   User's primary group ID (`dsAttrTypeStandard:PrimaryGroupID` or `dsAttrTypeNative:gid`), which is stored in the user's record, is the same as a group's gid (`dsAttrTypeStandard:PrimaryGroupID` or `dsAttrTypeNative:gid`)

▸   User's short name is listed as a member in the group record (`dsAttrTypeStandard:Group Membership` or `dsAttrTtypeNative:users`)

▸   User's GUID is listed in the `dsAttrTypeStandard:GroupMembers` attribute

▸   User is in a group that is in turn a member of the group via the attribute `dsAttrTypeStandard:NestedGroups`, which lists GUIDs of member groups

▸   User's short name is listed in a group's entry in the BSD flat file /etc/group, and the use of BSD users and groups is enabled

NOTE ▸ Accounts Preferences automatically adds a newly created user to the `staff` group (the group with `dsAttrTypeStandard:RealName Users` and `dsAttrTypeStandard:RecordName  staff`) by adding the user's short name to the `dsAttrTypeStandard:GroupMembership` attribute of the `staff` group. The name `staff` is legacy.

Creating and Editing Local Groups with Workgroup Manager

Because Workgroup Manager is a directory editor, you can use it to create and edit groups in the /Local/Default node. However, because it exposes functionality that is more appropriate for editing shared directory domains, you may find using Workgroup Manager for local groups to be quirky. Use Workgroup Manager in this section to explore local groups, but in your day-to-day administration use other tools like System Preferences or dsediteditgroup (which is covered in "Creating and Editing Local Groups with dseditgroup," below). The basic procedure for creating a group with Workgroup Manager follows:

1   Open Workgroup Manager in /Applications/Server/.

2   In the Server menu select View Directories, and dismiss the warning dialog if one appears.

3   Click the Accounts button in the toolbar.

4   Click the Groups button in the left section of Workgroup Manager.

5   Click the lock icon in the upper-right corner to authenticate as a local administrator.

6   Click the New Group button in the toolbar.

7   Specify a new group name and short name.

    Workgroup Manager automatically assigns a group ID; do not use a group ID less than 100, as these are reserved for system groups.

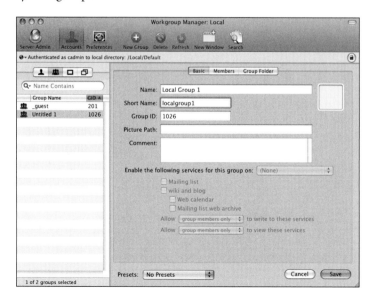

8   Click the Members button.

9   Click the Add button (+).

10   Drag a user from the drawer into the list of group members. You may find it useful to click twice on the UID column in the drawer to sort by UID, so that system users are separated from the other users.

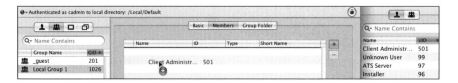

Creating and Editing Local Groups with dscl

In addition to using the Accounts Preferences pane or Workgroup Manager, you can use dscl to create, modify, and delete groups in the Local Default node. If you need to script the creation of groups, using dscl ensures that each time the script is run, the newly created group gets a unique GeneratedUID. The following example uses the create command of dscl to create a new group. This command sets up a new GeneratedUID for the group, but not much else:

```
bash-3.2# dscl . create /Groups/newgroup1
bash-3.2# dscl . read /Groups/newgroup1
AppleMetaNodeLocation: /Local/Default
GeneratedUID: B37BDB51-DBCA-46A3-AF2E-456528324722
RecordName: newgroup1
RecordType: dsRecTypeStandard:Groups
```

Remember that the append command of dscl appends a value to an existing attribute or sets an initial value if the attribute does not yet have one. To set the password as an asterisk, you must protect the shell from the asterisk, otherwise the shell will interpret the asterisk as the list of all the files in the current directory. Here's how you could use append to modify and review a local group record:

```
bash-3.2# dscl . append /Groups/newgroup1 GroupMembership cadmin
bash-3.2# dscl . append /Groups/newgroup1 Password "*"
```

```
bash-3.2# dscl . append /Groups/newgroup1 PrimaryGroupID 200
bash-3.2# dscl . append /Groups/newgroup1 RealName "New Group Number One"
bash-3.2# dscl . read /Groups/newgroup1
AppleMetaNodeLocation: /Local/Default
GeneratedUID: B37BDB51-DBCA-46A3-AF2E-456528324722
GroupMembership: cadmin
Password: *
PrimaryGroupID: 200
RealName:
 New Group Number One
RecordName: newgroup1
RecordType: dsRecTypeStandard:Groups
```

To remove a user from a group with `dscl`, use the `delete` command:

```
bash-3.2# dscl . delete /Groups/newgroup1 GroupMembership cadmin
```

Creating and Editing Local Groups with dseditgroup

Unlike `dscl`, which takes several steps to create a group and populate all the necessary attributes (at least `RecordName`, `PrimaryGroupID`, and `GroupMembership`), the `dseditgroup` tool provides a streamlined command-line interface for creating and editing group records. In fact, when using the command-line interface, all group edits are best done by using `dseditgroup` over any other tool, regardless if the groups are local or network based.

The synopsis is:

```
dseditgroup [options] [parameters] groupname
```

Combining several parameters lets you create a group and define several attributes with one command. The `man` page for `dseditgroup` lists a variety of options, including:

► `-o`—Operation

► `-p`—Prompt for authentication password

► `-q`—Disables interactive verification

► `-v`—Verbose logging to `stdout`

The available operations for the `-o` option are:

- ► read
- ► create
- ► delete
- ► edit
- ► checkmember

The available parameters are:

- ► `-m member`—User name for `checkmember` option
- ► `-n nodename`—Directory node location of group record
- ► `-u username`—Authenticate with administrator user name
- ► `-P password`—Authentication password
- ► `-a recordname`—Name of the record to add
- ► `-d recordname`—Name of the record to delete
- ► `-t recordtype`—Type of the record to add or delete
- ► `-i gid`—GID to add or replace
- ► `-g guid`—GUID to add or replace
- ► `-S sid`—SID to add or replace
- ► `-r realname`—Realname to add or replace
- ► `-k keyword`—Keyword to add
- ► `-c comment`—Comment to add or replace
- ► `-s timetolive`—Seconds to live to add or replace
- ► `-f n | l`—Change the group's format; n for the new group format and l for the legacy group format

If you do not provide any options, the default operation is to read; the default node is the /Search node; and the default user is the currently logged-in user. Therefore, `dseditgroup newgroup1` reads the first record found in the /Search node, with the credentials of the currently logged-in user.

NOTE ▶ For operations such as create, edit, and delete, the default node is /Local/default, also written as the period character.

The following example creates a group using dseditgroup. You need to provide an administrator's user name, and then authenticate with the password when prompted:

```
client17:~ cadmin$ dseditgroup -o create -u cadmin newgroup2
Please enter user password: [hidden]
```

Both dscl and the create operation of dseditgroup create a GeneratedUID. However, the dseditgroup create operation also creates a PrimaryGroupID. In the next example, you can see the PrimaryGroupID of 500, which was not specified when the group was created:

```
client17:~ cadmin$ dscl . read /Groups/newgroup2
AppleMetaNodeLocation: /Local/Default
GeneratedUID: B5621F0A-7E38-43B4-A4BF-C0A4402660A7
PrimaryGroupID: 500
RecordName: newgroup2
RecordType: dsRecTypeStandard:Groups
```

If you give no options to dseditgroup, it will read the record of the specified group. As you can see, the output of dseditgroup is more verbose than it is for dscl:

```
client17:~ cadmin$ dseditgroup newgroup2
Recordname <newgroup2>
5 attribute(s) found
Attribute[1] is <dsAttrTypeStandard:RecordType>
    Value[1] is <dsRecTypeStandard:Groups>
Attribute[2] is <dsAttrTypeStandard:RecordName>
    Value[1] is <newgroup2>
Attribute[3] is <dsAttrTypeStandard:GeneratedUID>
    Value[1] is <B5621F0A-7E38-43B4-A4BF-C0A4402660A7>
Attribute[4] is <dsAttrTypeStandard:PrimaryGroupID>
    Value[1] is <500>
Attribute[5] is <dsAttrTypeStandard:AppleMetaNodeLocation>
    Value[1] is </Local/Default>
```

With UNIX tools, no news is usually good news: The absence of an error message usually means there was no error. That's not always the case with dseditgroup, however. Look carefully at the error in the following example. Rather than the -o create option, the command contains the deliberate typo o create (without the dash character); there is no error message, but the command failed, as confirmed by a search with dscl:

```
client17:~ cadmin$ dseditgroup o create –u cadmin newgroup3
client17:~ cadmin$ dscl /Search read /Groups/newgroup3
<dscl_cmd> DS Error: -14136 (eDSRecordNotFound)
```

When you use dseditgroup to add a user as a member of a group, dseditgroup adds the user's short name to the GroupMembership attribute, and it also adds the user's GUID to the group's GroupMembers attribute. The following example adds the user imp1 to the group newgroup2. The group was created earlier and had no members. Notice that both GroupMembers and GroupMembership appear for the first time, and each has a value from the imp1 user record:

```
client17:~ cadmin$ dseditgroup -o edit -u cadmin -a imp1 -t user newgroup2
client17:~ cadmin$ dscl . read /Groups/newgroup2
AppleMetaNodeLocation: /Local/Default
GeneratedUID: B5621F0A-7E38-43B4-A4BF-C0A4402660A7
GroupMembers: 2151240B-09E9-47F0-8F4D-C4007C6C391F
GroupMembership: imp1
PrimaryGroupID: 500
RecordName: newgroup2
RecordType: dsRecTypeStandard:Groups
```

Use -t group instead of -t user to add a group to a group—for example, to add the group newgroup1 as a member of the group newgroup2. Note the addition of the previously empty attribute NestedGroups. The GeneratedUID listed is the GeneratedUID of newgroup1:

```
client17:~ cadmin$ dseditgroup -o edit -u admin -a newgroup1 -t group newgroup2
Please enter user password: [hidden]
client17:~ cadmin$ dseditgroup -o edit -u admin -a newgroup1 -t group newgroup2
client17:~ cadmin$ dscl . read /Groups/newgroup2
AppleMetaNodeLocation: /Local/Default
```

```
GeneratedUID: B5621F0A-7E38-43B4-A4BF-C0A4402660A7
GroupMembers: 2151240B-09E9-47F0-8F4D-C4007C6C391F
GroupMembership: imp1
NestedGroups: B37BDB51-DBCA-46A3-AF2E-456528324722
PrimaryGroupID: 500
RecordName: newgroup2
RecordType: dsRecTypeStandard:Groups
```

You can use the checkmember operation to verify that a user is a member of a group. The previous examples made user imp1 a member of the newgroup2 group, and the two commands below confirm this fact:

```
client17:~ cadmin$ dseditgroup -o checkmember -m imp1 newgroup1
no imp1 is NOT a member of newgroup1
client17:~ cadmin$ dseditgroup -o checkmember -m imp1 newgroup2
yes imp1 is a member of newgroup2
```

You can also use the dsimport command to import groups from a file. If you use the -T xDSStandardGroup option, your delimited import file should contain the following fields in order:

1. RecordName
2. Password
3. PrimaryGroupID
4. GroupMembership

(See the section on using dsimport, earlier in this chapter, for more details.)

Creating and Editing Local Groups with a Text Editor

Tools such as Workgroup Manager, dscl, and dseditgroup use calls to DirectoryService as a mediator for working with groups. However, you cannot circumvent DirectoryService by directly creating, removing, or editing files that contain records.

You can edit group records with a text editor. Each group in the Local Default node has an XML file to define it, and these files are located in /var/db/dslocal/nodes/Default/groups. Group records for the /BSD/local node are located in the flat file /etc/groups.

> **NOTE ▶** Mac OS X allows a user to be a member of any group in any node. A user may be a member of a group that is defined in the BSD Local node and a member of a group that is defined in the Local Default node. If both groups have the same gid, the first group found in the search path is the effective group.

Troubleshooting Directory Services

Earlier you reviewed some concepts behind directory services, then learned how to use various graphical and command-line tools to create and edit local users and groups in local nodes. Now you will learn some tools and techniques for troubleshooting directory services issues that can crop up when applications and the operating system make calls to DirectoryService to identify and authenticate users.

Using Logs

The Console application is a great log viewer; it also has a log browser to help you locate the appropriate log file. If you are familiar with a few common log locations, however, you can more easily troubleshoot directory issues. The /var/log/system.log is a good start, but you can also turn on additional DirectoryService logging from the command line.

There are two types of DirectoryService logging: debug logging and API logging.

DirectoryService debug logging provides an extremely detailed view of directory services activity. It includes information about which application is performing a request as well as the specific data contained in the request, or the question being asked. The log also contains data about the operations performed to service the request, such as the DirectoryService plug-in that is used for a given search (a single request might generate several searches based on the request type and directory services search path), the number of records found by a given search, and the result code of a search. The result code is a numeric value that represents a specific DirectoryService error (or lack of error). This is documented in the DirectoryService man page, and you can also use the command-line tool dserr as a shortcut for looking up DirectoryService error codes. Debug logging is written to /Library/Logs/DirectoryService/DirectoryService.debug.log.

DirectoryService API logging is less detailed and provides a summary view of transactions. These log entries include the client (requester) name, the request type (in the form of a DirectoryService function name), the DirectoryService plug-in that is used to perform that request, the result code (again in the form of a DirectoryService error code), and the time duration that was required to service the request. The timing information may be useful for performance troubleshooting, but the lack of details about the associated request in the API log means that you may need to cross-reference between the debug log and the API log to make sense of all the data. API logging is written to /var/log/system.log.

Sending the USR1 signal to DirectoryService toggles debug logging and sends log messages to /Library/Logs/DirectoryService/DirectoryService.debug.log. Use the following commands to send the signal:

```
sudo killall -USR1 DirectoryService
```

If you are troubleshooting issues at startup, create the file /Library/Preferences/ DirectoryService/.DSLogDebugAtStart, which forces debug logging at startup and sends log messages to /Library/Logs/DirectoryService/DirectoryService.debug.log.

Sending the USR2 signal to DirectoryService toggles API logging and sends log messages to /var/log/system.log. This API logging from USR2 is turned off automatically after 5 minutes. Here's how to send the signal:

```
sudo killall -USR2 DirectoryService
```

These logs are quite verbose. Unless you know the difference between routine and abnormal messages, the extra logging messages might not be useful to you. One strategy is to compare the log messages for a known-good login with log messages for a problematic login, perhaps viewing the logs with tail -f over an ssh connection.

> **TIP** ▸ You can change the Debug Logging Priority Level in /Library/Preferences/ DirectoryService/DirectoryServiceDebug.plist. See the syslog man page for priority levels.

Using dserr

As you examine the DirectoryService logs, you may see various error message numbers like -14138. When you see a mysterious error code like this, you can use the dserr command to get information about what the error signifies. The dserr command translates this numerical error into a slightly more informative text message:

```
client17:~ cadmin$ dserr 14120
-14120: eDSPermissionError
```

"eDSPermissionError" doesn't tell you why the error occurred, but it is a little more helpful than a number.

Resolving User Name Collision with Two Directories

A common dilemma is to have more than one user record with the same record name in various directories. Under normal circumstances, the first user record that DirectoryService finds in the authentication search path is the record that it uses for authentication; Open Directory will attempt authentication only against the first user that it finds in the authentication search path. The default authentication search path is /Local/Default then /BSD/local.

For example, suppose that you have two users named user1: one in the Local Default node with the password localpw, and one in the BSD Local node with the password bsdpw. You could use the dirt command twice: first with the password for user1 in the Local Default node, then with the password for user1 in the BSD Local node. In both examples below, dirt shows that there are two user records in the authentication search path that match the user name (returned count = 2) and that there are no errors (eDSNoErr: (0)).

> NOTE ▶ In this example, the "Use User and Group records in BSD Local node" is enabled in Directory Utility.

In this first example (with the correct password for user1 in the Local Default node), checkpw is successful and authentication against the Local Default node succeeds, but authentication against the BSD Local node fails as expected:

```
client17:~ cadmin$ dirt -u user1 -p localpw -u
Call to dsGetRecordList returned count = 2 with Status : eDSNoErr : (0)
Call to checkpw(): Success
path: /Local/Default
Username: user1
Password: localpw
Success
path: /BSD/local
Username: user1
Password: localpw
Error : eDSAuthFailed : (-14090)
```

In this second example, with the correct password for user1 in the BSD Local node, checkpw fails (checkpw never works with the BSD Local node) and authentication against the Local Default user record fails, but authentication against the BSD Local user record succeeds:

```
client17:~ cadmin$ dirt -u user1 -p bsdpw
Call to dsGetRecordList returned count = 2 with Status : eDSNoErr : (0)
Call to checkpw(): Bad Password
path: /Local/Default
Username: user1
Password: bsdpw
Error : eDSAuthFailed : (-14090)
path: /BSD/local
Username: user1
Password: bsdpw
Success
```

If you were to attempt to log in at the login window with the password for the BSD Local user record (bsdpw), the login would fail, because the Local Default node comes before the BSD Local node in the authentication search path. The only way to log in as user1 with the BSD Local password in this case would be to delete the user1 account from the Local Default node.

> **TIP** ▶ The login window does not display users in the BSD Local node. See the section "Logging in with >console" to log in as a user from the BSD Local node.

Logging in with >console

When troubleshooting login issues, you may want to skip the process of setting up the user's graphical environment. It is possible to log in with a text-based interface rather than the graphical window. If the login window displays the name and password fields, you can enter >console in the user name field and press Return, and the login window will be replaced by a black screen. You may need to press the Return key again to get the login: prompt. If the login is not successful, you may briefly see some error messages, but then the graphical window will reappear.

TIP ▶ If the login window displays a list of users, you can press any arrow key, then press Option-Return. If the user Other is listed, you can select it to get login window to display the user name and password fields, then type >console in the user name field.

Logging in as the System Administrator

In Mac OS X, the System Administrator, or root user, does not have a defined password. You can use the dsenableroot command to set a password for the System Administrator account, and you can also use it to disable the account.

NOTE ▶ It is a best practice to not use the root account to log in at the login window, because the root account has access to all files, and you could inadvertently make changes that adversely impact the system.

What You've Learned

▶ The term *directory services* refers to collections of processes, protocols, and data stores that provide a method for requesting data and receiving that data in a scalable, centralized, and distributable manner.

▶ Open Directory is Apple's architecture for directory services on Mac OS X and Mac OS X Server. Open Directory uses a plug-in architecture to access various directory nodes.

▶ DirectoryService is the Open Directory process that handles requests from directory services.

▶ Programs and processes that use API calls to Open Directory do not need to make any assumptions or have any knowledge about the data structure of the directories they are accessing.

▶ Programs and processes that circumvent Open Directory to edit or access directory information are not supported and may result in instability or stale information.

▶ DirectoryService does not normally run in single-user mode, but it is possible to use a text editor to create, modify, and delete user and group records.

▶ There are two ways of referring to attributes: `dsAttrTypeStandard` and `dsAttrTypeNative`. Some attributes may have the same name for both, similar names, or completely different names.

▶ The main local directory is the Local Default, or /Local/Default, node. Records are stored as XML text files in `/var/db/dslocal/nodes/Default/`.

▶ You can use the command-line tools `dscl`, `dsimport`, and `dseditgroup` to create, edit, and troubleshoot user and group records.

▶ You can use `su` and `dirt` to test user authentication.

▶ Workgroup Manager is a directory editor for creating and editing user and group records in any node, including the Local Default node, where it has limited functionality, but its Inspector is useful for examining records and their attributes.

▶ BSD user, group, and DNS records are stored in legacy flat files. The BSD Local node (/BSD/local) is always active and in the search path, but `DirectoryService` ignores BSD users and groups by default.

▶ The search path always includes /Local/Default and /BSD/local, in that order. These two nodes cannot be disabled or rearranged in the search path.

▶ Entries added to /etc/hosts are immediately available to tools that use standard APIs for DNS information.

▶ Various logging options are available to gather information for troubleshooting. The logging can be quite verbose.

References

Documentation

▶ Mac OS X Server User Management for Version 10.5 Leopard
http://images.apple.com/server/macosx/docs/User_Management_v10.5.mnl.pdf

▶ Mac OS X Server Open Directory Administration for Version 10.5 Leopard, Second Edition
http://images.apple.com/server/macosx/docs/Open_Directory_Admin_v10.5.pdf

▶ Mac OS X Server Command-Line Administration for Version 10.5 Leopard
http://images.apple.com/server/macosx/docs/Command_Line_Admin_v10.5.pdf

Developer Notes

▶ Directory Services for Mac OS X Server v10.5 Release Notes
http://developer.apple.com/releasenotes/MacOSXServer/RN-DirectoryServices/

▶ Mac OS X Manual Page for DirectoryServiceAttributes
http://developer.apple.com/documentation/Darwin/Reference/ManPages/man7/
DirectoryServiceAttributes.7.html

Review Quiz

1. What are the two local directory nodes in Mac OS X, and where are the files that store the underlying user and group records for these nodes?

2. Is the password for the first user created in Mac OS X stored in the user's record?

3. What's the difference between a group's `dsAttrTypeNative:GroupMembership` and `dsAttrTypeNative:GroupMember` attributes?

4. Which command should you use to edit users in the BSD Local node?

5. Why might you want to remove the file `.DSLogDebugAtStart` from /Library/Preferences/ DirectoryService after you are done troubleshooting?

6. Why shouldn't you directly edit a user record in /var/db/dslocal/nodes/Default/users with a text editor?

7. What's the difference between creating a group with `dscl` and creating a group with `dseditgroup -o create newgroup`?

Answers

1. The Local Default and the BSD Local nodes are the default nodes. The Local Default files are XML text files stored in `/var/db/dslocal/nodes/Default/users` and `/var/db/ dslocal/nodes/Default/groups`. The BSD Local files are `/etc/passwd`, `/etc/master.passwd`, and `/etc/group`.

2. No, the password is stored in a secure file that is readable with root credentials only. This shadow hash is in /var/db/shadow/hash, with the user's 128 bit GeneratedUID as the filename.

3. `GroupMembership` can contain a list of short names of users in the group. `GroupMembers` can contain the GeneratedUID of each user in the group.

4. You should use `vipw` to edit users in the BSD Local node.

5. /Library/Preferences/DirectoryService/.DSLogDebugAtStart will constantly log messages, taking up space on the local hard drive and backup media.

6. Open Directory doesn't know about changes to Local Default directory data if you edit the underlying data directly.

7. Both assign a GeneratedUID for the group, but `dseditgroup -o create newgroup` assigns a PrimaryGroupID to the new group. You can use additional options with `dseditgroup` to populate various attributes for the group.

2

Time This chapter takes approximately 3 hours to complete.

Goals Configure a Mac OS X computer to bind to an Open Directory server
Configure directory service search paths
Troubleshoot binding issues
Troubleshoot login issues

Chapter 2

Accessing an Open Directory Server

In Chapter 1 you examined users and groups in the two local directory nodes. Although the local directory is certainly fascinating on its own, you may be more productive if you take advantage of Mac OS X's ability to use directory services to access network user accounts and network home folders.

This chapter examines the process of binding Mac OS X to Mac OS X Server to gain access to the identification and authentication services offered by an Open Directory server. You'll investigate how a search path defines which nodes to use when searching for various records in the available directory nodes, and learn troubleshooting techniques for problems with binding Mac OS X to an Open Directory server, as well as for problems with logging in with a network user account.

Configuring Open Directory Clients

To *bind* is to set up a connection between a computer and a directory domain for the purpose of getting identification, authorization, and other administrative data. A computer can be bound to more than one directory domain at the same time. This chapter focuses on binding Mac OS X to a directory domain hosted by an Open Directory server (an Open Directory master or an Open Directory replica) running on Mac OS X Server, in order to allow a network user to log in on that bound computer and use such network services as managed preferences and network home folder storage.

An Open Directory server hosted by Mac OS X Server offers three key services to client computers that are bound to it:

▶   *LDAP* provides identification services for key records like users and groups, and also records containing configuration information.

▶   *Kerberos* provides authentication services for users and also for computers.

> **MORE INFO** ▶ For more information for Kerberos, go to the "Troubleshooting Login Issues" section in this chapter.

▶   *Password Server* provides user authentication services for services that are not compatible with Kerberos.

Using Directory Utility to Bind to an Open Directory Master

On other operating systems, it may be quite a chore to set up all the configuration files necessary to use an LDAP server, a Kerberos Key Distribution Center (KDC), and a Password Server. However, binding Mac OS X to an Open Directory server hosted by Mac OS X Server is simple: Use Directory Utility on Mac OS X to specify the name or IP address of the Open Directory server. Directory Utility then automatically performs all the necessary configuration to get full use of the three key services offered by an Open Directory server.

> **NOTE** ▶ The following instructions assume the Open Directory server is running in an Advanced configuration. If the Open Directory server is in a Standard or Workgroup configuration, it will advertise its directory services via Bonjour, and you have to supply only a network user's name and password.

1   Open Directory Utility in /Applications/Utilities.

2   Click the lock in the lower-left corner and authenticate as an administrator.

3   Click the Add button (+) in the lower-left corner.

4   In the "Server Name or IP Address" field, type the server name or IP address of the Mac OS X Server that hosts the Open Directory server. Do not click the checkbox labeled "Encrypt using SSL" unless the Open Directory server has been set up to allow SSL and your client has been configured to trust the certificate used by your Open Directory server, or you will be unable to communicate with the LDAP service. This is covered in Chapter 5, in the section "Managing Data Stored in an Open Directory Master."

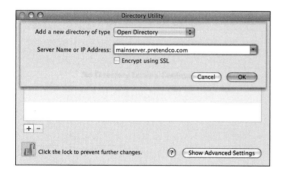

5   Click OK.

Confirming Mac OS X Is Bound to an Open Directory Server

One method for confirming that you are correctly bound to an Open Directory master is to try to log in as a network user. However, this involves logging out, and if something goes wrong and the login doesn't work, you have to log back in as a local administrator to troubleshoot and resolve the issue.

Instead, you can use Directory Utility to quickly confirm that you are bound to an Open Directory master. The main Directory Utility window shows the status, but this status indicates only the reachability of the server; it does not indicate if the server is in your authentication search path. For example, here mainserver.pretendco.com is listed as an Open Directory server; the status indicator is green; and the text on the right indicates that the server is responding normally:

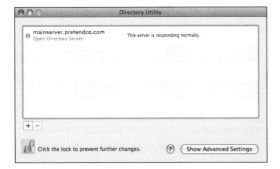

The server name appears exactly as you enter it in Directory Utility's "Server Name or IP Address" field when performing the initial bind. For example, if you specified 10.1.0.1 rather than mainserver.pretendco.com, the Directory Utility would list the status of 10.1.0.1.

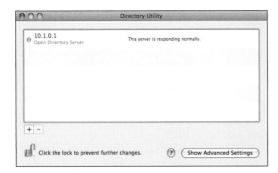

Similarly, you could specify mainserver.local and Directory Utility would display the status of mainserver.local.

Follow these steps to make sure that the new Open Directory server has been automatically added to your Authentication search path:

1   In Directory Utility, click Show Advanced Settings to reveal the toolbar, if necessary.

2   Click Search Policy.

3   Click Authentication.

4   Confirm that /LDAPv3/mainserver.pretendco.com is listed in the list of directory domains.

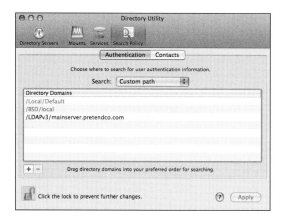

Using id to Confirm Binding

Finally, from the command line you can use the `id` command to confirm that your client computer is bound as well as to identify a network user using directory services. In the following example, `diradmin` is a known network user record, and the `-u` option specifies to return only the user's user ID, which simplifies the output. The user ID is returned, indicating a successful search:

```
client17:~ cadmin$ id -u diradmin
1000
```

If the `id` command returned `id: diradmin: no such user`, even though you know that user account is defined in the Open Directory shared domain, this would indicate that you have a problem with your bind to the Open Directory server; see the "Troubleshooting Binding Issues" section later in this chapter.

Setting Up Trusted Binding with an Open Directory Master

With a default bind to an Open Directory server, such as you created earlier, Mac OS X's communication with the services of the Open Directory server generates a mix of unencrypted and encrypted network traffic:

▶   All LDAP traffic between Mac OS and the Open Directory server is sent in clear text, potentially allowing snoopers with access to your physical network to inspect your LDAP requests and the replies from the Open Directory server. Note that by default all of the data in your Open Directory server's LDAP database is anonymously viewable, so there is no additional information exposed by the unencrypted traffic.

▶   Kerberos authentication traffic is never exposed in clear text.

▶   The Password Server does not authenticate clear text traffic by default, but you can enable an authentication method with the command line at the server.

Additionally, by default, Mac OS X does not ensure that an LDAP server that it uses is not an imposter. A mischief-maker, using a man-in-the-middle attack or otherwise tampering with the network, could set up a rogue computer to provide bogus replies to LDAP requests, including requests for configuration information. Fortunately, it is much more difficult for a Kerberos or Password Server to be impersonated, and service authentication is built into the associated protocols for Kerberos and the Password Server. Authenticated directory binding, often referred to as *Trusted Binding*, helps alleviate the problem of not knowing whether to trust the LDAP services of an Open Directory server.

Trusted Binding is a mutually authenticated connection between a computer and a directory domain. Trusted Binding requires Mac OS X v10.4 or later, and it is not compatible with the insecure practice of using DHCP to supply the LDAP server. In the Directory Utility application, Click the Bind button to set up Trusted Binding. Clicking the Unbind button removes the trusted bind.

> **NOTE** ▶ The Bind and Unbind buttons refer to Trusted Binding, not regular binding to a directory. Sometimes the word *bind* refers to a trusted bind.

Using Directory Utility to Set Up Trusted Binding

Follow these steps to configure Mac OS X to bind to an Open Directory server with Trusted Binding:

1   Open Directory Utility and authenticate if necessary.

> **NOTE** ▶ The Directory Utility application asks for directory administrator credentials for some operations even though network account credentials may suffice.

2   Click Show Advanced Settings if necessary.

3   Click Services.

4   In the list of services, select LDAPv3 and click the Edit button ✎.

5   Select the server configuration for the Open Directory server.

6   Click Edit.

If the Bind button does not appear, the Open Directory server does not support
Trusted Binding and you cannot complete the exercise. For now just read along with
the exercises until the next section, "Configuring Directory Services Search Paths." You
will learn how to configure an Open Directory server to enable and disable Trusted
Binding in Chapter 5.

7   Click the Bind button, then do the following:

▶   Enter the Computer ID from the Bonjour name. If the Computer ID is not what
you would like it to be, you can change it here. To keep the Bonjour name consistent
with the Computer ID that will be stored in the directory, click Cancel, change it with
the Network preference pane, and then click Bind again. The Computer ID must not
be in use by another computer for Trusted Binding or other network services. If you
see an alert saying that a computer record exists, click Cancel to go back and change
the computer name, or click Overwrite to replace the existing computer record.
The existing computer record might be abandoned, or it might belong to another
computer. If you overwrite an existing computer record, notify the LDAP directory
administrator in case replacing the record disables another computer.

▶   Enter the name and password of a network user or a directory administrator
from the Open Directory shared domain. Some documentation may state that a
directory administrator is required, but by default an Open Directory network user
has the ability to create a computer record in the shared domain, which is required
behind the scenes to set up Trusted Binding.

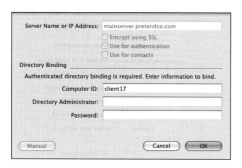

NOTE ▶ The Open Directory administrator guide notes that your Computer ID should not contain a hyphen.

8   Click OK.

9   Click OK or Apply in any Directory Utility window.

10 Quit Directory Utility.

NOTE ▶ The Directory Utility may indicate that "Authenticated directory binding is required." This may or may not be true; directory binding may be optional. If authenticated directory binding is required, when you click OK but do not provide authentication information, Directory Utility does not proceed and returns your cursor to the User Name field.

After you set up Trusted Binding, all Open Directory traffic should be encrypted between the trusted client and the Open Directory server. The process of setting up Trusted Binding creates a computer record in the Open Directory server's LDAP directory, and Open Directory uses that computer record to set up Kerberos on the trusted client. Kerberos is then used to set up a shared key (shared secret) that encrypts packets used for communications with the Open Directory server.

NOTE ▶ Do not use Trusted Binding with Mac OS X computers that were imaged from the same disk image. In early versions of Mac OS X v10.5 and Mac OS X Server v10.5, setting up Trusted Binding created three computer account records in the Open Directory server's LDAP database, based on the following: the Computer ID, the computer's hostname, and the Local KDC (LKDC). If you image multiple computers from the same disk image, the imaged computers will have the same LKDC name. When multiple computers try to create the same computer account record based on the duplicate LKDC name, this may cause problems. See *Mac OS X 10.5: Duplicate Computer Name Alert When Binding to Open Directory* (http://support.apple.com/kb/TS1245) for a solution.

Illustrating Clear Text Network Traffic

To better understand clear text network traffic for directory services queries and responses, you need to examine the difference between using LDAP requests through

Open Directory and querying the LDAP server directly. To do so, you'll use the `ldapsearch` command, which opens a connection to an LDAP server, binds the client computer to this server, and performs an LDAP search.

An LDAP directory is a very structured and hierarchical database. The `ldapsearch` tool provides functions that are relevant to hierarchical data, such as limiting the scope of a search to a particular branch of the directory tree. `ldapsearch` also provides access to standard database facilities for selecting records by name, attributes, or attribute values. When you use `ldapsearch`, it represents the bulk of the search logic in an LDAP search filter. The search filter is composed of one or more expressions that contain any of a wide variety of operators (such as = for equality or ! for negation) that are useful for searching text and numeric data.

You specify what you want to search for and which attributes you want returned in the results. See the `man` page for `ldapsearch` for more details, but the syntax is as follows:

```
ldapsearch [options] filter [attributes]
```

Some of the more common options are:

▶ `-LLL`—Displays search results in a simple version of LDAP Data Interchange Format (LDIF)

▶ `-x`—Binds with a simple authentication instead of SASL (Simple Authentication and Security Layer)

▶ `-h`—The LDAP server host

▶ `-b`—The LDAP search base, or where in the LDAP tree to start searching

▶ `-s`—The scope of the search; options are `base`, `one`, `sub`, or `children`

NOTE ▶ The `sub` scope searches at the level of the search base and all child objects below it. The default scope is `sub`.

The LDAP search filter defines what to search for. The pipe symbol (|) is used for a logical OR, and the ampersand (&) is used for a logical AND. Case is ignored. Often a search base specifies to search for strings in attribute values. Here are some search filters:

▶ `"(objectClass=*)"`—This returns any record with any value in its `objectClass` attribute. This is the default if no search filter is provided; it typically returns many records.

▶ `"(uidNumber=1025)"`—This returns any record with the `uidNumber` of 1025.

▶ `"(uid=is*)"`—This returns any record with a `uid` that starts with the characters "is". For example, Isadora and Istvan would be returned, but Chris and Christine would not.

▶ `"(|(uid=*son)(uid=*sen))"`—This returns any record with a `uid` that ends with the characters "son" *or* "sen". This would match both Hansen and Hanson.

▶ `"(&(uid=d*)(postalCode=*))"`—This returns any record that has both a `uid` that starts with the character "d" *and* has a `postalCode` that is not empty. It will not match a record that does not satisfy both requirements.

▶ `"(modifyTimeStamp>=20080322012311Z)"`—This returns any record with a `modifyTimeStamp` attribute that contains a timestamp greater than or equal to the timestamp stored in the attribute.

The last part of the `ldapsearch` command specifies the attributes that `ldapsearch` must return, and it is optional. If no attributes are specified, all of the record's attributes that relate to users are returned. With `ldapsearch`, you must specify Native rather than Standard. For example, Open Directory uses the Standard `NFSHomeDirectory` attribute, but LDAP stores the attribute with the name `homeDirectory`, so an `ldapsearch` query for `NFSHomeDirectory` will not return any matches.

If any objects are found, `ldapsearch` returns the `dn` (distinguished name, a unique identifier for an object in an LDAP tree) for each object that matches the search filter, followed by the object's requested attributes and their values. `ldapsearch` will not display an error if you request it to return an attribute that is not populated with data.

The following `ldapsearch` command requests a search for a user record that has a short name of `sally`. The command also requests to show the attributes `loginshell`, `uidNumber`, and `homeDirectory` of any found object. The result contains the `dn` of the object, then the requested attributes and their values:

```
client17:~ cadmin$ ldapsearch -LLL -x -h mainserver.pretendco.com -b cn=users,dc=main
server,dc=pretendco,dc=com "(uid=sally)" loginShell uidNumber
dn: uid=sally,cn=users,dc=mainserver,dc=pretendco,dc=com
uidNumber: 1025
loginShell: /bin/bash
```

Confirming Open Directory Traffic Is Secured

To illustrate the difference between secure and insecure LDAP traffic, you can use `tcpdump` to capture packets of a query from two different methods. Use `dscl`, which works through Open Directory, to perform some queries, and then use `ldapsearch`, which does not work through Open Directory, to perform some queries; `ldapsearch` queries the LDAP service directly without intervention from Open Directory. If authenticated directory binding is set up, searches initiated by Open Directory (the test queries via `dscl`) will have packets of traffic that have encrypted contents. Searches that do not go through Open Directory (the test queries via `ldapsearch`) will have packets with clear text contents.

The example below uses a query for the `macosxodconfig` record in the `config` portion of the Open Directory server's LDAP directory, because the record contains a large amount of text and it should be easy to spot when scrolling through the output of `tcpdump`, although any record should have similar results. Each step below has one single line of code to be entered:

1   In your main Terminal window, use `tcpdump` to show packets. `-A` shows each packet in ASCII; `-s0` captures the entire packet rather than the default first portion only; `-ien0` specifies the network interface to use (yours may be different); and the rest of the com-mand specifies to capture packets only with the source of `mainserver.pretendco.com`'s port for LDAP traffic:

```
client17:~ cadmin$ sudo tcpdump -A -s0 -ien0 src mainserver.pretendco.com
and port ldap
```

2   In a second Terminal window, use `ldapsearch` to search for the `macosxodconfig` record. `-x` specifies to use simple authentication, which allows an anonymous bind; `-H ldap://mainserver.pretendco.com` specifies the URI of the LDAP server; `-b cn=config,dc=mainserver,dc=pretendco,dc=com` specifies the search base; and `ou=macosxodconfig` speci-fies the record name to find:

```
client17:~ cadmin$ ldapsearch -x -H ldap://mainserver.pretendco.com -b cn=config,
dc=mainserver,dc=pretendco,dc=com ou=macosxodconfig
```

3   In the Terminal window with `tcpdump` running, scroll back and look for the clear text results. There will be many packets, but you will see the clear text of the `macosxodconfig` record over several of the packets.

4 In the same Terminal window with `tcpdump` running, press Command-K or choose View > Clear Scrollback to clear the results and prepare for the next query.

5 In the second Terminal window, use `dscl` to search for the `macosxodconfig` record:

```
client17:~ cadmin$ dscl /LDAPv3/mainserver.pretendco.com read /Config/macosxodconfig
```

6 In the first Terminal window with `tcpdump` running, scroll back and look for the clear text results. If authenticated directory binding is correctly set up, you will not be able to see the text of the `macosxodconfig` record in any of the packets.

7 In the `tcpdump` Terminal window, press Control-C to quit `tcpdump`. Quit Terminal.

Configuring Directory Services Search Paths

After you bind to an Open Directory server, you should confirm that it is in your search path, to ensure that your computer will use that node for identification and authentication services. In the context of directory services, the *search path* is a configurable list of directory nodes that Open Directory must use when searching for a record. Open Directory allows you to query many directories of varying kinds. `DirectoryService` doesn't search all the directories at the same time when looking for a record; it searches one directory at a time, and the search path determines the order in which directories are searched.

The search path is an ordered list of nodes, starting with /Local/Default and followed by /BSD/local. These first two nodes are always in the search path, in that order, and cannot be removed from the search path. Other directory nodes can be added, reordered, and removed from the search path.

> **NOTE ▶** Even though the /BSD/local node cannot be removed from the search path, user and group records from the /BSD/local node are not used by default.

The search path is also referred to as the *authentication search path*, even though Open Directory also uses the authentication search path for record queries that do not involve authentication, such as for mount and configuration records. The second type of search path is the *contacts search path*, which works with specific applications only. The next few sections look at each type in more detail, starting with authentication search paths.

NOTE ▶ In earlier versions of Mac OS X, you had to manually add new nodes to the authentication and contacts search paths; the operating system did not add them automatically. Mac OS X v10.4 introduced automatic addition of nodes to the authentication search path, and this behavior is brought forward in Mac OS X v10.5.

Understanding the Authentication Search Path

When Open Directory is used for authentication, authentication is tested only against the first record that Open Directory finds. In this context, once DirectoryService finds a match in one node, the search is complete and DirectoryService does not consult the next node in the search path. If DirectoryService does not find a match in the first node, it performs a search in the second node, then the next, and so on, until it either finds a match or exhausts all the nodes in the search path.

When DirectoryService finds a matching record for authentication, if the user does not authenticate correctly against that record, DirectoryService will not move on to another node and allow another attempt at authentication. This ensures that local users always take precedence over network users.

For other record queries that do not involve authentication, however, Open Directory may gather the results of all the directory nodes in the authentication search path. For example, all the mount records for automount in the search path will be used, not just the first mount record that Open Directory finds.

Understanding the Contacts Search Path

The contacts search path is used only by applications that are programmed to use it, such as Address Book, Mail, and Directory.

To use the Address Book to search with the contacts search path:

1 Open /Applications/Address Book.

2 Select Directories in the Group column.

3 Enter a query in the Search field.

In the figure below, Address Book displays a record from the Contacts search path that matches the text entered into the search field.

Although you can use the Address Book Preferences to manually specify an LDAP server to use, the Directories entry in the Group column of Address Book uses the contacts search path. Address Book will not show any entries in this category until you type characters in the search field.

Configuring Search Paths with Directory Utility

You can also configure search paths with Directory Utility. To do so, click the Search Policy button to gain access to the Authentication and Contacts buttons.

> **NOTE** ▶ The Search Policy button is not revealed in Directory Utility unless Advanced Settings are visible. After you click the Show Advanced Settings button in the lower-right corner of Directory Utility, a toolbar appears with Search Policy as an option.

You can set each search path separately by clicking the appropriate button, and you have a choice of three options for each search path:

▶ Automatic—Include only the LDAP server(s) assigned by the DHCP server. This option is not compatible with Trusted Binding.

▶ Local directory—Use only /Local/Default and /BSD/local.

▶ Custom path—Add, reorder, and remove directory nodes.

Choosing "Custom path" allows the most flexibility.

The following figure illustrates the authentication search path set to use Custom path.

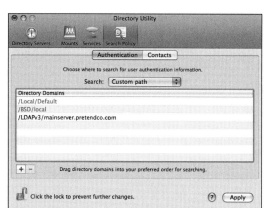

Note that there is an Add (+) button in the lower-left corner; if you press that button, you will see a list of directory nodes to which the computer is bound, but which are not yet in the search path. In this dialog you can add existing nodes only; if you want to define additional nodes, you must return to Services in Directory Utility. In the following figure, two additional directory nodes are defined but not yet added to the search path:

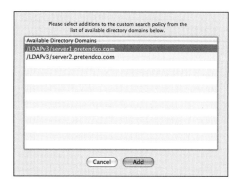

To remove a directory from a search path, use the Remove button (-) in the lower-left corner. If you remove a directory node from a search path, Directory Utility does not unbind from the node; it simply removes the node from the search path. If you remove or unbind from a node (using the Services button in Directory Utility, for example) before removing that node from the search path, the node will appear in red in the search path.

To reconfigure the directory node search order, simply drag and drop—but remember, the first two nodes cannot be removed or reordered. In the following figure, the last entry is about to be moved to the third position:

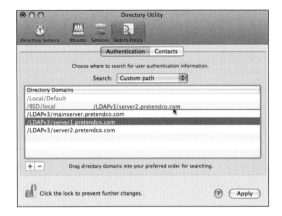

NOTE ▶ If you remove a directory node from your search path, it does not automatically get removed from the list in Services.

Examining and Modifying the Authentication Search Path with dscl

For troubleshooting and scripting, you can use dscl to examine and modify the authentication search path. Table 2.1 lists the three entries that correspond to the Search pop-up menu in the Search Policy section of Directory Utility.

Table 2.1   Search Path Options

Directory Utility Option	Listing in dscl	Notes
Automatic	NSPSearchPath	Network Search Path (DHCP-supplied LDAP servers)
Local directory	LSPSearchPath	Local Search Path (local nodes only)
Custom path	CSPSearchPath	Custom Search Path

The example below uses `dscl localhost read /Search` to inspect the authentication search path: `localhost` is the data source; `read` is the command; and `/Search` is the path. In the results, `DHCPLDAPDefault: off` signifies that the checkbox for "Add DHCP-supplied LDAP servers to automatic search policies" is not enabled in Directory Utility. Note that each of the three options listed in Table 2.1—`NSPSearchPath`, `LSPSearchPath`, and `CSPSearchPath`— are listed below. The `SearchPolicy` specifies to use `CSPSearchPath` (Custom). Finally, the contents of the `CSPSearchPath` are contained in `SearchPath` (`/Local/Default /BSD/local /LDAPv3/mainserver.pretendco.com`):

```
client17:~ cadmin$ dscl localhost read /Search
CSPSearchPath: /Local/Default /BSD/local /LDAPv3/mainserver.pretendco.com
DHCPLDAPDefault: off
LSPSearchPath: /Local/Default /BSD/local
NSPSearchPath: /Local/Default /BSD/local
ReadOnlyNode: ReadOnly
SearchPath: /Local/Default /BSD/local /LDAPv3/mainserver.pretendco.com
SearchPolicy: dsAttrTypeStandard:CSPSearchPath
```

You can use `dscl` to modify the contents of `CSPSearchPath`, but don't attempt to modify `LSPSearchPath` or `NSPSearchPath`, as these are read-only policies. To add a node to the authentication search path, use the `append` command of `dscl` (assuming the node has already been defined but not has not yet been added to the search path). There is no output from the following command; it simply adds the node:

```
client17:~cadmin$ sudo dscl /Search append / CSPSearchPath /LDAPv3/server3.pretendco.com
```

To confirm that the change took place, use `dscl` again. The result is all one line, though it is wrapped:

```
client17:~cadmin$ dscl /Search read / CSPSearchPath
CSPSearchPath: /Local/Default /BSD/local /LDAPv3/mainserver.pretendco.com
/LDAPv3/server3.pretendco.com
```

Troubleshooting Binding Issues

If you encounter problems binding to an Open Directory server, investigate the simplest possible reasons before moving to the more complex:

▶ Use Network Utility or `ping` to confirm that a stable network connection exists to the Mac OS X Server that is the Open Directory server.

▶ Use Network Utility or `host` to ensure that DNS resolution is available.

More complex problems could involve SSL, Access Control Lists, or missing or corrupted configuration files, to name a few. The following sections will help you troubleshoot these sorts of binding issues.

Using DHCP-Supplied LDAP Server to Bind to an Open Directory Master

Mac OS X will automatically connect to DHCP-supplied directory servers and add them to the search path only if Mac OS X is in the postinstall Setup Assistant phase of configuration. This policy facilitates fully automatic out-of-the-box configuration while also minimizing the threat of accidentally trusting a rogue directory service. Be forewarned that it is trivial for a mischief-maker to set up a rogue DHCP server to hand out the address of a rogue LDAP server.

Understanding the Processes and Files Involved with Binding

To set up the configuration files for using LDAP and Kerberos, `DirectoryService` performs a series of LDAP queries for configuration information, gathers the necessary information, and sets up local configuration files, many in /Library/Preferences/DirectoryService.

The first query that Directory Utility performs helps bootstrap the rest of the LDAP queries: `supportedSASLMechanisms`, `namingContexts`, `dnsHostName`, and `krbName`. You can reproduce Directory Utility's first query with the `ldapsearch` command. As you will see in the command output, the results include the search base, which is particularly important because it is required to construct other LDAP queries. You can bind to the LDAP service anonymously, but the results indicate that you could also bind to the LDAP directory using CRAM-MD5 (a challenge-response authentication method used by the Password Server) or GSSAPI (Generic Security Services Application Programming Interface, a generic API for client-server authentication that supports Kerberos). `krbName`, Kerberos name, is a service principal used for Kerberos authentication.

```
client17:~ cadmin$ ldapsearch -LLL -x -h mainserver.pretendco.com -b "" -s base
"(objectclass=*)" supportedSASLMechanisms namingContexts dnsHostName krbName
dn:
namingContexts: dc=mainserver,dc=pretendco,dc=com
supportedSASLMechanisms: CRAM-MD5
supportedSASLMechanisms: GSSAPI
dNSHostName: mainserver.pretendco.com
krbName: ldap/mainserver.pretendco.com@MAINSERVER.PRETENDCO.COM
```

Directory Utility then performs a few other searches to gather information about the object classes supported by the Open Directory server. Specifically, Directory Utility searches for these important records or objects:

▶ `macosxodconfig`—Configuration information about how to map the Open Directory Standard records and attributes to the Native records and attributes stored in the LDAP directory.

▶ `macosxodpolicy`—Policy and security settings, such as No Clear Text Authentication, that you can set with Directory Utility.

▶ `ldapreplicas`—Addresses of the Open Directory master and any Open Directory replicas.

▶ `KerberosClient`—Contains the default realm and the KDC.

Using the information that it gathered from the LDAP queries, `DirectoryService` modifies several files in the directory /Library/Preferences/DirectoryService. Do not edit these files directly with a text editor; that would circumvent Open Directory. Instead, use tools such a Directory Utility or `dscl`, which make Open Directory calls, to edit the contents of the files.

> **NOTE** ▶ You can edit these files directly with a text editor in special circumstances, such as when booted in single-user mode.

Some of the more important files that `DirectoryService` modifies are listed below. Unless otherwise noted, they are in /Library/Preferences/DirectoryService/.

▶ DSLDAPv3PluginConfig.plist—This contains mapping information about how to map Open Directory Standard records and attributes to the Native records and attributes stored in the Open Directory server's LDAP directory; configured security levels; Kerberos service principals to create; and other configuration information.

▶   SearchNodeConfig.plist—This contains a list of the directory nodes currently in the authentication search path. /Local/Default and /BSD/local are not listed here even though they are always in the authentication search path.

▶   ContactsNodeConfig.plist—This contains a list of the directory nodes currently in the contacts search path. /Local/Default and /BSD/local are not listed here even though they are always in the contacts search path.

▶   /Library/Preferences/edu.mit.Kerberos—This is a Kerberos configuration file. It contains information about the default realm and the KDC.

▶   /var/db/dslocal/nodes/Default/config/Kerberos:*REALM*.plist—This is another Kerberos configuration file, where `REALM` is your Kerberos realm.

Information about what happened during the bind is logged to the following log files:

▶   /var/log/system.log

▶   /Library/Logs/SingleSignOnTools.log

After setting up Trusted Binding, many files are also updated or created, but because they are more appropriate for Mac OS X Server than for Mac OS X, they are covered in Chapter 7.

Comparing dscl Data with ldapsearch Data

When you use tools such as `ldapsearch` that do not make `DirectoryService` calls, it is important to know the Native name of the attribute you are searching for, otherwise your search will not return the results you expect.

The following example searches for the text that stores the path to a user's home folder with both `dscl` and `ldapsearch`. `dscl` can use either the Standard or Native attribute, but `ldapsearch` can use only the Native attribute, so you need to know the Native attribute if you use `ldapsearch`. This becomes even more important in Chapter 3, where you integrate Mac OS X with a third-party directory service.

> **NOTE** ▶ The terms *home folder* and *home directory* are used interchangeably; this book refers to *home folder* to distinguish a file system folder from a directory services directory. Application windows and command-line output often use the term *home directory*.

The first command shows NFSHomeDirectory, which is the Standard name of the attribute that Open Directory uses to store the path to the home folder:

```
client17:~ cadmin$ dscl /Search read /Users/diradmin NFSHomeDirectory
NFSHomeDirectory: /Users/diradmin
```

In addition, you can use dscl to search for Native attributes. homeDirectory is the Native attribute name that the LDAP directory uses; NFSHomeDirectory is mapped to homeDirectory:

```
client17:~ cadmin$ dscl /Search read /Users/diradmin homeDirectory
dsAttrTypeNative:homeDirectory: /Users/diradmin
```

The ldapsearch results contain the same general information: /Users/diradmin. However, the output is a little different from the output of dscl; it contains the dn (distinguished name, which uniquely identifies the entry in the LDAP database) of the user, the requested Native attribute name, and the value contained in that attribute.

```
client17:~ cadmin$ ldapsearch -LLL -x -h mainserver.pretendco.com -b
  "cn=users,dc=mainserver,dc=pretendco,dc=com" -s sub "(uid=diradmin)" homeDirectory
dn: uid=diradmin,cn=users,dc=mainserver,dc=pretendco,dc=com
homeDirectory: /Users/diradmin
```

Finally, the following ldapsearch for the Standard attribute, which is not used by or stored in the LDAP directory, does not return a value. Note that the output contains the user dn, and there is no error message.

```
client17:~ cadmin$ ldapsearch -LLL -x -h mainserver.pretendco.com -b
  "cn=users,dc=mainserver,dc=pretendco,dc=com" -s sub "(uid=diradmin)" NFSHomeDirectory
dn: uid=diradmin,cn=users,dc=mainserver,dc=pretendco,dc=com
```

Setting Up Binding at the Command Line

Directory Utility is a great tool to bind Mac OS X to an Open Directory server. However, if you run into problems binding with Directory Utility, you might try the approach of replicating each action that Directory Utility performs, to see if you run into any problems with each step. Once you understand all the steps that Directory Utility takes, you have the added benefit of possessing the knowledge necessary to script the binding process, rather than relying on using the graphical utility.

Here is the general flow of events:

1. Enable the LDAPv3 plug-in.

2. Bind to the Open Directory server.

3. Add the LDAP server to the authentication search path.

4. Join the Kerberos realm.

To bind using the command line follow these steps:

1   Ensure that LDAPv3 is enabled (it should be by default). Use the `defaults` command, which modifies `DirectoryService` configuration settings in XML files, then kill `DirectoryService` and ensure that it notices the new setting.

```
client17:~ cadmin$ sudo defaults write '/Library/Preferences/DirectoryService/
DirectoryService' 'LDAPv3' 'Active'

client17:~ cadmin$ sudo killall DirectoryService
```

2   Use `dsconfigldap` to add the Open Directory master's LDAP service to the list of LDAP servers and perform the bind. The -v option specifies verbose output; the -a option adds a new server.

```
client17:~ cadmin$ sudo dsconfigldap -v -a mainserver.pretendco.com
```

3   Use `dscl` to add the new LDAP server to the authentication search path.

```
client17:~ cadmin$ sudo dscl /Search append / CSPSearchPath /LDAPv3/mainserver.
pretendco.com
```

4   Use `kerberosautoconfig` to set up Mac OS X as a client of the Open Directory server's Kerberos realm. `kerberosautoconfig` uses the `KerberosClient` record, which is stored in the Open Directory server's `cn=Config` portion of the LDAP directory, (this is covered in the section "Managing Data Stored in an Open Directory Master" in Chapter 5). The -f option tells `kerberosautoconfig` to look in the specified Open Directory node for the `KerberosClient` config record. This sets up the Kerberos configuration files /Library/Preferences/edu.mit.Kerberos and /var/db/dslocal/nodes/Default/config/Kerberos:MAINSERVER.PRETENDCO.COM.plist.

```
client17:~ cadmin$ sudo kerberosautoconfig -f /LDAPv3/mainserver.pretendco.com
```

Setting up Trusted Binding from the command line is just a little more involved. The only difference is the syntax of `dsconfigldap` to join with authenticated binding. Following are the options to use:

▶ `-f`—Forces authenticated binding

▶ `-v`—Specifies verbose mode

▶ `-a mainserver.pretendco.com`—Adds the LDAP server

▶ `-n`—Name given to the LDAP server configuration

▶ `-c `hostname -s``—Retrieves the host name of the computer, and then removes the domain information

> **NOTE** ▶ Put the `hostname` command in backticks (`) as shown so that `dsconfigldap` can use the result of the `hostname` command.

▶ `-u diradmin`—Name of a directory administrator

▶ `-p diradminpassword`—Password for the directory administrator specified above

▶ `-l cadmin`—Local administrator

▶ `-q localpassword`—Password for the local administrator specified above

Here is the command:

```
client17:~ cadmin$ sudo dsconfigldap -fv -a mainserver.pretendco.com -n mainserver.
pretendco.com -c `hostname -s` -u diradmin -p diradminpassword -l cadmin -q
localpassword
```

Using dscl to Verify Binding to an Open Directory Master

You can use `dscl` to verify that a computer is bound and the connection is functioning. If you run into a problem at any step along the way, resolve the problem before continuing.

1 In the `dscl` interactive mode, use `ls` to list the plug-ins.

```
client17:~ cadmin$ dscl localhost

 > ls

BSD

LDAPv3
```

```
Local

Search

Contact
```

2 Use `cd` to go into the directory that represents the `LDAPv3` plug-in.

```
> cd LDAPv3
```

3 Use `cd` again to enter the directory that represents the mainserver.pretendco.com LDAPv3 node.

4 Use `ls` to see the kinds of information stored in the shared LDAP directory.

If you do not see the server listed with the following command, perhaps the server has not been added to the authentication path:

```
/LDAPv3 > ls
mainserver.pretendco.com
```

If you are not able to use `cd` with the server's name as in

```
/LDAPv3 > cd mainserver.pretendco.com
```

Possible causes to investigate are:

▶ There is a problem with underlying network connectivity to the server.

▶ The server's LDAP service is not running.

▶ SSL is required but not set up.

▶ Custom Access Control Lists are preventing access.

Once inside the directory representing the LDAP server, use the `list` command of `dscl` to see the types of records that Open Directory makes available from the available LDAP records. In the interest of space, some of the output is deleted in the following example:

```
/LDAPv3/mainserver.pretendco.com > list
AccessControls
Augments
```

```
Automount
AutomountMap
AutoServerSetup
[results deleted]
Printers
Resources
Users
```

If you can `cd` to the directory that represents the server, but do not see a long list of these categories of records that are available, it is possible that:

▶   The record that sets up the automatic mapping of Standard Open Directory records to Native LDAP server records is corrupted or missing (`macosxodconfig`).

▶   The local file where this information is stored is corrupted or missing (DSLDAPv3PlugInConfig.plist in /Library/Preferences/DirectoryService/).

Understanding the Computer Record Created When Establishing Trusted Binding

The process of setting up Trusted Binding creates at least one computer record for your Mac OS X computer in the Open Directory shared domain. Directory services on your client computer use information in this computer record to obtain a Kerberos ticket for LDAP operations. An understanding of the computer record can help you troubleshoot binding problems. Use Workgroup Manager and `dscl` to inspect the computer records in the shared domain.

In the example below, the computer record for this Mac OS X computer is `client17$`. The trailing dollar symbol is a convention to indicate that the record is a *computer* record rather than a *user* record.

1   Open Workgroup Manager, in /Applications/Server/.

2   From the Server menu, select View Directories and dismiss the warning dialog if one appears.

3   Click the Globe icon in the upper-left corner of Workgroup Manager and choose /LDAPv3/mainserver.pretendco.com. If that choice is not available, choose Other, navigate to /LDAPv3/mainserver.pretendco.com, and then click OK to dismiss the directory node selection window.

4 Click the Computer button.

5 Look at the list of computers.

There may be only one computer record for your Mac OS X computer, but if you installed an earlier version of Mac OS X Server and updated it to the currently available version, you may see that there are three computer records created. In the figure below, there are three computer records listed for your Mac OS X computer. The names are based on your Mac OS X computer's hostname (if there are no DNS records available, this record name would be *computername.local$*), your computer name, and your Local KDC. The important computer record is the one based on your computer name, which contains the other names in its Comment attribute. In the figure below, this record is `client17$`.

6 Click the computer record for `client17$`, and note that the names of the other computer records are listed in the Comments field (`client17.pretendco.com$` and the record starting with `LKDC`).

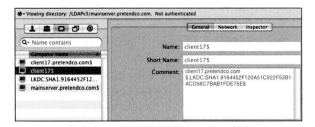

7 Prepare to inspect the attributes of the computer record with the Inspector pane. If you have not already done so, from the Workgroup Manager menu, choose Preferences, enable the option "Show 'All Records' tab and inspector," then click OK to dismiss the Preferences window.

8   Click the Inspector tab.

Because you do not have directory administrator credentials to mainserver's Open Directory shared domain, you cannot resize the columns in the Inspector view.

9   To get a clearer view of the attribute names, click the Options button in the lower-left of the Inspector pane.

10   Configure this window so that the only enabled options are "Show Standard Attributes" and "Show Native Attributes," then click OK.

11   Look at the partial list of attributes and their partial values. Note that the computer record has an `AuthenticationAuthority` attribute with two values. When this computer boots up, it attempts to obtain a Kerberos ticket-granting ticket (TGT) and then a service-granting ticket for the LDAP service. Also note that the computer record has the attribute `apple-ownerguid`, which is the GUID of the user that was used to set up the trusted bind. Only this user, or a directory administrator, can modify the computer record.

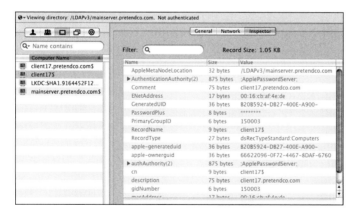

12   To reset Workgroup Manager to display Native attribute prefixes again, click the Options button in the lower-left of the Inspector pane.

13   Configure this window so that all options are enabled except "Show Standard Prefix." Click OK to dismiss the Options window.

14   In a Terminal window, use dscl to get a complete listing of your computer record's attributes and their values. You can use values for the AuthenticationAuthority to help troubleshooting problems authenticating the computer to the Open Directory server, and you can use the value of the apple-ownwerguid to help determine who has the ability to remove the computer record.

```
client17:~ cadmin$ dscl /LDAPv3/mainserver.pretendco.com read /Computers/client17$
```

Troubleshooting Login Issues

Once you have confirmed that your computer is bound to an Open Directory server, you may run into problems logging in with a network user account. Verify that you are able to identify the network user account and authenticate as the network user account. Again, start with the simple and move to the complex. This section walks you through troubleshooting steps to make sure that you can see the user record, obtain Kerberos tickets, and confirm that the home folder is available.

Identifying the Network User Account with Directory Services

Use id or dscl to get a quick confirmation that you can identify the network user account. Use the id command to confirm that DirectoryService sees the network user record. The -u option returns the user ID only, omitting the group information that is not necessarily useful for this quick test:

```
client17:~ cadmin$ id -u sally
1025
```

The following `dscl` command displays the user record and all of its attributes. For the sake of brevity, the command output is not displayed:

```
client17:~ cadmin$ dscl /Search read /Users/sally
```

Verifying Authentication Against the Password Server

You can use the `su` command to verify that you can identify and authenticate as a given user. The `su` command allows you to attempt to substitute the identity of the currently logged-in user for another user identity. The `su` command takes the form of

```
su [-] [-flm] [login [args]]
```

You will use `su` and specify only the `login`, the name of the user to switch to. `su` asks you for the password of user you specify and executes a shell as that user. Do not issue the `su` command with root privileges, because `su` will not request the password, defeating the purpose of using `su` to verify the user's password.

Before you issue the `su` command, be sure that you are in a directory that the user in question has access to be in, otherwise you will get this error:

```
shell-init: erorr retrieving current directory: getcwd: cannot access parent
directories: Permission denied
```

The above message is not a big problem, because you can `cd` to a different directory that the user should have access to, like /Users/Shared.

```
client17:~ cadmin$ su sally
Password: [password smith typed in but hidden]
bash-3.2$
```

The change in the shell prompt signals that you have successfully authenticated as the user and opened a new shell with that user's identify. Exit the shell to return to the local administrator's shell:

```
bash-3.2$ exit
client17:~ cadmin$
```

Be aware, however, that you have no indication of which node you authenticate against. For example, if you are authenticating local user named "sally," su attempts to authenticate against the user record from the local node first, even if you meant to verify authentication against the Open Directory network node.

The dirt command is another option for verifying a user's password. The advantage of dirt is that it attempts to authenticate using every directory node, whereas su attempts to authenticate only against the *first* directory node that contains a user record matching the user that you specify. For a user record in the Open Directory shared directory, dirt attempts to authenticate against the Password Server (rather than the KDC). Be forewarned that dirt not only shows the attempted password in clear text, but it also logs the attempted password in clear text to /var/log/system.log (although normally, nonadministrators do not have read access to this log).

```
client17:~ cadmin$ dirt -u sally
User password: [password smith typed in but hidden]
2008-03-25 17:17:45.606 dirt [799.10b] password is : smith
Call to dsGetRecordList returned count = 1 with Status : eDSNoErr : (0)
Call to checkpw(): Success
path: /LDAPv3/mainserver.pretendco.com
Username: sally
Password: smith
Success
```

Verifying Kerberos Authentication

When you log in as an Open Directory network user, Mac OS X and your Open Directory server work behind the scenes to grant access to all Kerberized services on the network, without requiring you to provide your user name and password again while you are logged in. This feature is called *single sign-on*. When Kerberos is working properly, you will not notice anything. If there are problems, however, you may have to provide your authentication credentials each time you attempt to access network services. Problems with Kerberos could be symptoms of bigger underlying issues involving DNS or time synchronization.

Understanding Kerberos Authentication

There are three main players in a Kerberos transaction:

▶   The user or computer that wants to access a service

▶ The network service that the user or computer wants to access

▶ The KDC

When you bind to an Open Directory server, the `DirectoryService` and `kerberosautoconfig` processes set up your Kerberos configuration files so that your Mac OS X computer can participate in the Open Directory server's Kerberos *realm* (roughly speaking, an authentication domain that includes users and services).

This allows network users to enjoy a single sign-on solution in which they provide their passwords once at login, and then automatically gain access to any Kerberized service in the Open Directory server's realm.

When network users log in on a bound client, they should automatically get a TGT that enables them to access all the Kerberized services in the Kerberos realm without providing their passwords again; instead of asking for the user's password, Mac OS X works in the background to use the TGT.

Kerberos will not work if the system clock on one computer is more than 5 minutes apart from the system clock of the computer hosting the KDC. Kerberos translates the local time to Coordinated Universal Time (UTC), so differences in time zone do not pose a problem. However, even if computers are synchronized to a time server, you can still run into problems: if one computer does not calculate daylight saving time correctly, it will be an hour out of sync; and if one computer's clock is set to the correct local time, but its time zone is incorrectly set, Kerberos will not work.

> **MORE INFO** ▶ For more information about Kerberos, see "Troubleshooting Authentication Issues" in Chapter 7 of this book, pages 220–224 of *Mac OS X Server Essentials, Second Edition,* and http://web.mit.edu/Kerberos.

When troubleshooting login problems, login as a local user and attempt to obtain a TGT as a network user to confirm that Kerberos authentication is working as expected. To do this, use either the Kerberos application or the `klist` and `kinit` commands, which are covered next.

Using the Kerberos Application

The Kerberos application is located in /System/Library/CoreServices. When the Kerberos application launches, the user can see immediately whether or not they have any tickets. It is possible for a local user to store a password for Kerberos in the keychain and specify a network volume from a Kerberized server in the login items. Under normal circumstances, on a computer bound to an Open Directory server, a local user should have no tickets—unless they obtained Kerberos tickets from accessing network services.

To determine if Open Directory set up your Kerberos realm correctly when you bound to the Open Directory server, click the New button in the toolbar, which results in a challenge to provide your credentials in the Kerberos realm.

In the "Authenticate to Kerberos" dialog, the Open Directory server's realm should already be specified in the Realm field. If the realm is not set up, this signals the computer may not have been bound correctly or that the Open Directory server was not set up correctly. To authenticate to the KDC and obtain a TGT, enter a user name and password from the Open Directory node, and then click OK.

TIP Do not select the "Remember this password in my keychain" checkbox. You do not want this local user account to be able to automatically obtain Kerberos tickets, especially if you plan to use this account for troubleshooting.

The following figure shows a successfully obtained TGT:

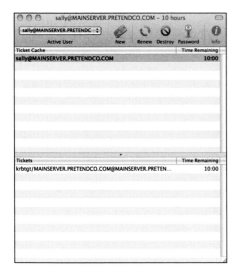

The Kerberos application displays useful error messages for many circumstances that prevent you from obtaining a TGT:

▶ Client not found in Kerberos database—The KDC can't find the user principal in its database.

▶ Password incorrect—The password that you entered doesn't match the password for the user in the KDC's database.

▶ Clock skew too big—Check your time, time zone, and daylight savings settings.

To resolve the first two problems, see "Troubleshooting Authentication Issues" in Chapter 7. To resolve the clock skew issue, check the settings specified in the error message on both the client and the server.

When you log out of Mac OS X, the operating system does not automatically destroy any tickets that the user possesses. If you log in as a different user in the intervening time, then log back in as the original local user before the tickets expire; the original user's tickets will still be valid. (The default ticket lifetime is 10 hours.) If you obtained any tickets in the course of troubleshooting, be sure to destroy them after you are done. An extra Kerberos ticket can cause confusion, especially if you start troubleshooting for more than one network user account. Click the Destroy button in the toolbar to destroy any tickets before moving on to the next section.

Using the klist and kinit Commands

One advantage of using `klist` and `kinit` is that you can use them to troubleshoot via a remote SSH session, rather than having to be in front of the computer. The `klist` command shows any Kerberos tickets that a user possesses. A local user should not see any tickets listed.

```
client17:~ cadmin$ klist
klist: No Kerberos 5 tickets in credentials cache
```

To obtain a TGT for a network user account, use `kinit` followed by the short name of the network user account:

```
client17:~ cadmin$ kinit sally
Please enter the password for sally@MAINSERVER.PRETENDCO.COM: [password typed but
hidden]
```

There is no feedback for a successful `kinit`. Use `klist` to confirm that a TGT was obtained:

```
client17:~ cadmin$ klist
Kerberos 5 ticket cache: 'API:Initial default cache'
Default principal: sally@MAINSERVER.PRETENDCO.COM
Valid starting    Expires       Service Principal
03/26/09 08:58:25 03/26/09 18:58:25 krbtgt/MAINSERVER.PRETENDCO.COM@MAINSERVER.
PRETENDCO.COM
        renew until 04/02/09 08:58:25
```

An unsuccessful `kinit` should contain information about why the operation failed. Some examples of failed attempts are:

▶   `Kerberos Login Failed: Password incorrect.`

▶   `Kerberos Login Failed: Client not found in Kerberos database.`

▶   `Kerberos Login Failed: Clock skew too big. Please check your time, time zone and daylight savings settings.`

The `kdestroy` command destroys any Kerberos tickets you have. Because it is possible to have tickets for more than one user at a time, use the `-a` option to delete all tickets. To prevent confusion from extra Kerberos tickets, use the following command to delete all obtained tickets, and then confirm that the user possesses no tickets:

```
client17:~ cadmin$ kdestroy -a; klist
klist: No Kerberos 5 tickets in credentials cache
```

Verifying Home Folder Access

Once you have confirmed that you can identify and authenticate the network user account, the next problem area to tackle is the automatic mounting of the network home folder. Before logging in with a network user account, verify that the following are true:

▶   The network user account has attributes set to define the network home folder.

▶   The Mac OS X computer can automatically mount the network volume that holds the home folder.

▶   The network user account has read and write access to the home folder.

Identifying the Home Folder attributes

There are two Open Directory Standard attributes that define a user's home folder: `NFSHomeDirectory` and `HomeDirectory`. The first, `dsAttrTypeStandard:NFSHomeDirectory`, defines the path in the local file system to the user's home folder. The second, `dsAttrTypeStandard:HomeDirectory`, contains an XML representation of a URL for the user's network home folder. This is used in conjunction with an automount record from the Open Directory domain that the Mac OS X automount processes use to automatically mount the network volume containing the user's network home folder.

> **NOTE ▶** It is possible to configure a user to have a Network File System (NFS) network home folder. NFS home folders do not require any help from the automounting processes, so they do not require the `dsAttrTypeStandard:HomeDirectory` attribute. However, Apple Filing Protocol has some features that make it a better choice for home folders, (a discussion that's outside the scope of this book).

The `dsAttrTypeStandard:NFSHomeDirectory` attribute name can be doubly confusing: first, even though the name contains "NFS," it usually applies to Apple Filing Protocol (AFP) home folders; second, it maps to the Native attribute `homeDirectory` in the Open Directory LDAP directory (note the first letter of `homeDirectory` is not capitalized). To make matters worse, it is easy to confuse the Native attribute `homeDirectory` with the Standard attribute `HomeDirectory` (which in turn maps to the Native attribute `apple-user-homeurl`).

> **TIP ▶** Native attribute names often have the first letter of the attribute name in lowercase.

If a network user's `NFSHomeDirectory` or `HomeDirectory` attribute doesn't exist or is misconfigured, you cannot log in as that network user because Mac OS X cannot access the AFP or SMB network home folder.

Use `dscl` to inspect the values of the Standard attributes `NFSHomeDirectory` and `HomeDirectory` for the user "sally".

```
client17:~ cadmin$ dscl /Search read /Users/sally NFSHomeDirectory HomeDirectory
HomeDirectory: <home_dir><url>afp://mainserver.pretendco.com/Users</url><path>sally
</path></home_dir>
NFSHomeDirectory: /Network/Servers/mainserver.pretendco.com/Users/sally
```

When you log in on any Mac OS X computer that is bound to the Open Directory server, using the credentials for the user "sally" that is defined in the Open Directory shared domain, Mac OS X tries to mount the network volume `afp://mainserver.pretendco.com/Users`, and to access the home folder in /Network/Servers/mainserver.pretendco.com/Users/sally.

Confirming Automount Records

It isn't enough for the user to have valid `dsAttrTypeStandard:NFSHomeDirectory` and `dsAttrTypeStandard:HomeDirectory` attributes. The Mac OS X computer must also have access to a mount record that enables *autofs* (a general term for the set of processes that automatically mount network volumes; also called *automount*) to prepare the network volume that holds the user's network home directory to be automatically mounted as necessary. The following search shows the list of automount records that are in the authentication search path:

```
client17:~ cadmin$ dscl /Search list /Mounts
mainserver.pretendco.com:/Users
```

If you get the following error, you may be facing a common situation: the administrator forgot to create the automount record for the volume that contains network user home folders.

```
list: Invalid Path
<dscl_cmd> DS Error: -14009 (eDSUnknownName)
```

To resolve the problem, see "Managing Data Stored in an Open Directory Master" in Chapter 5.

In the successful output of the `dscl` command above, the mount record's name is `mainserver.pretendco.com:/Users`, which has a special character, the forward slash. If you want to operate on that record, you have to escape the special character from `dscl`. You can put the entire record name in single or double quotes, or precede the forward slash with a backslash. Use the following `dscl` command to inspect the contents of the automount record:

```
client17:~ cadmin$ dscl /Search read /Mounts/mainserver.pretendco.com:\/Users
dsAttrTypeNative:cn: mainserver.pretendco.com:/Users
dsAttrTypeNative:mountDirectory: /Network/Servers/
```

```
dsAttrTypeNative:mountOption: net url==afp://;AUTH=NO%20USER%20AUTHENT@mainserver.
pretendco.com/Users
dsAttrTypeNative:mountType: url
dsAttrTypeNative:objectClass: mount top
AppleMetaNodeLocation: /LDAPv3/127.0.0.1
RecordName: mainserver.pretendco.com:/Users
RecordType: dsRecTypeStandard:Mounts
VFSLinkDir: /Network/Servers/
VFSOpts: net url==afp://;AUTH=NO%20USER%20AUTHENT@mainserver.pretendco.com/Users
VFSType: url
```

A full explanation of automount is outside the scope of this book, but the key attributes in the mount record above are RecordName, VFSLinkDir, and VFSOpts. When you navigate to the value of VFSLinkDir (/Network/Servers/), you will see the entries for the host portion of any RecordName attributes (mainserver.pretendco.com:/Users). Inside /Network/Servers/mainserver.pretendco.com you will see *mount points* (locations where the file system can mount network volumes) that correspond to the second portion of RecordName (mainserver.pretendco.com:/Users). The VFSOpts value url==afp://;AUTH=NO%20USER%20AUTHENT@mainserver.pretendco.com/Users specifies what to mount (mainserver.pretendco.com/Users) and how to mount it (as Guest; see the man page for mount_afp for more information about the complicated syntax).

When you navigate to the mount point Users, the automount processes attempt to mount the network share point. If you successfully changed to the Users folder, the prompt changes to reflect that fact. Use the df (display free disk space) command on /Network/Servers/mainserver.pretendco.com/Users to confirm that the Users directory is a mounted network volume; the line that starts with afp_ signals that this is an AFP network volume:

```
client17:mainserver.pretendco.com cadmin$ cd Users
client17:Users cadmin$ df /Network/Servers/mainserver.pretendco.com/Users
Filesystem        512-blocks    Used Available Capacity Mounted on
afp_47p9UA0002kB0000oM0000VU-1.2d000006   41943040 20368440 21574600  49%  /Network/
Servers/mainserver.pretendco.com/Users
```

It is possible that the AFP automatic mount will not take place. There are at least two possible errors that you might experience as a result of attempting to navigate to /Network/Servers/mainserver.pretendco.com/Users. The errors and possible steps toward resolution are:

▶ `-bash: cd: /Network/Servers/mainserver.pretendco.com/Users: Host is down`—The AFP service is not on or not available. Check basic network connectivity, DNS resolution, and firewall settings, and then make sure the AFP service is started on server hosting the network volume.

▶ `-bash: cd: /Network/Servers/mainserver.pretendco.com/Users: Unknown error: 118`—The AFP service does not allow guest access. Guest access is not required to support network home folders, but it does pose a problem if you attempt to troubleshoot by inspecting this path.

Understanding the Open Directory Value of 99

When inspecting the values that define a user's home folder, you may come across the value 99. If a user does not have a home folder set, Open Directory returns the value of 99 for `NFSHomeDirectory`. If some important attributes contain no data, Open Directory uses this value to prevent errors from operations that cannot deal with a null result. In the following example, the user "frank" does not have a home folder set, but Open Directory returns the value of 99 for `NFSHomeDirectory` anyway:

```
client17:~ cadmin$ dscl /Search read /Users/frank NFSHomeDirectory HomeDirectory
NFSHomeDirectory: 99
No such key: HomeDirectory
```

Confirming Access to the Network Home Folder

Once you have collected information about the home folder server and protocol, try to connect to the service, authenticating as a network user. The following example is for an AFP-based network home folder:

1   At a Mac OS X computer, log in as a local user.

2   Choose Go > Connect to Server.

3   Enter the URL for the home folder:

```
afp://mainserver.pretendco.com/
```

4   Enter the credentials for the network user "sally." You should see a list of all the volumes the user is authorized to access.

5   In the following figure, you see the default volumes for Mac OS X Server, but also a volume with the network user account's short name. You could select either the user's home folder or the share point that hosts it. For this example, select the volume with the user's short name.

The network volume that you selected opens in the Finder, and the server that hosts this network volume appears in the Finder sidebar with an Eject icon next to it. In the Mac OS X v10.5 Finder, network volumes do not appear on the desktop unless you change this setting in Preferences.

6   Click the Eject icon for the server in the Finder's sidebar.

7   Destroy any Kerberos tickets that you may have obtained, so you will not be confused by them if you log in as this user again.

Launch Terminal in /Applications/Utilities and issue the command `kdestroy`. If you don't have any Kerberos tickets, you can safely ignore the output "`kdestroy: No default credentials cache.`"

Confirming the Location of the Network Home Folder

After you successfully log in with a network user account, you can confirm that the home folder is located where you expect it to be, on a network volume:

1 Log in as a network user.

2 In the Finder, select Go > Home.

3 Press Command and click the user name in the Finder window toolbar.

 Command-clicking reveals the hierarchical path that reflects the value you found earlier with dscl. In the figure below, for example, it reflects the NFSHomeDirectory value of /Nework/Servers/mainserver.pretendco.com/Users/sally:

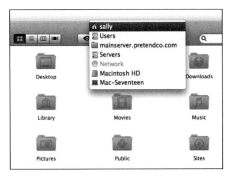

If the home folder is in the Users folder on the boot drive, rather than in /Network/Servers, it is possible that you are using a mobile account with a portable home folder; if this is the case, the fact that the home folder is on the boot drive is not a problem. It is also possible that you have a local user account with the same name and password as an Open Directory network user account. Because the local node is first in the authentication search path, Open Directory uses the local user account. If you have a local user account that conflicts with a network user account, you cannot use the network user account until you remove the local account, as detailed below. These steps preserve the files in the local home folder.

1 While logged in as the local user, connect to the file server hosting the network home folder, authenticate with the network user credentials, and then copy the files from the local home folder to the network home folder. Confirm that you have copied all the files that you intend to preserve. Use the command-line tool chmod or Finder's Get

Info window to ensure that the file permissions do not allow other users to read or write the files and folders in the network home folder.

MORE INFO ▶ For more information on using the `chmod` command, see pages 196–197 of *Mac OS X Support Essentials, Second Edition* and the `man` page for `chmod`.

2   Log out as the local user, and then log in as a local administrator.

3   Launch System Preferences, open the Accounts preferences, and then authenticate as a local administrator if necessary.

4   Confirm that the local user is indeed a local user and is not listed as "Managed, Mobile." If the user is listed as "Managed, Mobile," then you do not have to make any changes at the Mac OS X client computer, as Mobile users have a local home folder that may be synchronized with their network home folder.

MORE INFO ▶ Configuring mobile accounts and folder synchronization is outside the scope of this book; instead see Chapter 8 in *Mac OS X Server User Management for Version 10.5 Leopard*.

5   Select the user, then press the Remove (-) button. You will be prompted for what to do with the home folder. Select either "Save the home folder in a disk image" or "Delete the home folder."

MORE INFO ▶ See page 79 of *Mac OS X Support Essentials, Second Edition* for more information about deleting local users.

6   Log out as the local administrator, and then log in again as the network user. Follow the steps at the beginning of this section to confirm the location of the network home folder.

Understanding the Login Process

You can improve your login troubleshooting skills by understanding the processes involved in the seemingly simple task of logging in.

Before logging in, a user must access the `loginwindow` application, which is unique in its ability to run as both a background process and a GUI application. The `loginwindow` application displays the login window and is responsible for identifying and authenticating users. After the user successfully authenticates, `loginwindow` attempts to access the user's home folder, and then sets up the user's graphical environment.

MORE INFO ▶ See pages 553–558 of *Mac OS X Support Essentials, Second Edition* for more information about the loginwindow and related processes.

At the login window, a user must provide identification and authentication information, usually either a full name or short name, and a password. loginwindow searches for the user record in the nodes of the authentication search path and attempts to authenticate the user. If loginwindow is unable to identify and authenticate the user, or if loginwindow is unable to mount the network share point that hosts the user's home folder, then the login window shakes briefly and returns the user to an empty password field.

Understanding the Role of the AuthenticationAuthority Attribute in the Login Process

One important attribute of the user account record is the Standard attribute AuthenticationAuthority, which specifies how Open Directory should attempt to authenticate the user.

A local user's AuthenticationAuthority attribute normally includes ShadowHash, which indicates that hashes of the user's password are stored in a file readable only with root privileges and that Open Directory should attempt authentication against that hash file.

A network user in an Open Directory shared node normally has two values for AuthenticationAuthority: One value starts with ;ApplePasswordServer; and the other starts with ;Kerberosv5;. In this case, Open Directory attempts authentication against the Password Server. If authentication against the Password Server succeeds, loginwindow attempts to obtain a TGT from the KDC. If the user's AuthenticationAuthority attribute is missing or corrupted, the user may not be able to authenticate.

If the user has no AuthenticationAuthority attribute (an unusual situation), Open Directory will attempt to authenticate using Kerberos, with an educated guess of the user's Kerberos principal.

Mounting the Network Home Folder

If the network user account record specifies an AFP network home folder, the following requirements must be met in order for the user to use the AFP network home folder:

▶   The file service hosting the home folder must be running.

▶ The user must be authorized to access the service. Mac OS X Server has the ability to apply service Access Control Lists to allow only certain users and groups access to various services.

▶ The user must be authorized to access the share point that holds the home folder.

▶ The Open Directory shared domain must have an automount record set up for the network share point that holds the user's network home folder.

▶ The processes on your client computer related to automounting network volumes must be operational.

If any of the above requirements are not met, the login window shakes and returns the user to an empty password field or displays an error message similar to the ones below:

```
You are unable to log in to the user account "frank" at this time
Logging in to the account failed because an error occurred.
```

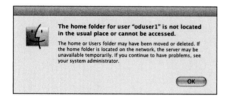

If the user authenticates correctly and has authorization to mount the home folder, `loginwindow` mounts the share point hosting the network home folder and sets up the user's graphical environment.

Using the >console Login for Troubleshooting

A common source of trouble with logging in and accessing a network home folder is that either the AFP service is not running or the share point is not set up. `loginwindow` does not offer any feedback to indicate either of these problems. If you log in with `>console`, however, you get some useful feedback.

MORE INFO ▶ See Chapter 1 for detailed instructions on how to use `>console` at the `loginwindow`.

In the following example, the network user "frank" does not have a network home folder assigned. When "frank" logs in with `>console`, Open Directory returns the value of 99 rather than null:

```
login: frank
Password: [hidden]
No home directory 99!
Logging in with home = "/".
```

In this example, "sally" logs in with `>console`, but the automount record has not yet been set up in the Open Directory shared domain:

```
login: sally
Password: [hidden]
No home directory /Network/Servers/mainserver.pretendco.com/Users/sally!
Logging in with home ="/".
```

For both of these examples, after either of these users successfully authenticates, the login window shakes and returns to a blank password field.

Viewing Log Files

To get a real-time view of the problems that Mac OS X experiences while you attempt to log in, you can open an SSH shell to your computer, watch the system.log, then attempt to log in at the computer. Follow these steps:

1   On the client computer, open System Preferences and open Sharing.

2   Enable Remote Login, then log out.

3   On another computer, `ssh` to the client computer with the credentials of an administrator local to the client computer.

4   Open Terminal and monitor the `system.log` with the `tail` command:

```
client16:~ ladmin$ ssh ladmin@client17.local

tail -f /var/log/system.log
```

5 At the client computer, attempt to log in as a network user.

You will see many log messages, but you are interested in anything that refers to the user's home directory. You may see messages like the following:

```
com.apple.loginwindow[248]: ParseOneArgument: Unable to access user's home
directory: "/Network/Servers/mainserver.pretendco.com/Users/kaelan".
```

It is not important that you understand exactly what the messages mean, but that you can see that there is a problem.

The /var/log/secure.log may also contain useful information. You will find that Open Directory server logs may contain more useful information, covered in Chapters 5 and 6.

What You've Learned

▶ You can bind a computer running Mac OS X to a Mac OS X Server hosting an Open Directory server to gain access to the identification and authentication services offered by the Open Directory server.

▶ You can use Directory Utility or `defaults` to modify the authentication and contacts search path.

▶ The Directory Utility application requires only the name or IP address of an Open Directory server to bind to it.

▶ Directory Utility uses configuration records stored in the LDAP directory to configure the computer to use the Open Directory server's LDAP and Kerberos services.

▶ Authenticated directory binding, also known as Trusted Binding, forces the client and Open Directory server to mutually authenticate to each other. It causes network traffic for Open Directory–related queries and replies to be encrypted.

▶ A search path specifies which directory nodes to use and the order in which to use them. *The authentication search path* is used for authentication and other administrative information. The *contacts search path* is used by applications that are programmed to use it, such as Address Book and Mail.

▶ `loginwindow` attempts to identify a user account against nodes in the authentication search path, then authenticate the user, mount the home folder specified in the user's record, and set up the user's environment, including the Finder.

▶ When troubleshooting binding or login problems, start with the simple and move toward the complex. Several tools are available, including Directory Utility and Kerberos, as well as `ldapsearch`, `dscl`, `id`, `kinit`, `su`, and `dirt`, to help identify a user account record and confirm authentication.

References

Apple Knowledge Base Articles

▶ Mac OS X 10.5: Duplicate Computer Name Alert when Binding to Open Directory http://support.apple.com/kb/TS1245.

Documentation

▶ Mac OS X Server User Management for Version 10.5 Leopard http://images.apple.com/server/macosx/docs/User_Management_v10.5.mnl.pdf

▶ Mac OS X Server Open Directory Administration for Version 10.5 Leopard http://images.apple.com/server/macosx/docs/Open_Directory_Admin_v10.5_2nd_Ed.pdf

Books

▶ Carter, Gerald. *LDAP System Administration* (O'Reilly, 2003).

▶ White, Kevin M. *Mac OS X Support Essentials, Second Edition* (Peachpit, 2008).

▶ Regan, Schoun, with Pugh, David. *Mac OS X Server Essentials, Second Edition* (Peachpit, 2008).

Review Quiz

1. After binding to an Open Directory server, what kinds of traffic are normally sent over the network in clear text?

2. When setting up Trusted Binding, if you get a message that the record already exists, why might it be a bad idea to overwrite the existing record?

3. Which directory nodes cannot be removed from the authentication search path?

4. What is one of the records that Open Directory looks for in the `cn=config` section of the Open Directory server LDAP directory, in order to set up local configuration files in /Library/Preferences/DirectoryService?

5. What is one way to see if Open Directory can identify or authenticate a network user record?

6. What is one way to open the Kerberos application?

7. What is the difference between the information returned by the `dscl` and the `ldapsearch` commands?

8. What two Standard attributes define a user's AFP network home folder?

Answers

1. LDAP queries and replies are sent in clear text unless authenticated Trusted Binding is used.

2. If you overwrite the computer record for another computer, you may disable Trusted Binding for the other computer that is using the computer record. This would break all directory service lookups for that other computer.

3. /Local/Default and /BSD/local

4. `macosxodconfig` and `macosxodpolicy`

5. Use the `id` or `dscl` command to identify the network user account; use the `su` or `dirt` commands to authenticate with the network user account's password; use the Kerberos application or the `kinit` command to authenticate and obtain a TGT.

6. Open the Kerberos application in /System/Library/CoreServices.

7. `ldapsearch` queries the LDAP service directly, circumventing Open Directory; `dscl` uses Open Directory to search for information. `ldapsearch` returns the actual data stored in the LDAP directory; `dscl` interprets the data, and in some cases, returns 99 if an attribute has no value stored in the underlying data store.

8. NFSHomeDirectory and HomeDirectory define a user's AFP home folder.

3

Time   This chapter takes approximately 3 hours to complete.

Goals   Populate an LDAP service with all the information required to support
Mac OS X network login

Configure Mac OS X to use an LDAP service for identification and
authentication

Troubleshoot binding issues with an LDAP server

## Chapter 3

Accessing a Third-Party LDAP Service

If your organization has a standard LDAP service that provides directory services, it is easy to integrate Mac OS X into your LDAP service. But what if your LDAP service doesn't have all the data required to enable users to log in to Mac OS X and automatically access a network home folder?

In this chapter you will consider two specific cases: standard installations of the LDAP service from the open source project OpenLDAP and standard installations of Novell's LDAP service eDirectory. You then can apply the processes you learn to any other LDAP service that follows the LDAP standards. (Microsoft's Active Directory also implements an LDAP service, but this is a special case and is covered in Chapter 4, "Accessing an Active Directory Service.")

You will learn the following techniques to integrate Mac OS X into your LDAP service:

▶ Edit the schema for your LDAP service to support additional object classes and attribute types.

▶ Repurpose unused attributes in your LDAP user records.

▶ Configure Mac OS X to use local mappings with static and dynamic variables.

▶ Use an auxiliary Open Directory server to provide records that do not exist in your LDAP service node.

Because each situation is different, you need to determine the solutions that are the most appropriate for your environment.

Populating an LDAP Server for Network Login

To figure out what is missing in your LDAP service, start by inspecting the data that it contains.

Inspecting Information from an LDAP Service

To understand the kinds of data that your LDAP service already contains, look at the records, record attributes, and attribute values populated in the LDAP service. Next, to determine the kinds of data that are *valid* for your LDAP service to contain, look at the *schema* (the rules that determine the object classes and attribute types allowed in your LDAP data store) for your LDAP service.

Before connecting to your LDAP service, determine the answers to the following questions:

▶ Is the LDAP service available at the default ports (389 for LDAP and 636 for LDAP over TLS/SSL)?

▶ Does the LDAP service require or allow a secure connection with SSL?

▶ Does the LDAP service allow anonymous binding, or do you need to provide a distinguished name (dn) and password?

▶ Does the LDAP service allow anonymous browsing of all the data, or does it return a limited set of objects and attributes?

You can find some of the answers through trial and error, but you may require help from the LDAP service administrator.

Inspecting Information from a Standard LDAP Service

You can choose among several applications to graphically interact with the LDAP directory. For this chapter, however, you will use LDAPManager, an open source application available from SourceForge.net (http://sourceforge.net/).

> **NOTE** ▶ The examples in this chapter use an Open Directory master that has a branch containing data as if the LDAP service was a standard implementation of OpenLDAP. User passwords are stored in an encrypted format in the directory, and the attributes necessary for logging in on Mac OS X are not present. The objects are located at `cn=openldap,dc=mainserver,dc=pretendco,dc=com`.

To use LDAPManager to inspect the data available from a standard LDAP service, follow these steps:

1   Download and install LDAPManager from http://sourceforge.net/projects/ldapmanager.

2   Open LDAPManager.

3   Complete the "Server Name or IP Address" field.

4   Complete the Search Base field, or click the Fetch Search Base button if you are unsure.

In this example, the main server has an OpenLDAP branch at `cn=openldap,dc=mainserver,dc=pretendco,dc=com`, so type this in the Search Base field, as shown in the figure.

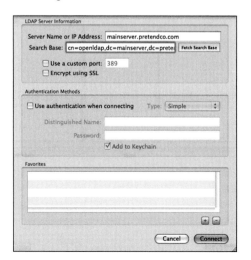

5 Click OK.

6 Browse records in the LDAP directory.

   TIP If you did not enter the search base, or if you mistyped it, LDAPManager will not display any records. You must close the search window and choose File > New to specify the LDAP service again.

7 Select a user. Note the attributes and the data stored in the attributes.

   Here's an example of a typical user stored in an LDAP data store, as seen with LDAPManager:

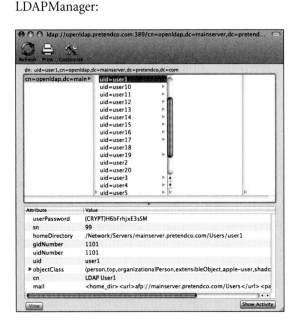

The figure above shows the attributes that are populated with values. If an attribute is not populated with a value, most graphical LDAP browsers do not display the attribute name. If an attribute is not displayed, how do you know whether that attribute is allowed? You need to learn more about the LDAP directory's schema. If you are using OpenLDAP, you can look at the schema files that are distributed with the LDAP service.

Inspecting the OpenLDAP Schema Files

The *schema* is the collection of rules that determine the object classes and attribute types allowed in your LDAP data store. Mac OS X supports OpenLDAP, and although Mac OS X does not run the LDAP service by default, each Mac OS X and Mac OS X Server computer has the schema files in /etc/openldap/schema. For example, with the file /etc/openldap/schema/nis.schema, Mac OS X Open Directory builds on the schema laid out in RFC 2307, "An Approach for Using LDAP as a Network Information Service," which specifies several object classes such as posixAccount, and attribute types such as uidNumber, gidNumber, and homeDirectory.

There are many schema files, and one may rely on the existence of another. Each file contains a list of all the object classes and attribute types available to an LDAP data store. Follow these steps to look in the nis.schema file for the homeDirectory attribute:

1   Open the Terminal application.

2   Navigate to the schema directory.

```
client17:~ cadmin$ cd /etc/openldap/schema
```

3   Edit the file nis.schema with your favorite text editor.

```
client17:schema cadmin$ nano nis.schema
```

4   Jump to the homeDirectory attribute: In the nano editor, press Control-W (for Where Is), type *homeDirectory*, and press Return to see the definition of the attribute, which is also shown below.

Lines in the description that start with the hash sign (#) are commented out and not used, so they are not displayed in the example below. The description (DESC), "The absolute path to the home directory," is clear, but SYNTAX is more cryptic. A *syntax* defines how an attribute's value must be encoded. The various syntaxes are listed in RFC 2252, "Lightweight Directory Access Protocol (v3): Attribute Syntax Definitions." In this case, 1.3.6.1.4.1.1466.115.121.1.15 is Directory String, which allows a broad range of characters.

```
attributetype ( 1.3.6.1.4.1.63.1000.1.1.1.1.99 NAME 'homeDirectory'
    DESC 'The absolute path to the home directory'
    EQUALITY caseExactMatch
    SYNTAX 1.3.6.1.4.1.1466.115.121.1.15 SINGLE-VALUE )
```

5   Press Control-X to exit nano or your text editor.

It is not important to understand the exact details of the homeDirectory attribute, but it is important to know that the schema is defined in definition files, and some additional information is available in various RFCs. The schema defines the records and attributes that the LDAP directory can contain, and the kind of data that the directory can store in those attributes.

Inspecting Information from an eDirectory Service

Novell's eDirectory also implements an LDAP service. eDirectory allows anonymous browsing, but only for a small set of attributes. An LDAP proxy user with no password can browse attributes that you specify; see Novell's documentation for instructions to create and configure the access for an LDAP proxy user. You could also bind as an eDirectory user to browse, but you do not want to send the LDAP bind password in clear text. See Novell's documentation on setting up SSL for LDAP.

To inspect the data, Novell offers graphical tools such as iManager, which enables you to securely use a Web browser to inspect and modify directory information (see below). The Attribute field in the lower-right corner of the window contains all the attributes that are allowed for a record of the User object class, displaying only a few at a time (in this figure, Higher Privileges, Home Directory, homePhone, and homePostalAddress).

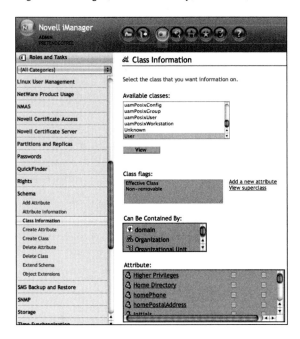

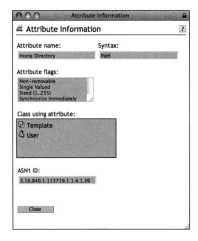

When you click a listed attribute, iManager opens a window with details for that attribute. The figure at left shows the window for the attribute Home Directory. The Syntax field defines the type of data that the attribute can contain—in this case, Path.

If your eDirectory is running on Linux, the schema files are located in /opt/novell/eDirectory/lib/ nds-schema. See the eDirectory documentation for locations of schema files for eDirectory running on other operating systems. As with OpenLDAP schema files, you can use a text editor to browse and inspect eDirectory schema files.

In these last few sections you learned how to determine which data is available from your LDAP service. This is important to help figure out how to enable your LDAP data store to hold the information it needs to support Mac OS X network user records that use network home folders. In the next section you will learn which attributes are required.

Identifying Required Network User Attributes

With an Open Directory server, we take for granted that all the necessary records and attributes are available. However, now that you are working with a standard LDAP service instead, it makes sense to list and examine the information that Open Directory uses from a server's LDAP directory, so you can determine the objects and attributes that you want the standard LDAP service to support.

Open Directory expects a record to have certain attributes available for a network user account to log in to and access a network home folder. Table 3.1 lists the required attributes and how these Standard attributes are mapped to the Native attributes in an Open Directory server's LDAP data store.

Table 3.1   User Record Attributes Required for Network Login

Open Directory Standard Attribute	LDAP Native Attribute	Description
RecordName	uid and cn	List of names for the user, such as mbartosh and Michael Bartosh
[RecordName]	uid	Short name, up to 16 values
RealName	cn	Full name, or long name, like Michael Bartosh
UniqueID	uidNumber	Integer, for example 1025
PrimaryGroupID	gidNumber	Integer, for example 20
NFSHomeDirectory	homeDirectory	Absolute path to home folder
HomeDirectory	apple-user-homeurl	\<home_dir>\<url>afp://*fqdn*/Users\</url>\<path>mbartosh\</path>\</home_dir> Delimited representation of the URL for the user's home folder

NOTE ▶ Table 3.1 is not exhaustive. For example, it does not list GeneratedUID, UserShell, MCXFlags, and MCXSettings because although these can enhance the user experience, they are not required.

Your LDAP directory may not have some of the attributes listed in Table 3.1. For example, your directory may have the Standard attributes cn and homeDirectory, but it probably does not have the apple-user-homeurl attribute, because that is specific to Mac OS X (unless, of course, your schema has been extended).

Rather than storing passwords in user records, Open Directory network users have an AuthenticationAuthority attribute that references an Open Directory server's Password Server and Kerberos Key Distribution Center (KDC).

Understanding Similar LDAP Attributes

Keep these differences in mind when you decide which Native attributes of your LDAP service to use for mapping to Standard Open Directory attributes:

▶ `RecordName` and `RealName`—Open Directory maps the Standard attribute `RecordName` to two Native attributes, one for any short names for the user (`uid`) and another for the full name of the user (`cn`). The Standard attribute `RealName` maps to the full name (`cn`). Apple's documentation states that the first attribute that you map to `RealName` must not be the same as the first attribute that you map to `RecordName`. In Table 3.1, `RecordName` maps to `uid` first, then to `cn` second; `RealName` maps to `cn`.

▶ `RecordName` and `UniqueID`—Open Directory maps the Standard attribute `RecordName` to the Native attributes `uid` and `cn`. An Open Directory server's LDAP service uses `uid` for a user's short name or names, but other UNIX systems use `uid` to refer to an integer rather than a string. When using an LDAP service, make sure that the attributes you choose to map for `RecordName` do not contain an integer; however, the attribute you choose to map for `UniqueID` must contain an integer.

▶ `NFSHomeDirectory` and `HomeDirectory`—The Standard attribute name `HomeDirectory` looks very similar to the Native attribute name `homeDirectory`, but they contain very different data. The Standard attribute `HomeDirectory` maps to the Native attribute `apple-user-homeurl`, which contains a tagged entry that specifies a URL for the share point as well as a path from that share point to the user's home folder. The Standard attribute `NFSHomeDirectory` maps to the Native attribute `homeDirectory`, which contains a file system path to the user's home folder.

If your LDAP implementation includes the RFC 2307 schema additions, your LDAP directory has most of the attributes necessary for a network user account to log in to Mac OS X. The biggest problem is the Open Directory Standard attribute `HomeDirectory`. The Native attribute that you select to map for `HomeDirectory` must be able to contain delimited text that defines a URL to the user's share point as well as the path to the home folder within that share point. You may have to use local mappings or extend the schema to provide for the Standard attribute `HomeDirectory`. The next section covers extending your schema, while local mappings are covered in the section "Augmenting LDAP Data with Local Static and Variable Mappings."

Editing Your Directory Schema

An LDAP service's schema is a description of the types of object classes and attribute types allowed. Adding additional object classes and attribute types to your schema is referred to as *extending* your schema. Although the mechanics of editing your particular LDAP directory are outside the scope of this book, you can use the schema files in /etc/openldap/schema/apple.schema when planning to add object classes and attribute types to your directory.

Appendix A, "Mac OS X Directory Data," in *Open Directory Administration for Version 10.5 Leopard, Second Edition* presents useful explanatory information to help you plan your schema changes. That appendix also includes:

▶ "Open Directory Extensions to LDAP Schema"—Provides the information contained in the apple.schema file, as well as some details that do not exist in the file, such as a brief explanation of an attribute's purpose.

▶ "Mapping Standard Record Types and Attributes to LDAP and Active Directory"— Specifies how the LDAPv3 plug-in maps Open Directory record types to LDAP object classes, maps Open Directory attributes to LDAP attributes, and lists similar information for the Active Directory plug-in.

▶ "Standard Open Directory Record Types and Attributes"—Specifies the format required for various attributes and adds detailed examples for some key attributes.

MacEnterprise.org (http://macenterprise.org/) has Novell eDirectory schema extension files and instructions available for download.

Reusing Existing, Unused Attributes

You can choose to reuse "spare" attributes that are already supported by your LDAP schema, but be sure that the attributes can support the required format. For example, the Standard attribute `HomeDirectory` (Native attribute `apple-user-homeurl`) needs to support UTF-8 XML text. If your LDAP directory has an unused Native attribute `countryName`, you may be tempted to reuse `countryName` for `HomeDirectory`. The `countryName` attribute, however, is limited to two characters, which is not enough to hold the necessary value for `HomeDirectory`. Also, be aware that you may need to use these attributes in the future for a different purpose.

Consult Appendix A in *Open Directory Administration for Version 10.5 Leopard, Second Edition* for guidance on what kind of data each Standard attribute is required to support. However, your LDAP service's schema is the final authority on what is allowed and what is not.

If at all possible, extend your LDAP's schema rather than reusing attributes; extending the schema is a much more stable solution.

> **TIP** If you make changes to the schema, be sure to document your reuse of attributes or extensions so that you or a subsequent administrator will later know what was done.

Providing Records for Automount

If your network user record has valid data in its attributes for NFSHomeDirectory and HomeDirectory, but the Mac OS X computer cannot find a network mount record corresponding to the file server and share point specified in the user record attributes, your network user will not be able to log in and access the network home folder.

Each mount record contains information that Mac OS X uses to perform on-demand connections to a given file server and share point. The trigger for activating the network mount is typically a local file system path, based on the existence of an associated mount record. Whenever that file system path is accessed, Mac OS X mounts the remote network volume at that local file system path. In Mac OS X, automatic connections to network mounts are handled by the autofsd daemon, which relies on other tools and daemons. The language can be a bit confusing at times, because the network mount records are commonly referred to as *automount records*, and the general process of automatically mounting network volumes is referred to as *automount* or *autofs*.

In order to extend your LDAP directory's schema to support automount records, you need to:

▶ Create the attributes required for the mount object.

▶ Create a mount object class that contains the mount record attributes.

▶ Create a new mount object in your LDAP directory and specify the new attributes listed below.

▶ Map the Open Directory Standard record type mount to the Native object class you created in your LDAP directory.

The processes that handle automount have been significantly improved with Mac OS X v10.5, and they now handle disconnected network volumes. The record format to support automount has not changed. Table 3.2 describes the necessary attributes for a mount record, with the Open Directory Standard attribute name, the LDAP Native attribute, its purpose, and a sample value for each attribute.

Table 3.2   Attributes for a Mount Record

Open Directory Standard Attribute	LDAP Native Attribute	Purpose	Example Value
RecordName	cn	Server FQDN and full path to shared folder	mainserver.pretendco.com:/Volumes/Disk2/UsersAG
VFSLinkDir	mountDirectory	Path to location where client will mount network volume	/Network/Servers
VFSType	mountType	Mount type: url for AFP; nfs for NFS	url
VFSOpts	mountOption	Mount options: net for dynamically mounted share points; AFP requires afp://[user[;AUTH=uamname][:password]@]host/volumename	Two values: net and url==afp://;AUTH=NO%20USER%20AUTHENT@mainserver.pretendco.com/UsersAG

Appendix A of *Open Directory Administration for Version 10.5 Leopard, Second Edition* contains useful information about the exact requirements for the new mount object and attributes.

The following steps set up a mount record for the share point on server17.pretendco.com at /Volumes/Disk2/Homes, assuming your LDAP service's schema supports the `mount` object class and associated attributes. The tools you should use to edit data in your LDAP data store will vary depending on your situation.

1   Create an new `mount` record. Start with the `RecordName`.

    This is the Fully Qualified Domain Name (FQDN) for the server, followed by the full path to the share point from the point of view of the server:

    `server17.pretendco.com:/Volumes/Disk2/Homes`

2   Add the attribute for `VFSLinkDir` with the value `/Network/Servers`.

3   Add the attribute for `VFSType` with the value `url`.

4   For dynamic mount points, add the attribute for `VFSOpts` with the value `net`.

5   For AFP mount points, add another value for the attribute for `VFSOpts`.

    This is the most complicated step. The value takes the form of
    `url==URLtype://[user[;AUTH=uamname][:password]@]host/volumename`

    The authentication type for guest access is `NO USER AUTHENT`, but you have to insert `%20` in place of spaces. You specify the `volumename` rather than the path to the volume name. The value is:

    `url==afp://;AUTH=NO%20USER%20AUTHENT@server17.pretendco.com/Homes`

As soon as you create the record, Mac OS X clients that are bound to the directory node can use it.

Modifying Your LDAP Workflow

After you modify your schema or decide on which attributes to reuse, be sure to reevaluate your workflow for creating and editing user accounts in your LDAP directory. How will you populate your newly created attributes for existing and new users? It might be possible to use Workgroup Manager to edit records in your LDAP node, but you will need to test this with a nonproduction copy of your directory.

After you've updated your LDAP directory, you need to configure your Mac OS X client computer to use the changes you have made. The next section prepares you for this task and tackles some other ways of providing data to Mac OS X to support network login and automatic access to a home folder.

Configuring Mac OS X to Log In Using a Standard LDAP Server

Now that you know what information to add to your LDAP service to support login and access from a network user account, you're ready to learn how to configure Open Directory to use these new objects and attributes from your LDAP service. Because you may choose not to store *all* the necessary objects and attributes in your LDAP service, you will learn how to use Directory Utility to configure Open Directory to construct its own values for attributes with local mappings that are static or dynamic. You will also learn how to augment the information available from your LDAP service with information available from an Open Directory server.

Understanding How a User Authenticates at the Login Window

Regardless of the directory node where a network user record is located, that record has to be identified and authenticated in order for the user to log in. The Open Directory process responsible for allowing users to log in, `loginwindow`, identifies the user by searching through the authentication search path to find the user record, and then it attempts to authenticate the user. When trying to authenticate a user, `loginwindow` tries various ways to provide authentication:

▶ If the user record contains the `AuthenticationAuthority` Standard attribute, `loginwindow` uses it. (Only users defined in an Open Directory shared domain are likely to have this attribute defined, but it is included here for the sake of completeness.) This could simply contain the encrypted password or contain information that specifies the user's Kerberos and Password Server information.

▶ If there is a mapping for the attribute `dsAttrTypeStandard:Password`, Mac OS X attempts to authenticate with the password that is stored in the LDAP directory. The password can be stored in clear text (a bad idea) or in an encrypted format (which is still not very secure) in your LDAP service.

▶ If the record does not have a mapping for either attribute dsAttrTypeStandard:Password or dsAttrTypeStandard:AuthenticationAuthority, Mac OS X attempts an LDAP bind to authenticate the user. Mac OS X attempts Kerberos authentication (using an educated guess of the user's Kerberos principal) if the LDAP service supports the Generic Security Services Application Programming Interface (GSSAPI), otherwise Mac OS X attempts CRAM-MD5 before sending the password in clear text. If your LDAP service does not support GSSAPI or CRAM-MD5, you should use SSL to encrypt your communications with the LDAP service to avoid sending the password in clear text.

If your LDAP service does not store an encrypted password in the user record and is not integrated with Kerberos, or the LDAP service will not allow authenticated binds, your network user will not be able to authenticate.

You should be aware how and whether Mac OS X users will see administratively defined password policies. The LDAPv3 plug-in's password policy support varies by vendor and does not currently support either Novell or Microsoft directories.

After a user is successfully authenticated, loginwindow continues with the login process, mounting a share point for the network home folder and checking to see if there are any records for managed preferences.

Understanding MCX Records

Earlier in this chapter you examined mount records, which exist specifically to support automatically mounting network home folders. MCX (Managed Client for X) records are similar in that they support a specific Mac OS X function: Managed preferences, also referred to as Managed Client for X. Workgroup Manager lets you easily manage preferences for users, computers, groups of computers, and workgroups. Managed preferences, which allow you to customize the user experience, are stored as XML lists in the appropriate LDAP record (user, computer, computer group, and workgroup).

Records that specify managed preferences have two main attributes: MCXFlags and MCXSettings. MCXSettings can have multiple values, one per broad type of managed setting. Each of those values is a plist. Table 3.3 provides a summary.

Table 3.3   Attributes for Managed Client for X (MCX)

Open Directory Standard Attribute	LDAP Native Attribute	Purpose
MCXFlags	apple-mcxflags	Whether MCX settings exist (also whether a user can simultaneously log in)
MCXSettings	apple-mcxsettings	XML formatted plist for each category of managed settings

Here's a view of the MCXFlags attribute value for a sample user. This plist specifies that the user has MCX settings, and that the user can log in simultaneously to more than one computer:

```
client17:~ cadmin$ dscl /Search read /Users/mcxuser1 MCXFlags
<?xml version="1.0" encoding="UTF-8"?>
<!DOCTYPE plist PUBLIC "-//Apple//DTD PLIST 1.0//EN" "http://www.apple.com/DTDs/
PropertyList-1.0.dtd">
<plist version="1.0">
<dict>
    <key>has_mcx_settings</key>
    <true/>
    <key>simultaneous_login_enabled</key>
    <true/>
</dict>
</plist>
```

The MCXSettings attribute usually contains much more data. For example, consider the MCXSettings data for this sample user with management settings for the Dock (appear on the left), Parental Controls (set a limit on time the computer can be used), and Printing (print a footer on each page). To see the amount of data, perform a dscl query for the user's MCXSettings attribute, but send the results to the word count command wc with the option -l to give the number of lines. The dscl command is one line, and the result of 233 lines shows that the MCXSettings data is quite large:

```
client17:~ cadmin $ dscl /Search read /Users/mcxuser1 MCXSettings | wc -l
    233
```

You can return to a graphical application such as Workgroup Manager or LDAPManager to illustrate the attribute values. The data begin with some header information (XML version, DOCTYPE, plist version) and then finally get to the dictionary. The figure below illustrates the user's MCX data for management of the Dock. The second to the last line, orientation, is a key with the value left to specify that the user's Dock appears on the left side of the screen.

The MCXFlags and MCXSettings attributes contain plists that define MCX settings for a user, but these attributes can exist for computer, computer group, and group records as well.

Modifying your LDAP schema so that the appropriate object classes can handle these additional attributes is one way of enabling MCX, but we will explore other creative ways to enable MCX later in this chapter.

Mapping Records and Attributes

Open Directory's LDAPv3 plug-in needs to know which object classes and attributes in an LDAP directory to use. This is called *mapping*: matching Open Directory records to LDAP object classes and matching Open Directory attributes to LDAP attributes.

For example, you can use the following steps to build on the basic set of mappings provided by the RFC 2307 template. You will map the Standard HomeDirectory attribute to the Native mail attribute, which has been repurposed in the LDAP data store to contain the necessary data for HomeDirectory (a delimited value that defines a URL for the share point and the path to the home folder from the share point). The steps are the same whether you specify a reused attribute or an attribute that you added to the LDAP schema.

1   Open Directory Utility and click the lock to authenticate as a local administrator.

2   Click Services in the toolbar, highlight the LDAPv3 service, and then click the Edit button 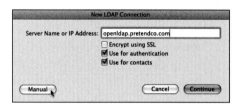.

3   Click New to specify a new standard LDAP service to bind to.

4   Enter the name of the server that hosts the LDAP service, in this case, openldap. pretendco.com. Click Manual to specify how Open Directory maps Standard objects and attributes to Native objects and attributes.

5   Type a descriptive name, in this case openldap, in the Configuration Name column.

6   Click LDAP Mappings and select RFC 2307 (Unix) from the pop-up menu.

This provides a base set of mappings from Standard objects and attributes to Native LDAP objects and attributes.

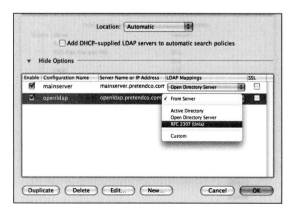

7   Type the search base location in the Search Base field—in this case *cn=openldap,*
    dc=mainserver,dc=pretendco,dc=com.

8   Click the Edit button to edit the mappings, and then click the Search & Mappings tab.

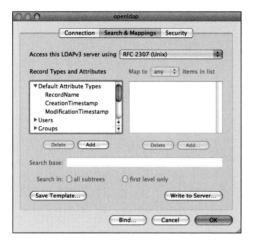

9   In the "Record Types and Attributes" list, click the disclosure triangle for Users.

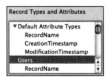

10 Scroll through the "Record Types and Attributes" list and notice there is no entry for
    HomeDirectory under Users.

11 Under "Record Types and Attributes," select Users. Note that this causes the search base to appear in the "Search base" field.

12 Under "Record Types and Attributes," click Add.

> **TIP** ▶ Notice that there are two Add buttons, one for "Record Types and Attributes" and one for "Map to any items in list." Be sure to click the proper one.

13 Prepare to map the Standard attribute HomeDirectory to the Native attribute mail. Select the Attribute Type HomeDirectory and click OK.

14 Under "Map to *any* items in list," click Add.

15 Type *mail.*

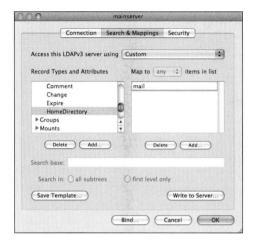

16 Click OK to dismiss the Search & Mappings window.

17 Click OK to dismiss the list of LDAP services and authenticate as a local administrator if prompted.

18 Click the Search Policy button in Directory Utility's toolbar.

19 If the LDAP service is not listed, click the Add button in the lower-left corner, choose the LDAP service you just defined, and then click Add.

20 Click Apply and then quit Directory Utility.

With the steps above, you mapped the Standard attribute HomeDirectory to the reused Native attribute mail. Use dscl to confirm that the change is in place:

```
client17:~ cadmin$ dscl /LDAPv3/openldap.pretendco.com read /Users/user1
HomeDirectory
HomeDirectory: <home_dir><url>afp://mainserver.pretendco.com/Users</url><path>user1
</path></home_dir>
```

Although you mapped HomeDirectory to mail, the attribute is still available on its own in the user record. Because you are reusing it, however, mail doesn't contain anything that has to do with mail:

```
client17:~ cadmin$ dscl /LDAPv3/openldap.pretendco.com read /Users/user1 mail
HomeDirectory: <home_dir><url>afp://mainserver.pretendco.com/Users</url><path>user1
</path></home_dir>
```

Again, because someone may later need to use the mail attribute for mail, reusing an attribute is not a very stable solution. In the next few sections you will learn other ways to provide necessary information for Open Directory Standard attributes.

Augmenting LDAP Data with Local Static and Variable Mappings

Local mappings are useful for allowing you to extend the data returned by Open Directory when the standard LDAP directory does not contain the data you need, especially if you can reliably predict your desired value for an attribute. There are two types of local mappings:

▶ Static mappings—Begin the attribute value with the hash sign (#) to force Open Directory to use the text that you specify as the value, instead of looking up the value from the directory node. For example, specify #20 for the Standard attribute PrimaryGroupID to force all users in that node to have a primary group ID of 20, regardless of what value is in their record, if any.

▶ Dynamic mappings—Wrap a Native attribute with the dollar sign ($) to force Open Directory to use the value of that attribute.

You can insert dynamic mappings into your static mappings. In the following example, you will remove the mapping you created in the previous section and use the dynamic mapping of uid inside a static map for dsAttrTypeStandard:HomeDirectory. This mapping causes every user that logs in to get a HomeDirectory value of <home_dir><url>afp:// mainserver.pretendco.com/Users</url><path>*uid*</path></home_dir> where *uid* is the user's dsAttrTypeNative:uid, which typically contains the user's short name.

This local mapping assumes that all users share the same home folder server and share point, and that the only difference is the path to their home folder, which happens to be their short name:

1   Open Directory Utility, click the lock in the lower-left corner, and then authenticate as a local administrator if necessary.

2   Click Services, choose LDAPv3, and then click the Edit button ✐ in the lower-left corner.

3   Select the entry for your LDAP service and click Edit.

4   Click the Search & Mappings tab, and then in the "Record Types and Attributes" list click the disclosure triangle for Users.

5   Choose the attributes `HomeDirectory` from the left column and `mail` from the right column, and then click Delete to remove the mapping you created in the last example.

6   In the right column, click Add.

7   Type the text below to create a static map:

`#<home_dir><url>afp://mainserver.pretendco.com/Users</url><path>$uid$</path></home_dir>`

For the static map, the URL for all users' home folder is the same, except for the sub-stitution of `uid`, which contains the short name.

8   Click OK to close the Search & Mappings window, and then click OK to close the list of LDAP services.

9   Quit Directory Utility.

Saving and Reusing a Mapping Template

It takes many steps to set up these mappings. This process is not scalable for many machines, especially when you have many mappings. To make matters easier, you can use Directory Utility to carefully set up the mappings, test your settings, and then save the mappings. By default, Directory Utility saves your mappings to your home folder in ~/Library/Application Support/Directory Access/LDAPv3/Templates. In very general terms, these are the steps necessary to share and then use a template of your customized mappings:

1   Use Directory Utility to create the mapping template.

2   Use standard tools to copy the template to another Mac OS X computer.

3   On the other Mac OS X computer, place the template in the folder /Library/
    Application Support/Directory Access/LDAPv3/Templates to make it available to
    all users of that computer.

4   On the other Mac OS X computer, use Directory Utility's LDAP Mappings pop-up
    menu and select the new template from the list.

Each step is explained in detail below.

Follow these instructions to save the template:

1   Open Directory Utility, click the lock in the lower-left corner, and then authenticate
    as a local administrator if necessary.

2   Select Services, choose LDAPv3, and then click the Edit button ✐ in the lower-left corner.

3   Select the entry for your LDAP service with your custom mappings.

4   Click Edit.

5   Click the Search & Mappings tab to reveal the Save Template button.

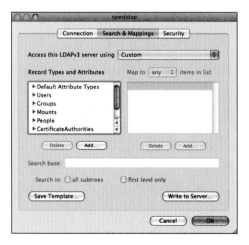

6 Click the Save Template button so that you can distribute these settings to other Mac OS X computers.

7 Type a name for the template, in this case, openldap-withstatic, and click Save.

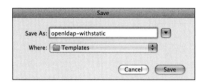

8 Click OK to close the Search & Mappings window, and then click OK again to close the list of LDAP services.

9 Quit Directory Utility.

10 In the Finder, confirm that your mappings template was saved in a plist file. Look in ~/Library/Application Support/Directory Access/LDAPv3/Templates.

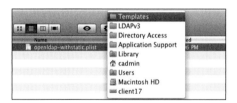

Copy the plist file to another computer, then follow the steps below to use the template on that other computer:

1 Create the folder structure /Library/Application Support/Directory Access/LDAPv3/ Templates.

Note that Directory Utility saves the file in your home folder, but you can place the file in a location accessible to all users of the computer. Also note that the directory name is Directory Access instead of Directory Utility.

2 Copy the file to /Library/Application Support/Directory Access/LDAPv3/Templates.

3   Open Directory Utility, click the lock in the lower-left corner, and then authenticate as a local administrator if necessary.

4   Click Services, choose LDAPv3, and then click the Edit button ✎ in the lower-left corner.

5   Click New, and then type the name of your LDAP service.

6   Click Manual, and then type a descriptive name in the Configuration Name column.

7   Click the pop-up menu in the LDAP Mappings column and select the entry for your new template.

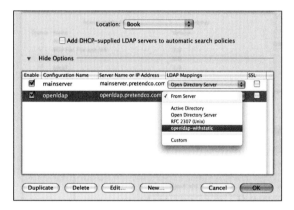

8   Type in the search base and click OK.

9   Click Edit to reveal the Search & Mappings tab.

10   Click the Search & Mappings tab.

11   Click the Disclosure tab for Users, scroll down, and then select HomeDirectory. Confirm that the local mapping is in place: The "Map to any items in list" column should contain the mapping that starts with the hash sign.

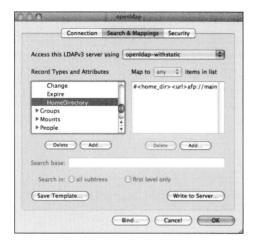

12 Click OK to close the Search & Mappings window, and then click OK again to close the list of LDAP services.

13 Quit Directory Utility.

See Help in Directory Utility for more information about using the Write to Server button to save your custom mappings to your Open Directory LDAP server's record `cn=macosxodconfig,cn=config,`*searchbase*.

Supplementing LDAP Data with Information from an Open Directory Server

Many organizations already have a well-tested procedure for creating, modifying, and deleting network user accounts when using an existing LDAP service. You can keep that infrastructure and its associated workflow in place, yet also take advantage of the features of an Open Directory server. This is sometimes referred to as the "Magic Triangle." Bind Mac OS X to both directories and put them both in the authentication search path:

▶ Bind Mac OS X to your other LDAP service for user identification and authentication.

▶ Bind Mac OS X to your Open Directory server for managed preferences for computer, computer group, and workgroup accounts, and for mount records for automounted network volumes.

In the figure below, the third-party LDAP service is on the left; the Xserve on the right represents the Open Directory server; and the Mac OS X computer in the center is bound to both directory services. The third-party LDAP service (left) provides user information, but the Open Directory server (right) provides mount records for automount, and provides MCX attributes for computer records, computer group records, and workgroup records.

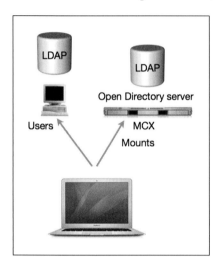

Make sure that both directory nodes are listed in the authentication search path, because the authentication search path is used not only for user records, but also for information such as mount records and Managed Preference attributes.

Mac OS X uses the first record it finds that matches the name you provide at the login window, so if it finds a user record in the third-party LDAP service, it will not consult the Open Directory server node for the user record. However, Mac OS X still uses the Open Directory server node for mount records and other information.

When you bind Mac OS X to two different directory nodes, it is possible to add user records from one node into the group membership list for a group in another node. (See Chapter 8 for instructions on how to do this with Workgroup Manager.) You also can make a standard LDAP user record a member of an Open Directory server workgroup. When you log in with that user record, you authenticate against the standard LDAP service; your home folder is automatically mounted with the help of mount records from an Open Directory server node; and you have Managed Preference settings applied for the workgroup that is defined on the Open Directory server. The "Troubleshooting Login Issues" section, later in this chapter, lists each step for a successful login using two directory nodes.

Configuring Mac OS X to Use a Third-Party Kerberos KDC

When you bind to an Open Directory server, Mac OS X uses the configuration information that it retrieves from the LDAP service to automatically configure the Kerberos environment. To use a third-party KDC, however, you need to create or modify the Kerberos configuration files.

The Kerberos application provides an easy way to specify a third-party KDC. The key is to understand where the configuration files are and when you can safely edit them.

> **NOTE ▶** The /Default/Local directory node in Mac OS v10.5 now contains Kerberos configuration information in /var/db/dslocal/nodes/Default/config/Kerberos:REALM.plist, where REALM is the name of the Kerberos realm.

Understanding Kerberos Configuration Files

Mac OS X uses the Native attribute `apple-xmlplist` of `cn=KerberosClient,cn=config,dc=mainserver,dc=pretendco,dc=com` to create and update the Kerberos configuration file /Library/Preferences/edu.mit.Kerberos. The file contains configuration information that includes the default realm and the locations of any KDCs within it. The file begins with this warning:

```
# WARNING This file is automatically created, if you wish to make changes
# delete the next two lines
# autogenerated from : /LDAPv3/10.1.0.1
# generation_id : 833361258
```

The `generation_id` above comes from the `generationID` that is part of the `apple-xmlplist` value. Mac OS X Server changes the value of the `generationID` when you make changes to the Kerberos environment, such as adding a new Open Directory replica (which adds a new KDC).

If Mac OS X is bound to an Open Directory server, when it reboots it checks to see if the autogeneration lines are still at the beginning of the file /Library/Preferences/edu.mit. Kerberos. If this file is missing, Mac OS X creates a new copy. If the autogeneration lines are not in the file, then the file is not modified. If the autogeneration lines do exist, then Mac OS X checks to see if a newer configuration is available by comparing it to the value of `generationID` that is available from the LDAP service, with the value stored in /Library/Preferences/edu.mit.Kerberos. If the `generationID` is the same on both sources, no change is made. If the `generationID` from the LDAP service is newer, then the entire /Library/Preferences/edu.mit.Kerberos file is regenerated, discarding any previous modifications.

You can prevent Mac OS X from overwriting your modifications by removing the first four lines of edu.mit.Kerberos—but after you do this, Mac OS X will not automatically be aware of any new KDCs or other changes.

The default location for the Kerberos configuration file is /Library/Preferences/edu.mit. Kerberos, but there are a few possible locations for this information. The files are listed below in order of precedence; Mac OS X uses the first Kerberos configuration file it finds in this list and ignores the others:

▶   ~/Library/Preferences/edu.mit.Kerberos

▶   /Library/Preferences/edu.mit.Kerberos

▶   /etc/krb5.conf

Mac OS X autogenerates the Kerberos configuration file at /Library/Preferences/edu.mit. Kerberos only. If a user has a custom ~/Library/Preferences/edu.mit.Kerberos file, any automatic or manual changes to the /Library/Preferences/edu.mit.Kerberos file will not take effect, because personal configuration files take precedence.

If you are bound to multiple Open Directory domains and you unbind from one Open Directory domain while the autogeneration lines still exist in /Library/Preferences/edu. mit.Kerberos, Mac OS X removes the entries for that Open Directory domain. If you unbind from the last Open Directory domain and the autogeneration lines are still in the file, Mac OS X removes the entire file /Library/Preferences/edu.mit.Kerberos.

You can use the Kerberos application to specify an additional KDC. When you do this, the application:

▶   Creates the file /Library/Preferences/edu.mit.Kerberos if it does not already exist

▶   Removes the autogeneration header from /Library/Preferences/edu.mit.Kerberos so that Mac OS X does not overwrite the file and destroy the changes you made

▶   Adds the new KDC to the list of Favorite Realms in your personal preference file ~/Library/Preferences/edu.mit.KerberosLogin.plist

To use the Kerberos application to specify a new KDC, follow these steps:

1   Open the Kerberos application (in /System/Library/CoreServices).

2   From the Edit menu, choose Edit Realms.

3   Click the Add (+) button in the lower-left corner of the Edit Realms window.

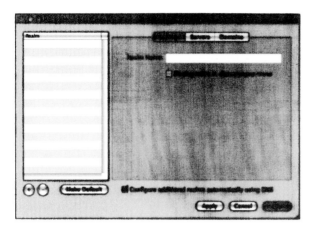

4   Type the realm name in the **Realm Name** field.

TIP It is customary, but not necessary, for realm names be written in all upper-case characters to distinguish Kerberos realms from DNS names.

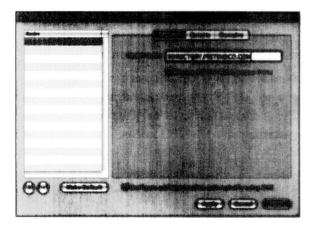

5   Click the Servers button.

6   Click the Add (+) button in the lower-left corner of the Servers pane.

7 Type the FQDN or IP address of the KDC in the Server field.

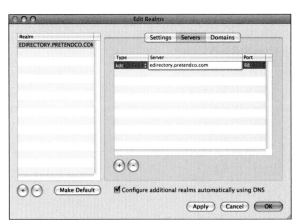

8 Click the Make Default button to make this the default KDC, and then click OK.

9 Click the New button in the Kerberos application's toolbar.

10 Notice that the Realm field contains the newly defined realm, EDIRECTORY.PRETENDCO. COM. Click Cancel to cancel, or type a password and network user account from the new realm, and then click OK.

11 Quit the Kerberos application.

An alternative to using the Kerberos application is to edit the /Library/Preferences/edu. mit.Kerberos file with a text editor. See the man page for krb5.conf for more details about the various options available for a Kerberos configuration file.

After you edit the Kerberos configuration file, all applications that use Kerberos will use the new KDC, including `loginwindow`. You may need to kill `DirectoryService` for directory services to be aware of the changes that you made to the configuration.

Troubleshooting Binding Issues

If you are having problems binding to the LDAP service, follow the troubleshooting tips in this section.

First, check the obvious: Verify underlying network connectivity. Can you ping the IP address of the computer hosting the LDAP service?

You'll also want to check the DNS service. Can you ping the FQDN for the computer hosting the LDAP service?

Make sure your LDAP service uses port 389 for LDAP, or use Directory Utility to change the port that Mac OS X uses for LDAP. Follow these steps:

1 Open Directory Utility.

2 Take the appropriate steps to edit your LDAP service.

3 Click the Connection tab.

4 Click the "Use custom port" checkbox and type 389 in the Custom Port field.

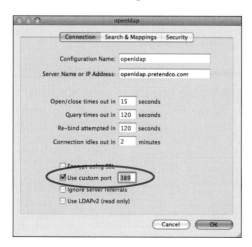

Make sure anonymous binding is allowed, or supply the correct credentials in Directory Utility. If you must provide credentials, supply the full distinguished name (dn), in addition to the password. The figure below shows a common setup with eDirectory, an LDAP proxy user that has no password. An LDAP bind with this user has no more rights than an anonymous LDAP bind.

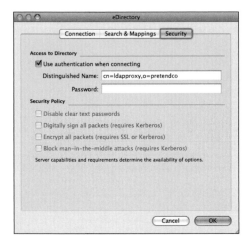

If you use authenticated binding, make sure that the user that you specify to bind with has read access to all the necessary attributes. If you extend your eDirectory schema, you must also update the access control list (ACL) for the new object classes and attributes to allow users to access them.

If TLS/SSL is required to bind to the LDAP service, enable it with Directory Utility. The checkbox for this appears in two locations. There is a checkbox to the right of each defined LDAP service, as shown here:

If you check the box for the LDAP service above, it will also be reflected in the checkbox under the Connection tab for the LDAP service:

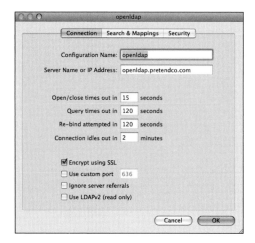

Check the search base. Use a graphical application such as LDAPManager, use `ldapsearch`, or ask your LDAP administrator. The following example searches the LDAP base for the `namingContexts`, and the result is `dc=openldap,dc=pretendco,dc=com`:

```
client17:~ cadmin$ ldapsearch -LLL -x -H ldap://openldap.pretendco.com -s base
namingContexts
dn:
namingContexts: dc=openldap,dc=pretendco,dc=com
```

Check the methods available for encrypting LDAP traffic with `ldapsearch`, or ask your LDAP administrator.

```
client17:~ cadmin$ ldapsearch -LLL -x -H ldap://edirectory.pretendco.com -s base
supportedSASLMechanisms
dn:
supportedSASLMechanisms: NMAS_LOGIN
```

If your LDAP service returns only a limited set of attributes for anonymous requests, use Directory Utility to provide user authentication. Note that many implementations of eDirectory use an "ldapproxy" user that doesn't have a password, but has access to various records and attributes.

Before attempting to log in with a network user, use `dscl` to make sure Open Directory can see the full user record. Here is an example:

```
client17:~ cadmin$ dscl /LDAPv3/openldap.pretendco.com read /Users/user1
[the output is not shown for the sake of brevity]
```

Troubleshooting Login Issues

You can try the same troubleshooting techniques that you learned in the "Troubleshooting Login Issues" section in Chapter 2, but if you use more than one directory node, your troubleshooting can get more complex. When troubleshooting your directory integration, take a step back and observe the chain of events in a successful login. This will help you troubleshoot issues that may crop up along the way.

In the following scenario, a Mac OS X computer is bound to both a standard LDAP directory and an Open Directory server. The LDAP directory contains the user record cscott with an encrypted password stored in the record. The Open Directory server contains a mount record for a share point hosted on the Open Directory server, which is also an AFP file server. The Open Directory server has a workgroup with managed preferences settings, and the user from the LDAP directory is a member of this workgroup.

Each section includes a number of steps followed by a figure illustrating those steps. The sections trace the events involved in logging in as the user "cscott," selecting a workgroup, and then gaining access to the user's home folder.

Booting and Using Mount Records

1. When Mac OS X boots up, Directory Services uses the configuration files in /Library/ Preferences/DirectoryService to get a list of directory nodes to use in the authentication search path.

2. Mac OS X searches for mount and computer records in all the nodes of the authentication search path.

3. The standard LDAP directory does not contain any mount records; the Open Directory server node returns the mount and computer records. The automount processes take care of mounting any static mounts and preparing for dynamic mounts. Mac OS X applies the MCX settings contained in the computer record.

4. Mac OS X displays the login window.

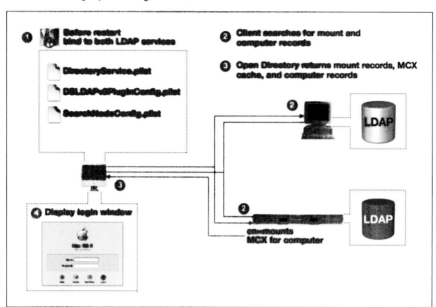

Identifying and Authenticating the User

If the login window displays a list of users, you select a user or select Other. If the login window displays user name and password fields, provide a user's short name, full name, or Kerberos principal, and then provide a password and click the "Log in" button. If the login window does not accept the login, see "Troubleshooting Login Issues" in Chapter 2. Here are the steps:

1. Provide the short name cscott and the correct password.

2. Mac OS X searches for a user record that matches the name that you selected or provided, using the authentication search path. DirectoryService first searches for the user record in the /Local/Default node but does not find it there. You did not enable BSD Users and Groups, so Mac OS X skips that directory node.

3. Mac OS X continues its attempt to identify the user record. dsAttrTypeStandard:Recordname is mapped to both dsAttrTypeNative:cn and dsAttrTypeNative:uid, so DirectoryService sends an LDAP request for a user whose attribute cn or uid has the value of cscott.

4. The LDAP node sends the user record to Mac OS X. Because Mac OS X finds a matching user record, it moves on to the authentication stage. Mac OS X does not search for the user record in the Open Directory server node next, because it found it in the standard LDAP node first.

5. Mac OS X attempts to authenticate the user. This user has no AuthenticationAuthority. If Mac OS X were configured to use Kerberos, it would make an educated guess at the Kerberos principal; but in this case, Mac OS X attempts an LDAP bind as cscott, with the password you typed at the login window.

6. The LDAP bind succeeds and loginwindow proceeds with the login.

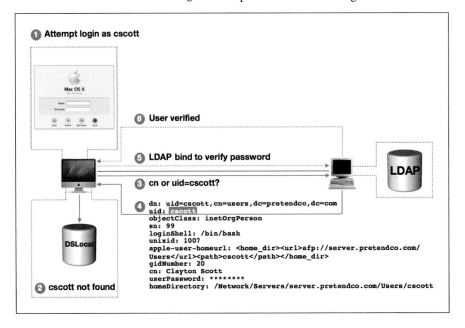

Applying Managed Preferences

After `loginwindow` identifies and authenticates the user, Mac OS X gets a list of workgroups that the user belongs to. The sequence of events follows:

1. The user is identified and authenticated.

2. Mac OS X queries all directory nodes in the authentication search path for group records that the user might belong to and that also have Managed Preference settings.

   A group that has managed preferences is called a *workgroup*. The standard LDAP node does not have any workgroups, but the Open Directory server node does. The figure below does not illustrate this, but Mac OS X also searches for the computer record or a guest computer record, and for records for groups of computers.

3. The Open Directory server returns a list of the user's workgroups to Mac OS X.

4. If the user belongs to more than one group with managed preferences, you must choose one workgroup for this login session. If there are no workgroups or if there is only one workgroup, you do not see the workgroup picker.

5. After you select a workgroup, the processes that handle Mac OS X's managed preferences combine the managed preference attributes for the user, computer, computer group, and workgroup records, along with locally cached managed preferences in the following locations:

   ▶ ~/Library/Preferences/com.apple.MCX.plist

   ▶ /Library/Managed Preferences/*username*

   ▶ /Library/Managed Preferences

   ▶ /var/db/dslocal/nodes/Default/config/mcx_cache.plist

   Managed preferences for users take precedence over managed preferences for computers, which take precedence over managed preferences for computer groups; managed preferences for workgroups have the lowest priority.

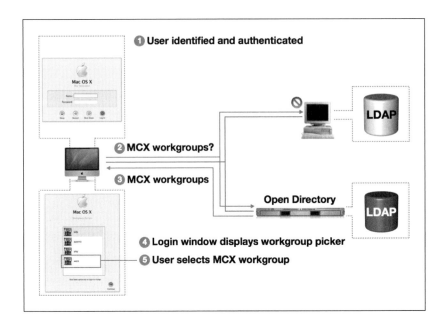

Mounting the Home Folder

Before users can do anything useful with the system, they need access to their home folder.

1. You select a managed group.

2. Mac OS X uses the Standard attribute `HomeDirectory` to mount the share point that hosts your network home folder. The `HomeDirectory` value for user `cscott` is `<home_dir><url>afp://bigdisk.pretendco.com/Users</url><path>cscott</path></home_dir>`. If there is a mount record for bigdisk.pretendco.com/Users, Mac OS X will use it to mount the share point. In this case, there is a record that includes `VFSLinkDir` of /Network/Servers, so the automount processes attempt to mount the share point at /Network/Servers.

3. Mac OS X attempts to mount the share point with the `cscott` credentials. The computer bigdisk.pretendco.com (the Open Directory server and AFP server) attempts to identify the user in its authentication search path, starting with /Local/Default, then moving to /BSD/local if enabled for users and groups, and finally its shared LDAP database.

4. bigdisk.pretendco.com continues searching for a record to identify the cscott user record, finding a match in the standard LDAP database. It eventually uses LDAP bind authentication with the user's password.

5. The LDAP service allows the bind authentication, which tells the AFP server that Mac OS X provided sufficient authentication.

6. The AFP server checks to make sure that "cscott" is authorized to use the AFP services, and then allows the Mac OS X computer to mount the share point. The user should see the Finder and have access to the home folder. The Standard attribute NFSHomeDirectory for "cscott" is /Network/Servers/bigdisk.pretendco.com/cscott, which is the local path to the home folder.

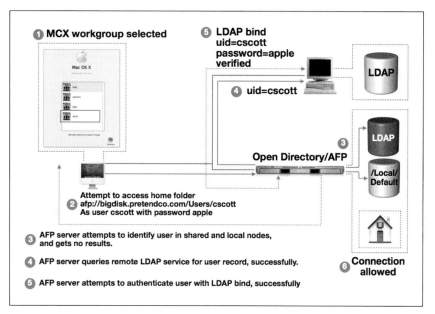

This complicated process usually happens quickly and is transparent to the user. Open Directory allows Mac OS X to use multiple directory sources to search for records to identify and authenticate users, find Managed Preference attributes, and mount the user's network home folder.

What You've Learned

▶ Several attributes are required for a network user to log in to Mac OS X and automatically access a network home folder.

▶ An LDAP directory's schema determines the object classes and attributes that the directory can handle. The schema also defines the kind of data that each attribute can store.

▶ An LDAP service that uses RFC 2307 schema definitions has many of the object classes and attributes required for a Mac OS X network user. The most important missing piece is the Standard `HomeDirectory` attribute, which is a delimited value that defines the share point and the path with the share point to a user's home folder. The Native attribute `homeDirectory` usually stores an absolute path, which is what the Standard attribute `NFSHomeDirectory` maps to.

▶ Mac OS X uses `AuthenticationAuthority` to attempt to authenticate a user. If there is no `AuthenticationAuthority` in a user record, Mac OS X does two things: It makes an educated guess of the Kerberos principal, and it attempts an LDAP bind with the user's password. If the LDAP plug-in is not set to use LDAP over SSL, the password is sent over the network in clear text.

▶ You can extend an LDAP directory's schema to add object classes and attributes to support requirements specific to Mac OS X, such as records that support automounting and attributes that support managed preferences. This is a more stable solution than repurposing otherwise unused attributes.

▶ Mac OS X can use local mappings, both static and dynamic—with the hash mark and the dollar sign (# and $), respectively—to generate values for attributes, such as a group ID of 20 for all users and a `HomeDirectory` value that varies only in the user's short name.

▶ Mac OS X uses Directory Utility to map Standard records and attributes to Native records and attributes available from LDAP services. You can save a template of your mappings to use again on another computer.

▶ Mac OS X can simultaneously use user records from one directory node and access mount records and Managed Preference attributes from an Open Directory server node, which is sometimes referred to as the "Magic Triangle."

▶ Even though your LDAP schema may not allow you to apply managed preferences at the user level, you can bind Mac OS X to an Open Directory server, add users from the LDAP service to Open Directory workgroups, and apply managed preferences at the computer and workgroup levels.

References

Documentation

▶ User Management for Version 10.5 Leopard
http://images.apple.com/server/macosx/docs/User_Management_v10.5.mnl.pdf

▶ Open Directory Administration for Version 10.5 Leopard, Second Edition
http://images.apple.com/server/macosx/docs/Open_Directory_Admin_v10.5.pdf

Books

▶ Carter, Gerald. *LDAP System Administration* (O'Reilly, 2003).

Websites

▶ LDAPManager Software
http://sourceforge.net/projects/ldapmanager

▶ OpenLDAP Project
http://www.openldap.org

▶ Lightweight Directory Access Protocol (v3)
http://ietf.org/rfc/rfc2251.txt

▶ Lightweight Directory Access Protocol (v3): Attribute Syntax Definitions
http://ietf.org/rfc/rfc2252.txt

▶ An Approach for Using LDAP as a Network Information Service
http://ietf.org/rfc/rfc2307.txt

▶ The LDAP Data Interchange Format (LDIF)—Technical Specification
http://ietf.org/rfc/rfc2849.txt

▶ [eDirectory] LDAP Directory Access over SSL, with Mac OS 10.5 Leopard
http://www.novell.com/coolsolutions/feature/19965.html

▶ Novell eDirectory 8.8 SP2 Administration Guide
http://download.novell.com

▶ Integrating Mac OS X and Novell eDirectory
http://macenterprise.org/dmdocuments/20041019-150_integrating-edir-osx10-3.pdf

Review Quiz

1. What are the attributes required to enable a user to log in to Mac OS X and automatically access an AFP network home folder?

2. What is the advantage of using an LDAP browser to test a connection to an LDAP service before using Directory Utility?

3. What are some choices for supplementing missing directory services data in a standard LDAP service, to successfully integrate Mac OS X with your LDAP service?

4. When integrating Mac OS X with a standard LDAP service, what attribute is commonly missing from the LDAP service?

5. Which Open Directory attribute contains the path, as seen on the local file system, to a user's home folder?

6. If you use Directory Utility to save your customized mappings as a template, where is that template saved?

7. What is the significance of RFC 2307?

Answers

1. The Standard Open Directory attributes are `RecordName`, `RealName`, `UniqueID`, `PrimaryGroupID`, `NFSHomeDirectory`, and `HomeDirectory`.

2. An LDAP browser can confirm that you have the correct settings and can establish a connection to the LDAP server. Once you can successfully access data, you can proceed with configuring Directory Utility with the settings you established as valid.

3. To supply data that is not available from a standard LDAP service, you could do the following: Repurpose existing fields; modify the schema of the directory; use local mappings with static or variable attributes; or bind to an Open Directory server that provides mount records.

4. Many directory services do not provide a default attribute for `dsAttrTypeStandard:Home Directory`, which is required for a Mac OS X AFP network home folder.

5. `dsAttrTypeStandard:NFSHomeDirectory`

6. The template is saved as a plist file in ~/Library/Application Support/Directory Access/LDAPv3/Templates.

7. RFC 2307 defines a series of Standard object classes and attribute types. If your standard LDAP directory contains the RFC 2307 schema definitions, it contains many attributes that are required to support Mac OS X login. The most important Open Directory attribute challenge is the `dsAttrTypeStandard:HomeDirectory` attribute, which should contain a delimited value that defines a URL for the share point and the path to the home folder from the share point.

4

Time   This chapter takes approximately 2 hours to complete.

Goals   Configure Mac OS X to log in using Active Directory
        Troubleshoot binding issues
        Troubleshoot login issues

Chapter 4
Accessing an Active Directory Service

Active Directory is Microsoft's directory services solution that provides LDAP and Kerberos services for identification and authentication. Many organizations with Windows computers use Active Directory because it provides these features:

▶ Security and policy management for Windows computers

▶ Tight integration with popular application servers such as Microsoft Exchange and Microsoft SQL Server

▶ High availability, with the ability to place multiple replica servers across geographic locations in a multimaster configuration

It is easy to integrate Mac OS X into an Active Directory environment. Although Mac OS X computers can access directory information provided by Active Directory via the LDAPv3 plug-in, you should use the Active Directory plug-in, which provides the following capabilities:

▶ Creating a computer account for secure communication with Active Directory services

▶ Configuring mappings of Open Directory objects and attributes to Active Directory objects and attributes

▶ Setting up the Kerberos environment for seamless integration with Active Directory

▶ Enabling SMB packet signing and packet encryption

▶ Support of Active Directory password policies

▶ Support of Active Directory Sites, which directs Windows and Mac OS X client computers to the most appropriate services based on their IP network

▶ Caching information from Active Directory services so that Mac OS X computers can use the information even if they are not connected to the network

In this chapter you will learn how to use both Directory Utility and the command line to bind to Active Directory, and to modify the default settings for the Active Directory plug-in to enable login and access to a network home folder. You will learn how to overcome problems with your initial bind to Active Directory, and you will learn troubleshooting techniques for login problems with an Active Directory user account.

Configuring Mac OS X to Log In Using Active Directory

You can either use Directory Utility or dsconfigad to bind a Mac OS X client computer to an Active Directory domain. dsconfigad allows you to configure some features that Directory Utility does not expose, but if you use dsconfigad you need to take some additional steps (such as enabling the Active Directory plug-in and adding the Active Directory node to your search paths). Before you can bind with either method, however, you need to know a few things about your Active Directory service.

Understanding Active Directory Terms

When you bind to Active Directory, you need to know the domain name and you must have the credentials of a user who has authorization to join computers to Active Directory.

A *domain* is the building block of Active Directory; it is a collection of directory objects such as users, groups, and computers. An Active Directory domain requires a *domain controller*, which can be a computer running any version of Windows Server 2000 through Windows Server 2008. A domain is identified by its DNS namespace; in this book the example server windows-server.pretendco.com hosts the domain pretendco.com. Active Directory relies on DNS records generated by a DNS service that is tightly integrated with Active Directory, so you should configure Mac OS X to use the DNS service associated with the Active Directory domain before attempting to bind.

A *tree* is one or more domains in a contiguous name space. A *forest* is a set of domain trees that have a common schema and *global catalog*, which is used to describe a best-effort collection of all the resources in a domain. The global catalog is commonly used for email address lookups.

Like standard Windows clients, Mac OS X binds to only one Active Directory domain at a time.

Understanding the Active Directory Computer Object
When you bind a Mac OS X client computer to Active Directory, you use or create a *computer object* for Mac OS X. Just like user objects, computer objects are used for identification, authentication, and authorization. The computer object has rights to do certain things, such as to bind and update its own DNS record.

When you bind a Mac OS X computer to Active Directory, Mac OS X uses the user credentials you supply to set up a computer account and password. This password is a shared secret between your Mac OS X computer and the Active Directory service. Your Mac OS X computer uses this password to authenticate to Active Directory and set up a secure channel to enable your Mac OS X computer to communicate with Active Directory. The password is randomly generated, and is unrelated to the user account you use to perform the bind. For more information, see "Confirming Your Active Directory Plug-in and the Samba Service Are Using the Same Active Directory Computer Password" in Chapter 8.

If you delete the computer object or reset the computer object password in Active Directory, you need to rebind Mac OS X to Active Directory in order for Mac OS X to access Active Directory.

When you use Directory Utility to bind to Active Directory, Directory Utility suggests a computer ID to use for the name of the Active Directory computer object. This computer ID is based on the computer name or Bonjour name that you set in the Sharing pane of System Preferences. If your computer name is longer than 15 characters, you may experience errors when binding to Active Directory. Also note that Directory Utility may replace any instance of a dash (-) with an underscore (_) and change capital letters to lowercase in the suggested computer ID. You should use the same Mac OS X computer name and Active Directory computer name to help keep track of computer names, unless you have a good reason not to do so.

Specifying a User to Create the Computer Object

When binding to Active Directory, you need to supply the credentials of an Active Directory administrator or user who is authorized to create computer objects. By default, you can use a regular active directory user to bind to Active Directory ten times, but after that you will encounter an error. "Troubleshooting Binding Issues," later in this chapter, offers some solutions for this problem.

Binding to Active Directory with Directory Utility

The simplest way to bind Mac OS X to Active Directory is to use Directory Utility with all the default settings in place. The steps are as follows:

1 Quit Directory Utility if it is open.

2 Use the Sharing preference in System Preferences to set your computer name to be the name of the computer object you want to create for binding to Active Directory.

3 Open Directory Utility.

4 If necessary, click the lock in the lower-left corner and provide credentials for a local administrator.

5 Click the Add (+) button in the lower-left corner.

6 Click the "Add a new directory of type" pop-up menu and choose Active Directory.

7 In the Active Directory Domain field, type the name of the Active Directory domain—in other words, "pretendco.com" not "windows-server.pretendco.com."

This can be any domain in the forest, but remember that the domain name is the DNS namespace of the domain, not the DNS name of the domain controller.

8 In the Computer ID field, type the name of the Active Directory computer object to use for this Mac OS X computer.

9 In the AD Administrator Username field, type the name of an Active Directory administrator or the name of an Active Directory user who can join a computer to the domain.

10 In the AD Administrator Password field, type the password for the user you specified in step 9.

11 Click OK.

Mac OS X attempts to bind to Active Directory with the default settings.

Logging In as an Active Directory User on Mac OS X

Once you bind your Mac OS X computer to Active Directory, you can log in with your Active Directory user account at your Mac OS X login window.

The following figure shows the default desktop for an Active Directory that logs in to a Mac OS X computer. Note that the home folder is located on the startup disk (Option-clicking the name of a folder in the title bar of a Finder window reveals the path to the folder). The user launched the Kerberos application (in /System/Library/CoreServices), which shows that Mac OS X obtained a Kerberos ticket-granting ticket (TGT) for the user as part of the login process.

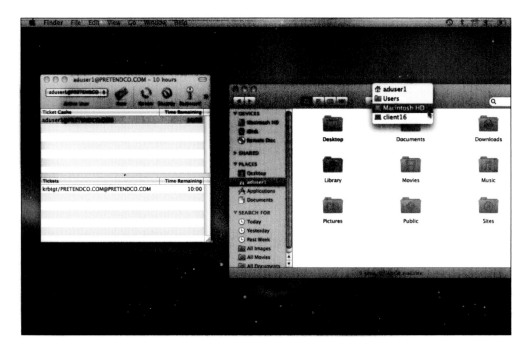

Specifying a User Name at the Login Screen

By default the Mac OS X login window displays the names of local user accounts and Other to allow you to specify a user name from a different directory node, as shown in this figure.

When you choose Other, the login window reveals a field for Name and Password.

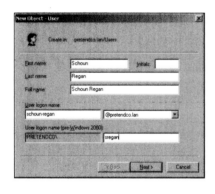

At the Mac OS X login window, you can use many combinations of the user identifiers "Full name," "User login name," or "User login name (Pre-Windows 2000)" from Active Directory, along with other elements of the domain name. Consider the figure at left, which shows a user created with Active Directory tools.

You can log in with any of the following names in the Name field in Mac OS X's login window:

▶   schoun-regan

▶   sregan

▶   Schoun Regan

▶   schoun-regan@pretendco.com

▶   sregan@pretendco.com

▶   Schoun Regan@pretendco.com

▶   PRETENDCO\schoun-regan

▶   PRETENDCO\sregan

▶   PRETENDCO\Schoun Regan

Understanding the Home Folder Default Behavior

When you log in with a user account for Active Directory, by default Mac OS X creates a home folder for the user on the startup disk in /Users/*usershortname*.

If a directory already exists with that name, Mac OS X will not create a new home folder. You may experience unexpected results because the Active Directory user does not have write permissions to the home folder.

See "Transitioning from a Local User to an Active Directory User," later in this chapter, if that is appropriate for your situation.

Understanding Home Folder Synchronization

The default settings do not configure Mac OS X to synchronize the local home folder with a network home folder. If you log in as the same Active Directory user on multiple Mac OS X computers that are configured with the default settings for the Active Directory plug-in, you will have a different home folder on each computer, and the contents will not be synchronized. To prevent this situation you can do the following:

▶ Configure mobile accounts and home folder synchronization. See "Understanding Mobile Accounts" for more on this.

▶ Deselect the option to force the creation of a local home folder, and use Active Directory tools to assign a network home folder for the Active Directory user account. See "Specifying a Network Home Folder" for details.

Changing the Active Directory Plug-in Default Settings

The Active Directory plug-in's default settings might not meet your needs. For instance, you may want to not force local home folders on the startup disk, or you may want to use custom mappings or to specify Active Directory groups to members that have local administrative access on your Mac OS X computer. In this section you will learn how to use Directory Utility and the command line to configure some of the advanced options of the Active Directory plug-in.

Follow these steps to use Directory Utility to access Active Directory Advanced Options:

1 Open Directory Utility. If necessary, click the lock in the lower-left corner and provide credentials for a local administrator. If necessary, click the Show Advanced Settings button in the lower-right corner of the Directory Utility window.

2 Click Services in the toolbar.

3 Make sure the Active Directory service checkbox is selected.

4 Select the Active Directory service.

5 Click the Edit button ✎ in the lower-left corner of the Directory Utility window.

6 Click the disclosure triangle next to Show Advanced Options.

Exploring the "User Experience" Advanced Options Pane

The default pane for Directory Utility's Advanced Options is the User Experience pane, shown in the figure to the left.

The first option, "Create mobile account at login," is disabled by default. A mobile account caches user credentials locally so they can be used when the computer is not connected to the directory node. See "Understanding Mobile Accounts" for more details about mobile accounts and synchronized home folders.

The "Force local home directory on startup disk" option is enabled by default. If you deselect this option, and an Active Directory user who does not have a network home folder defined logs in, Mac OS X creates a local home folder in /Users/*username* for the user when the user logs in (unless a local home folder already exists).

Specifying a Network Home Folder

There are two possible ways to specify a network home folder:

▶   If your Active Directory schema has been extended to support Apple objects and attributes, map dsAttrTypeStandard:HomeDirectory to an extended attribute in your user record, and use Workgroup Manager to specify the home folder.

▶ Enable the option "Use UNC path from Active Directory to derive network home location" and use Active Directory tools to populate the Home Folder field for an Active Directory user. The Active Directory plug-in maps `dsAttrTypeStandard:SMBHomeDirectory` to Active Directory's `dsAttrTypeNative:homeDirectory`. You can also specify this option with the `-uncpath` option of `dsconfigad`.

You must specify which file-sharing protocol to use: SMB or AFP (Apple Filing Protocol). SMB is the default setting, so it is easy to use Windows file services to host home folders for Active Directory users who log in to a Mac OS X computer.

New in Mac OS X v10.5 is full support for SMB packet signing, a security feature designed to prevent man-in-the-middle attacks, which is required by default on Windows Server 2003 SP1 and later. Many Windows Server administrators require client computers to use this option, which makes it impossible for computers using earlier versions of Mac OS X to access their SMB share points without installing third-party SMB client software.

AFP offers some advantages over SMB as a file service protocol for Mac OS X client computers: It is faster, native to Mac OS X, supports Time Machine and network Spotlight searching, has better auto-reconnect, and handles a wider range of file names in a mixed environment. Unfortunately, Windows servers do not offer AFP by default.

Although Windows Server 2000 and Windows Server 2003 can offer AFP via Services for Macintosh (SFM), the SFM version of AFP is not current. For example, SFM supports only 31 characters in a file name, which causes a problem when Mac OS X uses a long file name, such as ~/Library/Preferences/ByHost/com.apple.iCal.helper.0017f3e00523.plist. SFM is not recommended for Mac OS X network home folders. If you must use your Windows server for network home directories, consider running a third-party AFP file service, such as GroupLogic's ExtremeZ-IP, on your Windows server.

You can use a Mac OS X Server to host network home folders for Active Directory users, whether they log in to Mac OS X computers or Windows computers. You can use Mac OS X Server's AFP service for users who log in to Mac OS X computers, and Mac OS X Server's SMB service for users who log in to Windows computers. Discourage users from simultaneously logging in as the same user simultaneously on Mac OS X and Windows computers, because if they edit the same file over two different protocols simultaneously, this could corrupt the file.

For more information about offering file services from a Mac OS X Server, see Chapter 10 of *Mac OS X Advanced System Administration v10.5.*

Logging In with a Windows Home Folder

If you use Active Directory tools to define a network home folder (`dsAttrTypeNative:SMBHome`) for the user, as shown in the figure to the left, Mac OS X mounts the network volume that contains that Active Directory home folder. Unless you specify otherwise, by default the Active Directory plug-in creates a local home folder on the startup disk, so Mac OS X mounts the Windows home folder but does not use it as the user's home folder.

The network folder appears in the Dock, but the volume does not appear on the user's desktop by default. The default preference for the Finder in Mac OS X v10.5 is to not display mounted network volumes on the desktop. To change this in the Finder, select Finder > Preferences and select the checkbox for "Connected servers."

The next figure illustrates what the standard desktop looks like for an Active Directory user who has an Active Directory home folder defined. The user opened Finder preferences and enabled "Connected servers" so that the Windows share point appears on the desktop. Note also that the user's home folder is located on the startup disk, which is the default setting for the Active Directory plug-in.

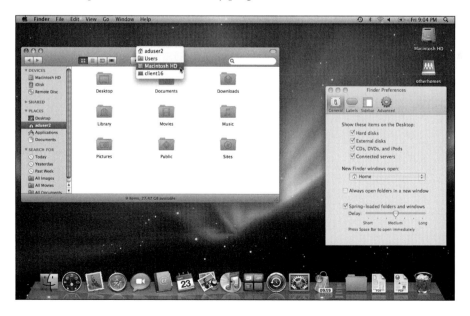

The figure below shows the desktop of an Active Directory user who has a Windows home folder set (`dsAttrTypeStandard:SMBHome`) and logs in to a Mac OS X computer that does not have the "force local home directory on startup disk" option enabled in the User Experience pane of the Active Directory plug-in.

Some things to note:

▶ The home folder is not on the startup disk.

▶ This user did not enable the option to show connected volumes on the desktop, so the volume containing the network home folder does not appear on the desktop.

▶ The user launched the Kerberos application to confirm that Mac OS X obtained a TGT, then the user closed the main window of the Kerberos application. The icon for the Kerberos application displays how much time is remaining (in hours and minutes) in the validity of the TGT. The usual TGT lifetime is 10 hours; after that time, the user can reauthenticate to renew the TGT.

▶ The question mark in the user's Dock represents the user's Documents folder, which has not yet been created. If the network home folder was hosted on a Mac OS X Server file service, Mac OS X Server would create the set of standard folders.

Changing User and Group Mappings

By default, the Active Directory plug-in generates a `dsAttrTypeStandard:UniqueID` for an Active Directory user record based on that user's GUID attribute. The calculated `UniqueID` is unique across the domain, yet consistent across every Mac OS X computer in the domain. Likewise, the Active Directory plug-in generates a unique integer for each Active Directory group record as well. If you have extended your Active Directory schema, you can use the Mappings pane to access the appropriate attributes from the Active Directory user and group records.

Be forewarned that if you change the mappings, users may lose access to files that they previously owned or could access.

The Mappings pane, shown below, allows you to change the mappings for the following:

▶   UID—`dsAttrTypeStandard:UniqueID`

▶   User GID—`dsAttrTypeStandard:PrimaryGroupID`

▶   Group GID—`dsAttrTypeStandard:PrimaryGroupID`

If the Active Directory schema were extended with Microsoft's Services for UNIX, the following would hold:

▶   Map UID to `msSFU-30-Uid-Number`

▶   Map both user GID and group GID to `msSFU-30-Gid-Number`

If the Active Directory schema were extended with RFC2307 or Apple object classes and attributes:

▶   Map UID to `uidNumber`

▶   Map both user GID and group GID to `gidNumber`

Exploring the "Administrative" Advanced Options Pane

The "Prefer this domain server" option shown in the figure below specifies a domain controller to use for the initial bind.

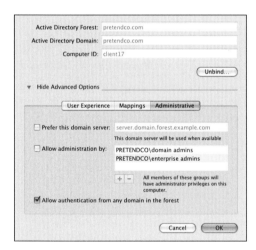

Use the "Allow administration by" option to enable any user of the Active Directory groups that you specify to be in the group of local administrators for this Mac OS X computer. This is useful if you create an Active Directory group and populate it with users who should have the authority to administer the Mac OS X computers in your organization.

When you add Active Directory to your search path, Directory Utility adds the node Active Directory/All Domains to your search path by default. If you want to restrict the authentication search path to use specific domains only in your forest, follow these steps:

1   Deselect the option "Allow authentication from any domain in the forest," then click OK to dismiss the Active Directory services pane.

2   Click Search Policy in the toolbar of Directory Utility, and then click the Authentication tab.

3   Select Active Directory/All Domains, click the Remove (-) button in the lower-left corner of the Directory Utility window, and then click OK at the confirmation dialog.

4   Click the Add (+) button in the lower-left corner of the Directory Utility window. Directory Utility displays a list of the domains in your forest. Select the domains that you want to enable in your authentication search path and click Add, as shown in this figure:

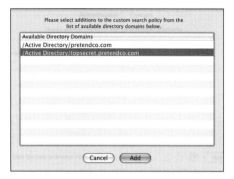

5   Click Apply to activate the change.

Creating the Computer Account in a Custom Location

Unless you specify otherwise, the Active Directory plug-in creates computer objects in CN=Computers with the domain that you specified to join. Depending on the configuration of your Domain Controller, this may not be correct. For example, some administrators have a special container (CN) for all Mac OS X computers, while others use organizational units (OU).

Follow the steps listed below to tell the Active Directory plug-in to add the computer to the container CN=MacComputers,DC=pretendco,DC=com. Rather than binding from the default pane in Directory Utility, you will bind from within the Active Directory services pane, which offers different binding options.

1   Open Directory Utility. If necessary, click the lock in the lower-left corner and provide credentials for a local administrator. If necessary, click the Show Advanced Settings button in the lower-right corner of the Directory Utility window.

2   If your Mac OS X computer is already bound to Active Directory, you must first unbind. See "Unbinding from Active Directory" for instructions.

3   Click Services in the toolbar.

4   Make sure the Active Directory service checkbox is selected.

5   Select the Active Directory service.

6   Click the Edit button ✏ in the lower-left corner of the Directory Utility window.

If you are not already bound to Active Directory, Directory Utility displays the dialog shown in the figure below. If you are already bound, you must first unbind in order to change the location of your computer account.

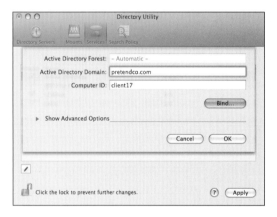

7   In the Active Directory Domain field, type the Active Directory domain.

8   In the Computer ID field, type the name of the Active Directory computer object to use for this Mac OS X computer.

9   Click Bind.

Directory Utility displays the authentication and Computer OU dialog shown in this figure:

10 In the Username field, type the name of an Active Directory administrator or the name of an Active Directory user who has authority to join a computer to the domain.

11 In the Password field, type the password for the user you specified in step 10.

12 In the Computer OU field, type the custom container in which to create the computer object for this Mac OS X computer to use.

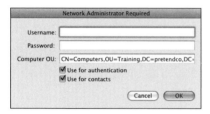

13 Click OK to start the bind process, and then click OK to dismiss the Active Directory services pane. Quit Directory Utility.

Binding to Active Directory with dsconfigad

The `dsconfigad` command is particularly useful for scripting the process of binding to Active Directory, and it offers a way to bind with custom settings in one step. This command has drawbacks, however: It does not enable the plug-in, nor does it add the Active Directory node to the search paths. You must also use the `defaults` and `dscl` commands to accomplish those tasks.

To bind a computer to Active Directory with `dsconfigad`, collect the following information for the following `dsconfigad` options:

▶ -a—Name of Active Directory computer object to use

▶ -domain—Fully Qualified Domain Name (FQDN) of Active Directory domain to join

▶ -u—Name of an Active Directory user who is authorized to add this computer to the domain

▶ -p—The password for the Active Directory user

▶ -lu—Name of a local administrator

▶ -lp—The password for the local administrator

The commands listed below enable the Active Directory plug-in, bind to Active Directory, and add the Active Directory node to the authentication and contacts search paths:

1 Use the `defaults` command to modify the settings of the file /Library/Preferences/DirectoryService/DirectoryService.plist:

```
client17:~ cadmin$ sudo defaults write \

/Library/Preferences/DirectoryService/DirectoryService \

"Active Directory" Active
```

2 Use `dsconfigad` to bind to Active Directory.

```
client17:~ cadmin$ dsconfigad -a client17 \

-domain pretendco.com \

-u Administrator -p ADadminpw \

-lu cadmin -lp cadmin

Computer was successfully Added to Active Directory.
```

3 For the authentication search path, use `dscl` to add "`Active Directory/All Domains`" to the custom search path (`CSPSearchPath`), and set the authentication search path to use `CSPSearchPath`:

```
client17:~ cadmin$ sudo dscl /Search -create / SearchPolicy CSPSearchPath
```

```
client17:~ cadmin$ sudo dscl /Search -append / CSPSearchPath "Active Directory/All Domains"
```

4 For the contacts search path, use `dscl` to add "`Active Directory/All Domains`" to the custom search path (`CSPSearchPath`), and set the contacts search path to use `CSPSearchPath`:

```
client17:~ cadmin$ sudo sudo dscl /Search/Contacts -create / SearchPolicy CSPSearchPath
```

```
client17:~ cadmin$ sudo sudo dscl /Search/Contacts -append / CSPSearchPath "Active Directory/All Domains"
```

5   Stop `DirectoryService`, which automatically starts up again with these new settings:

```
client17:~ cadmin$ sudo killall DirectoryService
```

6   Use `dscl` to confirm that the Active Directory node is in the search paths:

```
client17:~ cadmin$ dscl /Search -read / CSPSearchPath SearchPolicy

CSPSearchPath:

 /Local/Default

 /BSD/local

 Active Directory/All Domains

SearchPolicy: dsAttrTypeStandard:CSPSearchPath

client17:~ cadmin$ dscl /Search/Contacts -read / CSPSearchPath SearchPolicy

CSPSearchPath:

 /Local/Default

 /BSD/local

 Active Directory/All Domains

SearchPolicy: dsAttrTypeStandard:CSPSearchPath
```

7   Use `id` to confirm that Open Directory knows about an Active Directory user.

In this example, the user `aduser1` is an Active Directory user object. The `-p` option makes the output human readable:

```
client17:~ cadmin$ id -p aduser1

uid aduser1

groups      AD\domain users
```

If you issue the `id` command after binding and the result is `no such user`, wait a few seconds and then try again.

MORE INFO ▶ For more options, see the `man` page for `dsconfigad`.

Using Configuration Options Available Only with dsconfigad

dsconfigad offers much of the same functionality that Directory Utility offers: You can bind, unbind, set configuration options, and show the status of a bind. In addition, dsconfigad offers some functionality that Directory Utility does not offer, such as the following:

▶   -packetsign <disable | allow | require>—This supports packet signing options for both SMB and LDAP. SMB signing is required by default on Windows Server 2003 SP1 and later. This caused much frustration with earlier versions of Mac OS X. The default is to allow packet signing, a new feature in Mac OS X v10.5.

▶   -packetencrypt <disable | allow | require>—This supports packet encryption options for both SMB and LDAP. The default is to allow packet encryption, which is a new feature in Mac OS X v10.5.

▶   -namespace <forest | domain>—The forest option enables a user to log in even if there is another user account with an identical user name in the forest. Be forewarned that if you specify forest, the Active Directory plug-in calculates each Active Directory user's local home folder as /Users/DOMAIN\username instead of /Users/username. Toggling the namespace setting after Active Directory users have already logged in can cause confusion as Active Directory users perceive the contents of their home folder to be missing. The default is domain.

▶   -passinterval <days>—This specifies how often Mac OS X changes the Active Directory computer object password, measured in days. It is common for Active Directory administrators to use Active Directory tools to look for computers that have not recently changed their passwords. The default is for Mac OS X to change its computer object password every 14 days.

Providing Managed Preferences to Active Directory Users

Using Active Directory Group Policy Objects is the traditional method for managing users, groups, and computers, but Mac OS X is not compatible with Group Policy Objects. If you want to apply Managed Preferences to Mac OS X users, you could do any of the following:

▶   Augment Active Directory with an Open Directory server, and then make Active Directory users members of Open Directory groups to which you apply Managed Preferences. See "Using Workgroup Manager to Provide Managed Preferences in the Magic Triangle Configuration," in Chapter 8, for instructions.

▶ Use third-party software such as Thursby ADmitMac, Centrify DirectControl, or other similar user management utilities.

▶ Extend your Active Directory schema to handle Apple-specific object classes and attributes, and then use Workgroup Manager to manage preferences for objects in the Active Directory domain. See Appendix B.

Troubleshooting Binding Issues

For the most part, binding to Active Directory should just work. Some conditions, however, will prevent binding. This section introduces potential problem areas and provides instructions on how to resolve them.

Using Command-Line Tools to Confirm Binding

You can confirm that you are bound to Active Directory with the `dsconfigad -show` command and option, which also shows the status of many Active Directory plug-in options. You can also use the `dscl` or `id` commands to confirm that Mac OS X is bound to Active Directory. For example:

```
client17:~ cadmin$ dsconfigad -show
cadmin's Password: [password typed but hidden]
You are bound to Active Directory:
  Active Directory Forest      = pretendco.com
  Active Directory Domain      = pretendco.com
  Computer Account             = client17
Advanced Options - User Experience
  Create mobile account at login = Disabled
      Require confirmation       = Enabled
  Force home to startup disk     = Enabled
  Use Windows UNC path for home  = Disabled
      Network protocol to be used = smb:
  Default user Shell             = /bin/bash
Advanced Options - Mappings
  Mapping UID to attribute       = not set
  Mapping user GID to attribute  = not set
  Mapping group GID to attribute = not set
```

```
Advanced Options - Administrative
  Preferred Domain controller    = not set
  Allowed admin groups           = not set
  Authentication from any domain = Enabled
  Packet signing                 = allow
  Packet encryption              = allow
Advanced Options - Static maps
  None
client17:~ cadmin$ dscl /Active\ Directory/All\ Domains \
-list /Users
```
[a successful bind will display a list of users; not shown here]
```
client17:~ cadmin$ id -p aduser1
uid aduser1
groups      AD\domain users
```

Binding After Imaging

If you use a standard image for Mac OS X, do not bind the image model to Active Directory before making the master image that you will use to image multiple computers. All computers imaged from that master image will use the same computer object in Active Directory, which may cause problems. If you later remove the computer object, all of the Mac OS X computers will be unable to log in with Active Directory user accounts, and you will need to force an unbind, then rebind each computer to Active Directory.

Using System Logs

If the bind fails, check /var/log/system.log, which contains the progress for each step of the binding process listed here:

```
Step 1 of 6: Searching for Forest/Domain information
Step 2 of 6: Finding nearest Domain controllers
Step 3 of 6: Verifying credentials
Step 4 of 6: Searching for existing computer
Step 5 of 6: Joining new Domain
Step 6 of 6: Writing config
```

The binding process writes files to /var/db/dslocal/nodes/Default/config/, which only the root user can view.

Confirming DNS Service

The binding process is sensitive to DNS records, so make sure that you specify the Active Directory DNS service in the Network preference of System Preferences, and that port 53 (UDP and TCP, used for DNS requests and replies) to the DNS service is not blocked. If your Active Directory DNS is incorrectly configured, you may experience problems binding Mac OS X to Active Directory.

The Active Directory plug-in requires several DNS service records (SRV) in order to determine which hosts provide certain services on certain protocols. SRV records use the form _Service._Protocol.domain, and the requests are usually in lowercase text. Examples of the searches and replies for a few of the SRV records necessary to bind to Active Directory are shown below:

```
client17:~ cadmin$ host -t SRV _ldap._tcp.pretendco.com
_ldap._tcp.pretendco.com has SRV record 0 100 389 windows-server1.pretendco.com.
client17:~ cadmin$ host -t SRV _kerberos._tcp.pretendco.com
_kerberos._tcp.pretendco.com has SRV record 0 100 88 windows-server1.pretendco.com.
client17:~ cadmin$ host -t SRV _kpasswd._tcp.pretendco.com
_kpasswd._tcp.pretendco.com has SRV record 0 100 464 windows-server1.pretendco.com.
client17:~ cadmin$ host -t SRV _gc._tcp.pretendco.com
_gc._tcp.pretendco.com has SRV record 0 100 3268 windows-server1.pretendco.com.
```

The host option -t SRV specifies a search of type SRV, and the queries are for various services that are available via the protocol tcp (as opposed to udp) in the domain pretendco.com. The key thing to notice is the port number and host offering the service. This example forest is very simple, and the same host offers all the services (windows-server1.pretendco.com). However, the port number is different for each service, as shown here:

- ▶ 389   LDAP

- ▶ 88   Kerberos (used for obtaining Kerberos tickets)

- ▶ 464   Kpasswd (used for making Kerberos password changes)

- ▶ 3268   gc (used for Active Directory Global Catalog lookups)

Although it is possible to use a DNS service that isn't integrated with Active Directory, many SRV records are required, so it may be difficult to set up all the necessary records and keep them up-to-date.

Confirming Access to Service Ports

After performing SRV requests to find the hosts and ports that offer the required services, you can use telnet to open a connection to a specific port, to verify that you can make a basic connection to each service port. When you see a "Connected to" message from the service, type quit and press Return to end the connection. If you do not see the "Connected to" message, make sure there is no firewall blocking access, check underlying network connectivity, and make sure the service is running on the server.

> **NOTE ▶** There may be network monitoring processes that perceive as hostile the network traffic you generate to test access to the services, so coordinate with your network and Active Directory administrators before using these techniques.

Below are two examples of using telnet to connect to a port, and the replies from the service. The first connects to port 389 for LDAP service, followed by port 88 for Kerberos service. A failed attempt would stop at "Trying 10.1.0.5...," but each of these telnet sessions successfully connect to the service:

```
client17:~ cadmin$ telnet windows-server1.pretendco.com 389
Trying 10.1.0.5...
Connected to windows-server1.pretendco.com.
Escape character is '^]'.
quit
Connection closed by foreign host.
client17:~ cadmin$ telnet windows-server1.pretendco.com 88
Trying 10.1.0.5...
Connected to windows-server1.pretendco.com.
Escape character is '^]'.
quit
Connection closed by foreign host.
```

Understanding the Binding Process

Mac OS X fully supports Active Directory Sites, which allows directory administrators to associate specific domain controllers with specific networks. When you bind a Mac OS X client computer to an Active Directory domain, this kicks off a complicated series of events, shown in the next figure. Understanding the process can help you isolate any problem that might crop up.

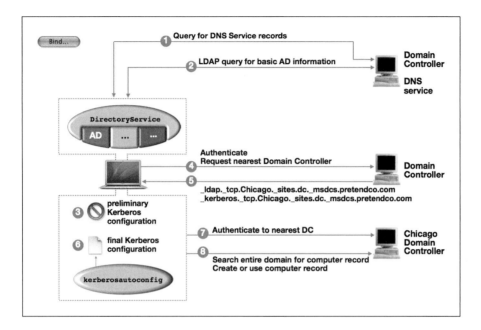

Here are the steps, in detail:

1.   Mac OS X performs a request for LDAP, Kerberos, and Kpasswd DNS service records in the domain. If Mac OS X is not using the DNS server that is integrated with Active Directory, the process will likely fail at this point.

2.   Mac OS X binds anonymously with LDAP and gathers basic Active Directory domain information.

3.   DirectoryService's Active Directory plug-in creates a preliminary Kerberos configuration.

4.   Mac OS X uses the Kerberos configuration, authenticates, and then requests the nearest Domain Controller.

5.   The Domain Controller returns a list of the nearest Domain Controllers, based on the IP subnet of the Mac OS X computer.

6.   Mac OS X confirms that it can connect to the LDAP and Kerberos services of the Domain Controller list from step 5, and DirectoryService and kerberosautoconfig create a final Kerberos configuration in /Library/Preferences/edu.mit.Kerberos and /var/db/dslocal/nodes/Default/config/Kerberos:*REALM*.plist.

7. Mac OS X connects to what it was told was the nearest Domain Controller.

8. Mac OS X searches the domain for an existing computer record, and it creates a new computer record to use if it cannot find one.

Specifying a User with Authorization to Bind

When binding, you must provide an Active Directory user name and password. You'll need to confirm that this user has write privileges for the container in which the computer object will be created or used. If the computer object already exists, the user whom you specify must have write access to the computer object. By default a regular Active Directory user can join and create a computer object only ten times. After that, you will get an error. Here are some workarounds for this limitation:

▶ Create the computer object in Active Directory and assign a user or group the ability to join the computer to a domain.

▶ Modify the number of times that a particular user can join computers to a domain.

▶ Give all authenticated users the unlimited ability to join computers to the domain.

▶ Use an administrator account to perform the bind.

Unbinding from Active Directory

You can unbind from Active Directory with either the Directory Utility application or the dsconfigad command with the -r option. If you cannot communicate with the Active Directory service, you can force the unbind. If you force the unbind and the computer object that Mac OS X was using still exists in Active Directory, you can use Active Directory tools to remove the computer object.

In rare circumstances, you may be unable to do a clean unbind from Active Directory. To get a fresh start with the Active Directory plug-in, remove the files that are associated with the Active Directory plug-in, kill DirectoryService, and then try your bind again.

In /Library/Preferences/DirectoryService the files are as follows:

▶ ActiveDirectory.plist

▶ ActiveDirectoryDomainCache.plist

▶ ActiveDirectoryDomainPolicies.plist

▶ ActiveDirectoryDynamicData.plist

/Library/Preferences/edu.mit.Kerberos will no longer include information about the Active Directory KDC, but do not remove this file if you are bound to any other Kerberos realm.

In /var/db/dslocal/nodes/Default/config/ you can remove these files:

▶ Kerberos:*REALM*.plist, where *REALM* is your Active Directory Kerberos realm

▶ AD DS Plugin.plist

You may also want to remove the following:

▶ The computer object in Active Directory that Mac OS X used

▶ The record for the Mac OS X computer that the Active Directory plug-in created and updated in the DNS service

If you unbind, change the computer name, and then rebind, you may notice Kerberos errors in /var/log/system.log that reference the old computer name. These occur because the name that you last used to bind to Active Directory may still be found in /Library/Preferences/SystemConfiguration/ in the preferences.plist file, which modifies com.apple.smb.server.plist. Do not modify these files, as the errors are harmless and appear only right after you bind.

If the computer object that Mac OS X uses has been deleted or reset, you will not be able to log in using an Active Directory user account. However, if you are troubleshooting, you should be aware that you will be able to obtain a Kerberos TGT for an Active Directory user. However, you will not be able to use su to switch to an Active Directory user, and dirt will return a dDSAuthFailed error even if you supply the correct password. In this case, you must unbind and rebind to Active Directory.

Binding to Active Directory and Open Directory

In any circumstance in which a user account is missing some attributes—for example, because you cannot extend the schema, or you do not have authority to edit the attributes you are interested in—you can always try using the Magic Triangle, in which you use an Open Directory node to supplement data available from the primary node. You learned about this configuration in Chapter 3, in "Augmenting LDAP Data with Information from an Open Directory Server," and it is illustrated in the figure below.

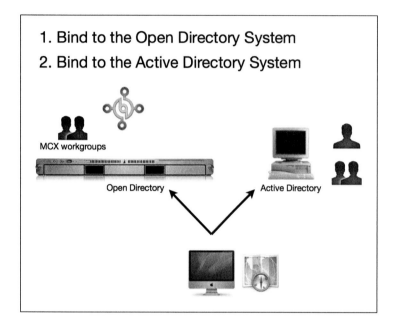

The Magic Triangle configuration lets you apply Managed Preferences to Open Directory computers and workgroups, and then add Active Directory groups and users to Open Directory workgroups to manage them. See the instructions in Chapter 8, in "Preparing Mac OS X Server for the Magic Triangle Configuration."

Because the Active Directory plug-in dynamically generates mount records for network home folders, you do not need to provide an additional directory node or mount object to automount an AFP home folder.

Troubleshooting Login Issues

The process for logging in with an Active Directory network user is similar to the process of logging in with a network user from other directory services. You can use the troubleshooting techniques in Chapters 2 and 3, which include scenarios in which Open Directory accesses user records from Active Directory and uses mount, computer, and group records (including attributes for Managed Preferences) from Open Directory.

This section discusses some common problems, but also covers issues that are specific to logging in with an Active Directory user record.

Before you begin, verify that you are not experiencing binding issues; for instructions, see the section "Troubleshooting Binding Issues" later in this chapter.

Try to determine if the login problem is related to identification, authentication, or authorization. Start with identification of the user record. To confirm that you can use the `id` or `dscl` commands to identify the user, use the following:

```
client17:~ cadmin$ dscl localhost read /Search/Users/aduser1
```

It is possible that `DirectoryService` is having problems communicating over LDAP to Active Directory. Use a graphical LDAP browser or an `ldapsearch` query to ensure that you can make LDAP requests authenticating as an Active Directory user:

```
client17:~ cadmin$ ldapsearch -x -D "cn=dcolville,CN=Users,DC=pretendco,DC=com" -W
-H ldap://windows-server.pretendco.com -b "CN=Users,DC=pretendco,DC=com" cn=dcolville
homeDirectory
[authentication information deleted]
dn: CN=dcolville,CN=Users,DC=pretendco,DC=com
homeDirectory: \\windows-server\smbhomes\dcolville
```

Verify that your Active Directory node is listed in your authentication search path.

Check to see if you can authenticate as the Active Directory user. Log in as a local user or local administrator, and then use `su` to switch identity to the Active Directory user.

Verify that your Kerberos configuration is set up for the Active Directory domain; the file /Library/Preferences/edu.mit.Kerberos should reference your Active Directory Kerberos domain.

Confirm that you can use `kinit` or the Kerberos application (in System/Library/CoreServices) to obtain a TGT from the Active Directory KDC.

Resolving Time Issues

If the clocks on the Active Directory domain controller and Mac OS X are more than 5 minutes apart, you cannot obtain a Kerberos ticket and you cannot log in. Make sure your Mac OS X computer is in the correct time zone, has the correct daylight saving time settings, and uses the same Network Time Protocol server as your Active Directory servers.

Using the Logs

Use the log file /var/log/system.log and the log files in /Library/Logs/DirectoryService/ DirectoryService to gather information if you are experiencing problems logging in. Refer to Chapter 1 for information about enabling DirectoryService logging by sending the USR1 or the USR2 signal to DirectoryService.

Transitioning from a Local User to an Active Directory User

If you want to transition from using an established local user account to a network account, yet continue to use the existing home folder, you must perform these steps:

1 On your Mac OS X computer, log in as a local administrator. Open System Preferences and choose the Accounts preference.

2 Click the lock in the lower-left corner to authenticate as a local administrator.

3 Choose the local account that conflicts with the Active Directory account.

4 Click the Remove (-) button in the lower-left corner.

5 When prompted, leave the default selected, "Do not change the home folder," then click OK.

6 If the short name of the local user differs from the short name of the Active Directory user, change the name of the home folder. The following command changes the name of the home folder from the local user short name "david" to the Active Directory user name "dcolville":

```
client17:~ cadmin$ sudo mv "/Users/david (Deleted)" /Users/dcolville
```

7   Change the ownership of the files in the preserved home folder so that the Active Directory user is the new owner. Open Terminal and issue the `chown` (change owner-ship) command, which takes the form of

```
chown [options] owner[:group] file
```

The option `-R` changes ownership recursively, so the command changes ownership for the entire home folder. The `chown` command below changes the owner and group associated with all the files in the home folder:

```
client17:~ cadmin$ sudo chown -R dcolville:"PRETENDCO\domain users" /Users/dcolville
```

8   Log out as the local administrator account, and then log in as the Active Directory account.

Understanding Mobile Accounts

A mobile account is a local copy of a network user account, with attributes and credentials synchronized at login if the network node is available. A mobile account allows you to log in even when the network directory node is not available. The mobile account concept is not specific to Active Directory, but the Active Directory plug-in provides a checkbox to enable Mac OS X to a create a mobile account when users log in. This enhances the user experience because it caches other information, such as group membership, about Active Directory. Mobile accounts work well when you synchronize the contents of the local home folder with a network home folder, but this is not automatic.

See "Exploring the 'User Experience' Advanced Options Pane," earlier in this chapter, for instructions on configuring the Active Directory plug-in to configure Mac OS X to create mobile accounts. For more information about home folder synchronization, see the section "Managing Mobile User Accounts," starting on page 502 of *Mac OS X Server Essentials, Second Edition,* or read Chapter 8, "Managing Portable Computers," of *Mac OS X Server User Management for Version 10.5 Leopard.*

Updating Active Directory Indexing

As do other directories, Active Directory indexes the values of commonly requested attri-butes in order to increase the speed of operations. If your Active Directory implementa-tion contains a large amount of Mac OS X clients, your Mac OS X computers may request attributes that Active Directory does not index. Microsoft provides a downloadable Server

Performance Advisor tool that lets you investigate whether there are any attribute queries that could be sped up by better indexing. Use this tool to determine if there are many requests for attributes that are not indexed, and then use Active Directory tools to add the unindexed attributes to the list of attributes to index.

Forcing Replication

If the computer object is created in one site but hasn't been replicated to another, you may not be able to log in until the replication takes place. You can force replication to take place with standard Active Directory tools.

What You've Learned

▶ Mac OS X's Open Directory has a specific Active Directory plug-in that uses Active Directory's LDAP and Kerberos services and enables extra functionality with the Active Directory domain, such as Dynamic DNS updates. The Active Directory plug-in comes with a default set of mappings for objects and attributes, which you can modify.

▶ You can use Directory Utility or dsconfigad to bind a Mac OS X computer to Active Directory. You must specify the Active Directory domain, the name of a computer object in Active Directory to use or create, and the user name and password of an Active Directory user who has the ability to create or that computer object.

▶ By default, Mac OS X assigns a home folder in /Users for Active Directory users. If the user also has an Active Directory network home folder assigned, the folder will appear in the Dock and the Network volume will be mounted, but by default Mac OS X does not display network volumes on the desktop.

▶ The Active Directory plug-in uses DNS extensively, including SRV records. You should configure Mac OS X to use the Active Directory DNS service or continually replicate the complicated set of records on another DNS service.

▶ Binding to an Active Directory domain takes several steps, and the progress is logged to /var/log/system.log.

▶ Mac OS X v10.5 supports packet signing, packet encryption, and dynamic DNS updates by default.

▶ The login process after binding to Active Directory is similar to the login process after binding to any other LDAP directory node.

References

Administration Guides

▶ Command-Line Administration
http://images.apple.com/server/macosx/docs/Command_Line_Admin_v10.5.pdf

▶ Open Directory Administration
http://images.apple.com/server/macosx/docs/Open_Directory_Admin_v10.5.pdf

Apple Knowledge Base Documents

▶ Mac OS X: Using the Active Directory plug-in in a multidomain controller environment
http://docs.info.apple.com/article.html?artnum=301010

▶ Using network homes with the Active Directory plug-in for Mac OS X 10.3.3 or later
http://docs.info.apple.com/article.html?artnum=107943

▶ Mac OS X 10.5: Active Directory—Name and password considerations when binding with Directory Utility or dsconfigad
http://support.apple.com/kb/TS1532

Books

▶ Allen, Robbie. *Active Directory Cookbook for Windows Server 2003 & Windows 2000* (O'Reilly Media, Inc., 2003).

▶ Allen, Robbie and Lowe-Norris, Alistair G. *Active Directory, Second Edition* (O'Reilly & Associates Inc., 2003).

▶ Kouti, Sakari and Seitsonen, Mika. *Inside Active Directory: A System Administrator's Guide, Second Edition* (Addison-Wesley, 2005).

▶ Marczak, Edward R. *Apple Training Series: Mac OS X Advanced System Administration v10.5* (Peachpit Press, 2009).

Websites

▶ Apple Professional Services Consulting Group
http://www.apple.com/services/consulting/

▶ Apple Education Professional Services
http://www.apple.com/education/services/

▶ Apple IT Pro—Integrating Mac OS X and Active Directory
http://images.apple.com/itpro/articles/adintegration/

▶ Leveraging Active Directory on Mac OS X, Leopard Edition
http://www.bombich.com/mactips/activedir.html

▶ Domain Users Cannot Join Workstation or Server to a Domain
http://support.microsoft.com/kb/251335/EN-US/

▶ Windows Server 2003 Active Directory
http://www.microsoft.com/windowsserver2003/technologies/directory/
activedirectory/default.mspx

▶ ExtremeZ-IP File Server
http://www.grouplogic.com/products/extreme/overview.cfm

▶ Thursby ADMit Mac
http://www.thursby.com/products/admitmac.html

▶ Centrify DirectControl for Mac OS X
http://www.centrify.com/directcontrol/mac_os_x.asp

▶ Likewise—Making Linux and Windows work well together
http://www.likewisesoftware.com

▶ SMB/CIFS Comparison
http://www.grouplogic.com/products/extremeZ-IP/?fa=smb-cifs-comparison

▶ Introduction to Microsoft Windows Services for UNIX 3.5
http://technet.microsoft.com/en-us/library/bb463212.aspx

▶ Microsoft® Windows Server™ 2003 Performance Advisor
http://www.microsoft.com/downloads/details.aspx?familyid=09115420-8c9d-46b9-
a9a5-9bffcd237da2&displaylang=en

Review Quiz

1. What protocol does the Active Directory plug-in use to retrieve directory data from an Active Directory service?

2. How does the Active Directory plug-in generate the numerical user ID by default?

3. What is the default location for an Active Directory user's home folder?

4.   When binding to Active Directory, what information do you need to supply?

5.   What are two ways to provide Managed Preferences for Active Directory users?

6.   What is the possible danger of making changes to an Active Directory schema?

7.   If you change the IP address of your Mac OS X computer, will it update the DNS record in Active Directory's DNS service?

Answers

1.   LDAP. The Active Directory plug-in also relies on DNS records.

2.   The Active Directory plug-in generates the numerical user ID based on the object-GUID in Active Directory.

3.   Unless you specify otherwise, an Active Directory user who logs in to Mac OS X gets a home folder created in the /Users folder of the startup disk.

4.   You need to supply the Active Directory domain name, a computer name for Mac OS X, and the name and password of a user who has permission to bind computers to the Active Directory domain.

5.   You can extend the Active Directory schema. You can bind a Mac OS X client computer to an ancillary Open Directory server; and you can provide Managed Preferences at the workgroup, computer and computer group level.

6.   It is difficult to undo schema changes to Active Directory. Windows Server 2003 offers more flexibility than Windows Server 2000. You can flag any schema changes you made as inactive with Windows Server 2003, but you can never delete them.

7.   Yes, Mac OS X v10.5 supports dynamic DNS updates.

5

Chapter Files   userforldapmodify.ldif

userforldapadd.ldif

These files are available at http://www.peachpit.com/
asca.directory-services/.

Time   This lesson takes approximately 3 hours to complete.

Goals   Configure Mac OS X Server as an Open Directory master

Configure Mac OS X Server as a Primary Domain Controller

Manage data stored in an Open Directory master

Troubleshoot issues when promoting a Mac OS X Server computer to an
Open Directory master

Chapter 5

Configuring Open Directory Server

The first four chapters of this book considered directory services on Mac OS X. The final four chapters shift the focus to offering, using, and integrating directory services with Mac OS X Server.

In this chapter you will learn how to configure an Open Directory server, including upgrading and migrating from a Mac OS X Server v10.4 Open Directory master, providing Windows NT domain services to Windows clients, and using various tools to manage the data stored in the Open Directory master. The chapter ends with troubleshooting techniques for promoting a Mac OS X Server to an Open Directory master.

Configuring Mac OS X Server as an Open Directory Master

After you install Mac OS X Server, the first application to run is the Server Assistant. Server Assistant offers three different configurations (also referred to as modes): Standard, Workgroup, and Advanced. When you set up your server to use with this book, choose the Advanced configuration. If you select the Standard or Workgroup configuration, the Server Assistant automatically configures an Open Directory master and other services, and you must use Server Preferences instead of Server Admin to administer your server. See Table 1.3, "Default-Enabled Services Per Configuration," on page 36 of *Mac OS X Server Essentials, Second Edition,* for a list of services that are automatically enabled and configured.

Unless otherwise indicated, this book uses Mac OS X Server in the Advanced configuration, because it offers more control than the Standard or Workgroup modes.

Using changeip to Confirm Your DNS Records

You *must* have DNS working in order to promote your Mac OS X Server to an Open Directory master, or the automatic process of configuring the Kerberos portion of your Open Directory master will fail. Even though you can add an entry for your host in /etc/hosts, and it will be immediately available to tools that use directory services like Server Admin and Workgroup Manager, you cannot fully promote to Open Directory master without access to forward and reverse DNS records.

You can use the changeip command's -checkhostname option:

```
server17:~ ladmin$ sudo changeip -checkhostname
```

The result should look something like the figure below:

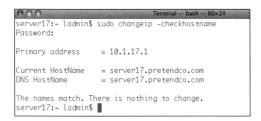

If there is a problem, `changeip` gives good advice, like this:

```
The DNS hostname is not available, please repair DNS and re-run this tool.
```

Upgrading from Earlier Versions of Mac OS X Server

If you have an Open Directory server running on an earlier version of Mac OS X Server and you want to move to Mac OS X Server v10.5, you need to decide whether you are going to *upgrade* or *migrate*:

▶ You can upgrade from Mac OS X Server versions 10.3 and 10.4, leaving your data and settings in place.

▶ You can migrate data and settings from a different computer running Mac OS X Server versions 10.2 to 10.5.

> **NOTE** ▶ *Mac OS X Server Upgrading and Migrating for Version 10.5 Leopard* contains information about upgrading and migrating from earlier versions of Mac OS X Server.

The advantages of upgrading are:

▶ You do not need to provision new hardware.

▶ You need make only minimal adjustments to the newly upgraded server settings.

The advantages of migrating are:

▶ You can use newer, faster computer hardware.

▶ You can take your old server offline, but keep it available to bring back online if you experience a problem with the new server. This enables you to offer clients minimal downtime.

The main disadvantage of upgrading is:

▶ Your Open Directory master must be offline while you run the installation. However, your replicas will continue to provide identification and authentication services.

The disadvantages of migrating are:

▶ You cannot use Workgroup Manager to export passwords. To preserve user passwords, you must make an archive of the old Open Directory master information, create a new Open Directory master on Mac OS X Server v10.5, and then restore the archive to the Open Directory master that you just created.

▶ There are many steps involved in a server migration, and you may forget to copy or restore data or settings.

▶ You will also have to rebuild all of your replica servers after you have established the new Open Directory master.

Whether you upgrade or migrate, you still need to boot from installation media and install Mac OS X Server 10.5. With an upgrade, you boot from installation media, run the installer, and choose to upgrade an earlier version of Mac OS X Server. With a migration, you install and configure a new copy of Mac OS X Server. In either case, be sure you have a reliable backup, and follow the steps detailed in *Mac OS X Server Upgrading and Migrating for Version 10.5 Leopard.*

Upgrading from Earlier Versions of Mac OS X Server

If you are upgrading from Mac OS X Server v10.3, you need to ensure that you are running version 10.3.9, or update it as needed. If you are upgrading from Mac OS X Server v10.4, you must be running version 10.4.10 at minimum.

Upgrading from an earlier version of Mac OS X Server requires these resources:

▶ Intel or PowerPC G5 or G4 processor, 1 gigahertz (GHz) or faster

▶ At least 1 gigabyte (GB) of RAM

▶ At least 20 GB of disk space available

If your Open Directory master has any replicas, follow these steps to upgrade to Mac OS X Server v10.5:

1 Upgrade the Open Directory master to version 10.5.

2 Upgrade each Open Directory replica to version 10.5.

3 Use Server Admin to connect to each replica and reconnect the replica to the master.

Depending on your situation, you may need to take a few more steps after upgrading to Mac OS X Server v10.5:

▶ If you upgrade from Mac OS X Server v10.4 to Mac OS X Server v10.5, you may need to change the authentication search path from Automatic to Custom, and then add the Open Directory master back to the search path.

▶ If you want to use the new group features available in Mac OS X Server v10.5, such as nested groups and stricter membership checking, you may need to upgrade your groups. To do this use Workgroup Manager to select the group, click "Upgrade legacy group," and then click Save.

▶ If you have a shared NetInfo directory and want to convert it to an LDAP directory, see the *Open Directory Administration* guide for further instructions. Mac OS X Server v10.5 does not support any NetInfo directory—not local, not shared.

▶ If your old Open Directory master did not have Kerberos properly set up, use the `slapconfig -kerberize` command to set up a new Key Distribution Center (KDC). If you have any users with password type *crypt*, use Workgroup Manager's Advanced button to convert the user to a user password type for Open Directory.

▶ If you had any custom LDAP Access Controls (DACs), you must manually move them from `AccessControls` to `OLCBDBConfig`. If any rules used the `set` directive, you must use the `group` directive instead. The details are outside the scope of this book, but you would use Workgroup Manager's Show All Records button or a series of `ldapmodify` commands to do this. Versions of Mac OS X Server before 10.5.3 do not replicate the DACs.

▶ If you updated the `slapd.conf` file when adding schema files, you must use the `slaptest` command to rebuild the `slapd.d` directory and make the change permanent. See page 24 of *Mac OS X Server Upgrading and Migrating for Mac OS X 10.5 Leopard* and the OpenLDAP documentation for full instructions.

▶ If a user previously had the ability to administer a portion of your directory, in Mac OS X Server v10.5 it will appear that the user has full administrative rights to the entire directory. In the Privileges pane for the user, the "Administration capabilities" pop-up menu contains the word "Full," and the status message for the user is "This user has full capabilities to make changes in Workgroup Manager." The user record's `AdminLimits` attribute is still intact, however, and Workgroup Manager will not let that user administer the entire directory, only the portions it had authority to administer before.

Consult *Mac OS X Server Upgrading and Migrating for Version 10.5 Leopard* before attempting to upgrade or migrate, and be sure you have a backup of your Mac OS X Server.

Restoring from an Open Directory Archive

When you move Mac OS X Server from one computer to another, you can use Server Admin or `slapconfig` to archive your Open Directory master data, and then restore it to a new instance of an Open Directory master. See "Using Server Admin to Archive Your Directory Information," later in this chapter, for more information about creating an archive.

Be aware that various checks might not be in place when you restore an archive, so if you have any existing users in the new directory, you can end up with duplicate users with the same `UniqueID`, which can lead to unexpected results.

> **NOTE** ▸ The instructions for creating and restoring from an archive of an Open Directory master are summarized here; for the complete process, see pages 192–195 in *Mac OS X Server Open Directory Administration for Version 10.5 Leopard, Second Edition.*

To restore an Open Directory archive with Server Admin:

1   Promote a standalone server to an Open Directory master before restoring from an archive. You cannot restore to a standalone server. See the next section, "Promoting a Standalone Server to Open Directory Master" for instructions.

2   Open Server Admin, select the Open Directory service, and then click the Archive button in the toolbar.

3   Type the path to the disk image that contains the archive, or click the Choose button and navigate to the archive.

4   Click the Restore button, enter the password for the archive (leave the password field blank if there is no password for the archive), and then click OK.

   You will not see a success message.

5   Quit Server Admin and use Workgroup Manager to confirm that the directory contains new records from the archive.

To restore an Open Directory archive with the command line:

1 Promote a standalone server to an Open Directory master before restoring from an archive. You cannot restore to a standalone server.

2 Use the `slapconfig` command with the `-restoredb` option. You must provide a path to the archive:

server17:~ ladmin$ `sudo slapconfig -restoredb /Volumes/Backup/TigerODArchive.`
`sparseimage`

3 Use `dscl` or Workgroup Manager to confirm that the directory contains new records from the archive:

server17:~ ladmin$ `dscl /LDAPv3/127.0.0.1 list /Search/Users`

[the list of users is not displayed here]

> **TIP** If you created any users in the new Open Directory master on Mac OS X Server v10.5 before restoring from an archive, you need to check for duplicate user IDs. In Workgroup Manager, view the Users, and then click the UID column to sort by `UniqueID`.

Promoting a Standalone Server to Open Directory Master

When you use Server Admin to promote a standalone Mac OS X Server in Advanced configuration to an Open Directory master, Server Admin initiates a `slapconfig` command, which in turn initiates a set of commands that set up the LDAP, Kerberos, and Password Server services. `slapconfig` logs its activity to /Library/Logs/slapconfig.log, which is the first log you should inspect if your new Open Directory master does not function properly.

Using Server Admin to Promote to Open Directory Master

If your Mac OS X Server is in the Advanced configuration, you can use Server Admin to promote to Open Directory Master by following these steps:

1 Open Server Admin. If necessary, click the Add button in the lower-left corner to select Add Service, and then select Open Directory to enable it.

2   Highlight the Open Directory service in the left column, and then click Settings in the toolbar.

3   Click Change, select Open Directory Master, and then click Continue, as shown in the figure below.

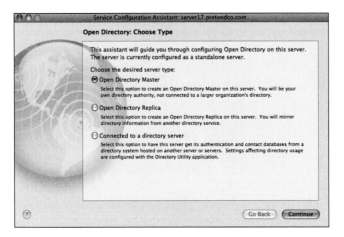

4   The Name, Short Name, and User ID fields all suggest values, but you must supply the password. Enter a password and click Continue, as shown below.

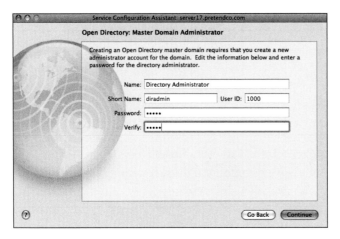

5 The Kerberos Realm and Search Base fields display default values based upon the
server's domain name. For example, a server with the domain name of server17.
pretendco.com should have a default search base of dc=server17,dc=pretendco,
dc=com and a Kerberos Realm of SERVER17.PRETENDCO.COM, as shown in the
figure below. If the Kerberos Realm field is empty, close the window, quit Server
Admin, and make sure you have forward and reverse DNS entries for your server
before starting over with step 1. Click Continue to move on once the Kerberos Realm
is automatically populated with information based on your server's domain name.

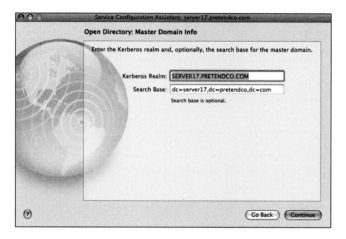

6 Click Continue at the Confirm Settings dialog, and then click Close at the dialog stat-
ing the change is complete.

7 Click Overview in the toolbar, and confirm that the overall status is "Open Directory
is: Open Directory master." Confirm that status for the LDAP Server, Password Server,
and Kerberos is Running, and the LDAP Search Base and Kerberos Realm are displayed, as shown in this figure.

NOTE ▶ If you already have a 10.5 Open Directory master and replica, and something terrible happens to the computer that hosts the Open Directory master, you can promote your replica to be the new master, as described in Chapter 6.

Preparing Mac OS X Server to Serve Home Folders

Throughout this book, you have used this server to test logging in as a network user with an Apple Filing Protocol (AFP) home folder. Login will fail if you do not do the following:

▶ Assign a network home folder for a user.

▶ Make a mount record available to a bound client computer, to support automatically mounting the network share point that contains the user home folder.

▶ Use Server Admin to configure the Users share point to be used for network home folders, and then start the AFP file-sharing service.

Configuring an Automount Record for User Home Folders

Before you begin, use dscl to confirm there are no mount records in any of the nodes in the authentication search path. Because there are no mount records yet, dscl returns an error:

```
server17:~ ladmin$ dscl /Search list /Mounts
list: Invalid Path
<dscl_cmd> DS Error: -14009 (eDSUnknownNodeName)
```

Use the following steps to create a mount record for the Users folder:

1 In Server Admin, click your server's name in the server list.

2 Click File Sharing in the toolbar.

3 Click Share Points.

4 Select the Users share point.

5   Click the Share Point tab in the lower pane of the Server Admin window, as shown here:

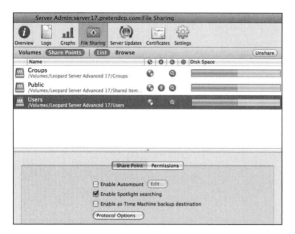

6   Click the Enable Automount checkbox. A dialog appears, prompting for automount configuration settings. Verify that the settings are correct as listed here and shown in the figure below:

Directory: /LDAPv3/127.0.0.1

Protocol: AFP

Use for: User home folders

7   Click OK.

8 An authentication dialog appears, prompting for administrator credentials for your server's LDAP domain. These credentials are required to create a new mount record in the LDAP database. Authenticate with the following information:

Name: `diradmin`

Password: `apple`

9 Click OK, and then click Save.

10 Perform the search again with `dscl` to confirm that you created the mount record:

server17:~ ladmin$ `dscl /Search list /Mounts`

server17.pretendco.com:/Users

11 Use `dscl` to view the mount record's attributes and their data. Note that the name of the record contains a colon, which you must escape with a backslash:

server17:~ ladmin$ `dscl /Search read /Mounts/server17.pretendco.com\:/Users`

dsAttrTypeNative:cn: server17.pretendco.com:/Users

dsAttrTypeNative:mountDirectory: /Network/Servers/

dsAttrTypeNative:mountOption: net url==afp://;AUTH=NO%20USER%20AUTHENT@server17.pretendco.com/Users

dsAttrTypeNative:mountType: url

dsAttrTypeNative:objectClass: mount top

AppleMetaNodeLocation: /LDAPv3/127.0.0.1

RecordName: server17.pretendco.com:/Users

RecordType: dsRecTypeStandard:Mounts

VFSLinkDir: /Network/Servers/

VFSOpts: net url==afp://;AUTH=NO%20USER%20AUTHENT@server17.pretendco.com/Users

VFSType: url

Starting Apple File Protocol (AFP)

Follow the steps below to use AFP to provide access to the network home folder. By default, the AFP server does not allow guest access; it will accept either Standard or Kerberos authentication.

1   In Server Admin, select your server's AFP service in the left column. If the AFP service is not listed, click Settings in the toolbar, click the Services tab, select AFP, click Save, and then select your server's AFP service in the left column.

2   Click Settings.

3   Click the Logging tab.

4   Select the "Enable access log" checkbox.

   AFP logs are useful for diagnosing home folder problems. On a busy server, you may choose to increase performance by not enabling Open File event logging.

5   Click Save to update the configuration for the AFP service.

6   Click Start AFP in the lower-left corner of Server Admin.

7   Quit Server Admin.

Securing LDAP Connections

Recall that when you set up Trusted Binding between a Mac OS X client computer and an Open Directory master, LDAP communications and any authentication traffic is encrypted: Before making an LDAP request, your computer obtains a Kerberos ticket-granting ticket (TGT) and then performs LDAP queries using the Generic Security Services Application Programming Interface (GSSAPI). If you did not configure your Mac OS X computer for Trusted Binding, another way to protect LDAP traffic between Mac OS X and your Open Directory master is to use Transport Layer Security (TLS), which is a minor update to SSL (Secure Sockets Layer).

The LDAP client in Mac OS X v10.5 is not integrated with the Keychain architecture, so you must edit the LDAP configuration file (/etc/ldap.conf) to get the LDAP client to trust any TLS certificates. In the next three sections, you will do the following:

1. Create a self-signed TLS certificate that you will use to secure your LDAP service.

2. Configure your Open Directory master to use the certificate to secure the LDAP service.

3. Configure LDAP to trust the certificate. You must perform this step for each computer that will use the LDAP service, including Open Directory servers.

   NOTE ▶ After configuring your LDAP service to accept LDAP requests using TLS, it still accepts nonsecure LDAP requests. You cannot use Server Admin to configure the LDAP service to reject non-TLS LDAP requests. It is possible to use command-line tools to configure your LDAP service to reject non-TLS LDAP requests, but at the moment this configuration causes unexpected results and is not supported or recommended.

Creating a Self-Signed TLS Certificate to Secure LDAP Service

When you use Server Admin to create a certificate, Server Admin writes the resulting files to /etc/certificates. To create a certificate, follow the steps listed here and illustrated in the figure below:

1 Open Server Admin, select your server in the left column, and then click Certificates in the toolbar.

2 Click the Add (+) button.

3 Fill out the fields. In the Common Name field, use the Fully Qualified Domain Name (FQDN) for your Open Directory master.

4 In the Private Key Passphrase field, type the password `apple`. Of course, in a production environment you should use a secure password.

   NOTE ▶ As of this writing, some Mac OS X Server services may not work with a TLS certificate that has a private-key passphrase, so be sure to verify that your services are working properly if you use this certificate for services other than LDAP.

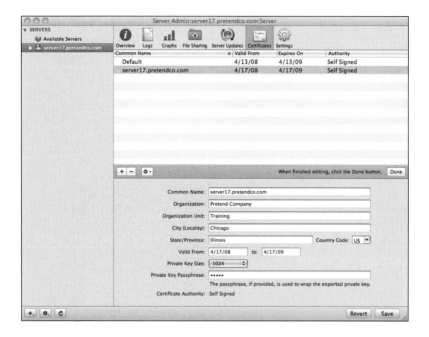

5   Click Save.

NOTE ▶ This procedure places the files related to the certificate in /etc/certificates.

Using Server Admin to Secure LDAP Service with TLS

Now that you have your certificate, follow these instructions to use Server Admin to configure the LDAP service to use the certificate:

1   Open Server Admin, select the Open Directory service in the left column, and then click Settings in the Toolbar.

2   Click the LDAP tab.

3   Select the Enable SSL checkbox.

4 Click the pop-up menu, and then select the certificate that you created in the last section (it should be your server's FQDN).

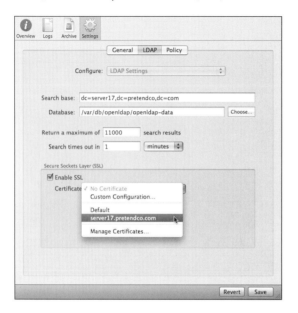

5 Click Save.

NOTE ▶ As of the current writing, if you choose Custom Configuration in the Certificate pop-up menu, Server Admin saves the passphrase in clear text to /etc/openldap/slapd_macosxserver.conf. Only the root user can read this file, but it is still preferable to select a certificate from the pop-up menu rather than choose Custom Configuration.

As soon as you specify the certificate to use and click the Save button, Server Admin updates /etc/openldap/slapd_macosxserver.conf and /System/Library/LaunchDaemons. org.openldap.slapd.plist, and the LDAP service starts accepting LDAP requests with TLS on port 636.

Configuring LDAP Client to Accept a TLS Certificate

The LDAP client in Mac OS X and Mac OS X Server is very strict by default. The LDAP client configuration file /etc/openldap/ldap.conf contains this directive:

```
TLS_REQCERT demand
```

This causes the LDAP client to reject all TLS certificates until you install and configure them specifically for the LDAP client.

> **NOTE** ▸ The default directive for Mac OS X v10.4 is `TLS_REQCERT never`.

You could change the directive `TLS_REQCERT` from `demand` to `never` so that the LDAP client ignores certificate validity, but that is probably not wise. A more prudent approach is to specify a directory that contains certificates that you want to trust, and then place the certificates in that directory. Perform the following steps on your Mac OS X Server computer first, so that its own LDAP client trusts its LDAP service over TLS, then repeat the steps on your Mac OS X client computers:

1   Perform an LDAP search using TLS to confirm that the LDAP client will not accept the self-signed certificate:

```
server17:~ ladmin$ ldapsearch -LLL -x -H ldaps://server17.pretendco.com -b
"dc=server17,dc=pretendco,dc=com"
```

The result should be an error message:

```
ldap_bind: Can't contact LDAP server (1)

    additional info: error:14090086:SSL routines:SSL3_GET_SERVER_CERTIFICATE:
certificate verify failed.
```

2   Create the directory to store the certificates:

```
server17:~ ladmin$ sudo mkdir /etc/openldap/certs
```

3   Copy the certificate to the new directory:

```
server17:~ ladmin$ sudo cp /etc/certificates/server17.pretendco.com.crt
/etc/openldap/certs
```

4   With root privileges, edit the /etc/openldap/ldap.conf configuration file and append the following line:

```
TLS_CACERTDIR          /etc/openldap/certs
```

5   Use the c_hash command to calculate a filename that the LDAP client can use. While you could rename the existing certificate to this new name, you may prefer to use a soft link in order to keep track of the certificate's original name. The new name of your certificate will not match the name in these instructions:

```
server17:~ ladmin$ cd /etc/openldap/certs

server17:certs ladmin$ /System/Library/OpenSSL/misc/c_hash /etc/openldap/certs/
server17.pretendco.com.crt

fb6e4467.0 => /etc/openldap/certs/server17.pretendco.com.crt

server17:certs ladmin$ sudo ln -s server17.pretendco.com.crt fb6e4467.0
```

6   Perform an LDAP search using TLS to confirm that the LDAP client trusts the certificate:

```
server17:certs ladmin$ ldapsearch -LLL -x -H ldaps://server17.pretendco.com -b
"dc=server17,dc=pretendco,dc=com"
```

The result should be the contents of your LDAP directory.

Configuring Mac OS X to Use TLS for LDAP Queries

Now that Mac OS X Server will accept and make LDAP queries using TLS, you need to configure your client computers to trust the certificates and make TLS LDAP requests, which requires distributing the changes on a large scale. Whether you use Apple Remote Desktop or other tools, here are the basic steps:

1   Create the certificates directory on your Mac OS X computer.

```
client17:~ cadmin$ sudo mkdir /etc/openldap/certs
```

2   Copy the certificates from Mac OS X Server to Mac OS X. You could use a USB drive, but the scp command is convenient. This command uses the Secure Shell protocol

(SSH) to securely copy files. You need a user name and password on the remote computer, which you know is `ladmin/apple`. The `-r` option used here recursively copies all files in a directory:

```
client17:~ cadmin$ sudo scp -r ladmin@server17.pretendco.com:/etc/openldap/certs
/etc/openldap/certs

Password: [type the password for sudo if prompted]

The authenticity of host 'server17.pretendco.com (10.1.17.1)' can't be established.

RSA key fingerprint is 8e:6c:d7:ec:50:0a:e0:b8:c3:3c:84:c9:b3:71:79:62.

Are you sure you want to continue connecting (yes/no)? yes

Warning: Permanently adding 'server17.pretendco.com,10.1.17.1' (RSA) to the list of
known hosts.

Password: [Type the password of the remote user, apple, here]

fb24467.0                           100% 960 0.9KB/s 00:00

server17.pretendco.com.crt          100% 960 0.9KB/s 00:00
```

3   With root privileges, edit the /etc/openldap/ldap.conf configuration file and append the following line:

```
TLS_CACERTDIR        /etc/openldap/certs
```

4   Use Directory Utility to enable SSL for server17.pretendco.com, as shown here:

Tuning Open Directory Master Performance and Security Settings

The LDAP and Policy panes of the Open Directory service in Server Admin contain several options that relate to both performance and security. The following figure illustrates the LDAP pane:

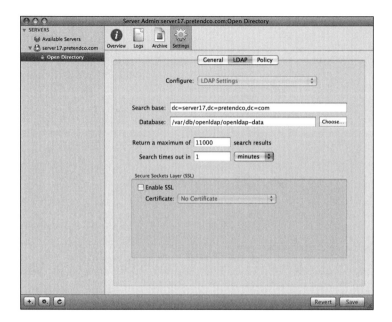

The LDAP pane lets you move the LDAP database to a different location. By default, the database resides on the boot volume. If you have a large amount of data, you may get better performance if you move the database to a different physical disk. Here are the general steps to do this:

1. Stop the LDAP service.

2. Specify a different location.

3. Move the directory to the new location.

4. Start the LDAP service.

You can prevent one type of denial-of-service attack by changing the "Search times out in" field to set a limit on the amount of time the server spends on each search of its shared LDAP directory domain. The default timeout is 1 minute, and you can change this to any number of seconds, minutes, or hours.

By default, your LDAP service returns a maximum of 11,000 search results. You can reduce this number to prevent random harvesting of information. Remember, this also affects such applications as Workgroup Manager: If you set the maximum number of search results to 50, for example, Workgroup Manager can show only 50 users at a time.

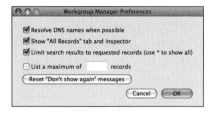

To improve Workgroup Manager's response time, you may want to enable the preference "Limit search results to requested records (use * to show all)," so that Workgroup Manager will not show any records unless you specifically search for them. This way you do not have to wait for Workgroup Manager to retrieve all the records in your directory.

Setting Global Password Policy

You can change the password policies for all nonadministrative users. The settings shown in the figure below apply globally, but any policy that you apply for a specific user may take precedence over the global policy that you set in the Passwords pane.

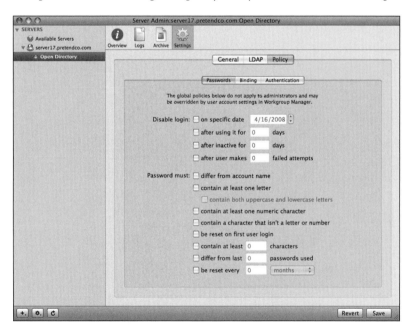

You can also use the `pwpolicy` command to set global and per-user password policies. For more information, see the "Setting Password Policy" section on page 134 of *Mac OS X Server Command-Line Administration* and the `man` page for `pwpolicy`.

Setting Binding Policy

Authenticated Trusted Binding, a mutually authenticated LDAP connection, is covered in Chapter 2. Most of the settings that you specify in the Binding Policy pane are advisory only, and they don't affect processes that ignore these settings. For example, if you enable "Require authenticated binding between directory and clients," Server Admin updates the settings in the macosxodconfig object in your LDAP service's config branch. Directory Utility in Mac OS X v10.5 and Directory Access in Mac OS X v10.4 use macosxodconfig to determine whether to demand authentication to continue with the binding process, but the setting "Require authenticated binding between directory and clients" does not affect any other LDAP clients. Versions of Mac OS X below version 10.4 cannot use Trusted Binding.

Similarly, enabling the "Disable clear text passwords" option *does not* prevent a noncompliant client from sending a clear text password.

> **NOTE ▶** If clients of your Open Directory server are also bound to other directory services that provide Kerberos, you should disable "Enable authenticated directory binding," because authenticated directory binding also makes use of Kerberos. For all practical purposes, you can use only one Kerberos realm at a time, otherwise you will run into unexpected authentication problems.

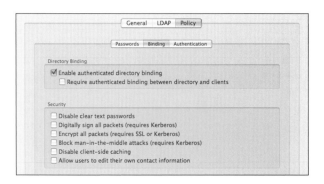

Allowing Users to Edit Their Own Contact Information

The "Allow users to edit their own contact information" option dynamically updates the Directory Access Controls (DACs) to allow or disallow users to edit any attribute that is listed as a possible attribute for the `apple-user-info` object class (which is defined in /etc/openldap/schema/apple.schema). These attributes are:

```
apple-namesuffix apple-phonecontacts apple-emailcontacts apple-postaladdresses
telephoneNumber mobile facsimileTelephoneNumber pager l st c postalCode postalAddress
street apple-imhandle loginShell jpegPhoto apple-user-picture description
```

The Directory application enables users to easily edit some of the attributes, such as `jpegPhoto`, which the Directory application (in /Applications/Utilities) uses for the user's image.

Changing the Types of Password Hashes Stored in the Password Server Database

Use the Authentication pane to change the type of hash methods that the Password Server uses to store passwords in its secure database. In simplified terms, a hash is the scrambled or encrypted text or password.

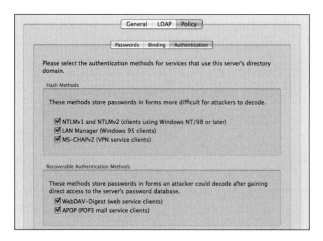

By default, Mac OS X Server stores an Open Directory user's password with a recoverable hash that an attacker could decode after gaining access to the Password Server database, including from a backup tape or an archive from Server Admin of the Open Directory master. You should disable each recoverable hash if you are not going to use their accompanying service.

It is not enough to simply deselect the boxes; the hashes are recalculated and modified in the Password Server database only once a user changes his or her password. You may want to make the authentication policy changes here first, before creating new users. If you make authentication policy changes after your users have already been created, you can use Workgroup Manager to select all users and force them to change their passwords at their next login:

1   Open Workgroup Manager, select Accounts in the toolbar, and select the Users icon in the left column.

2   Select all the users.

3   Click the Advanced button.

4   Click the Options button.

5   Select the "Password must be changed at next login" checkbox.

6   Click OK to close the Options pane.

7   Click Save in Workgroup Manager.

Disallowing Anonymous Binding

In previous versions of Mac OS X Server, you could simply update a value in one of the slapd (stand-alone LDAP daemon) configuration files and restart the slapd service. In Mac OS X Server 10.5, however, /etc/openldap/slapd.conf and /etc/openldap/slapd_macosxserver.conf are used only during the initial setup of the LDAP service and are not necessarily referred to again. The LDAP service does not notice any modifications to the .conf files, even after starting and stopping slapd. Additionally, early versions of Mac OS X Server (before 10.5.3) did not replicate some changes made to the live LDAP database.

As disallowing anonymous binding is not an available configuration in Server Admin, and is not a recommended or supported solution, this book does not contain instructions for that configuration.

Making Changes to the Berkeley DB Cache Size

In Mac OS X Server 10.4 and 10.5, the Berkeley DB cache size is determined by the amount of RAM installed on your computer when you promote to Open Directory master. If you later add memory, you may want to increase the cache size to increase performance. See the OpenLDAP documentation (listed in the "References" section at the end of the chapter) to determine an appropriate value. Once you determine the value:

1   With root privileges and your favorite text editor, edit the file /var/db/openldap/open-ldap-data/DB_CONFIG and change the `set_cachesize` entry to an appropriate value.

2   Stop and start the LDAP service with `launchctl`.

```
server17:~ ladmin$ sudo launchctl unload /System/Library/LaunchDaemons/org.openldap.
slapd.plist

server17:~ ladmin$ sudo launchctl load /System/Library/LaunchDaemons/org.openldap.
slapd.plist
```

There are many ways to modify the configuration for a new instance of an Open Directory master, but the defaults should be sufficient for most uses. The most common change is to use Server Admin to disable the storage of recoverable hashes for all users.

Configuring Mac OS X Server as a Primary Domain Controller (PDC)

If you have Windows computers in your network that are not already part of an Active Directory domain, you can provide them with directory services from Mac OS X Server. Mac OS X Server v10.5's PDC supports Windows 95 through Windows Vista (the latest shipping version of Windows at this writing). Your Open Directory master can be a Primary Domain Controller (PDC) for Windows computers, providing identification, authentication, and file services. You can log in on Windows computers with an Open Directory user, and even access the same network home folder from both Windows and Macintosh computers. This section does not attempt to duplicate the documentation that already exists for Windows NT domains; the focus is to help you get your PDC and Backup Domain Controllers (BDCs) up and running, then customize the user experience.

Mac OS X Server needs to be an Open Directory master in order to provide PDC services, and only an Open Directory replica can provide BDC services. If a PDC becomes unavailable, a BDC can still provide identification and authentication requests, but the BDC cannot write any updates back to the directory; the PDC must be available in order to update the directory.

Use the following steps to set up your PDC:

1 Open Server Admin. Add the SMB service to the list of services in the left column, then choose SMB in that list.

2 Choose Settings in the toolbar and click the General tab.

3 Change the Role from Standalone Server to Primary Domain Controller (PDC).

4 You can modify the Description and Computer Name fields, but it may make sense to leave the Computer Name field with its pre-populated name, which is from your computer name.

5 In the Domain field, choose and type a Windows domain name. This cannot be more than 15 characters long.

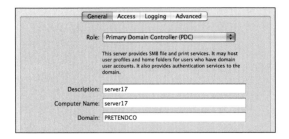

6 Click Save, then provide your directory administrator credentials.

7 Click the Start SMB button in the lower-left corner of Server Admin.

Providing WINS Services

The Windows Internet Name Service (WINS) provides name resolution like DNS, except rather than host name to IP resolution, WINS maps Windows NetBIOS names to network addresses. You can provide WINS services for your Windows clients to help older Windows clients find hosts on the network:

1   Open Server Admin, select the SMB service in the left column.

2   Click Settings in the toolbar.

3   Click the Advanced tab.

4   In the WINS Registration field, choose "Enable WINS server."

5   Click Save.

Providing Windows Roaming Profiles

A Windows roaming profile allows a Windows user to have the same profile when he or she logs in to the domain from any Windows computer. The roaming profile contains the My Documents folder, Internet Explorer favorites, desktop background settings, and other settings. By default Mac OS X Server's PDC stores all the roaming profiles in /Users/Profiles with a folder for each user. This is a special share point that does not appear in Workgroup Manager and is not available over any protocol other than SMB. You can change the roaming profile location per user in Workgroup Manager, as you will see in the next section.

Providing Windows Network Home Directories

When you start the SMB service, you start providing both PDC services (for identification and authentication) and SMB file services. Mac OS X Server has three share points enabled by default: Groups, Public, and Users. Each existing and new share point is automatically enabled for each of the following protocols: AFP, SMB, and FTP. Of course, it does not matter that a share point is enabled for that protocol until you enable the file service that is associated with that protocol.

TIP ▶ To control what share points are available, you may decide to disable sharing for all protocols for each of your share points, then selectively enable them at a later time.

Use Workgroup Manager to specify the Windows network home directory and roaming profile:

1   Open Workgroup Manager, select Accounts in the toolbar, and click the User icon in the left column.

2   Select a user.

3   Click the Windows tab.

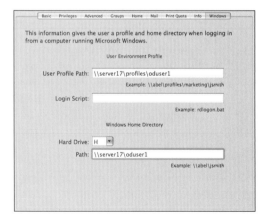

4 To fill in the User Profile Path field, choose one of three options:

▶ To use the default directory, leave this field blank. The default directory is the hidden SMB share point on the PDC: /Users/Profiles.

▶ To use a different network share point, type a Universal Naming Convention (UNC) path to the network share point. The UNC syntax is:

`\\`*servername*`\`*sharename*`\`*usershortname*

Here `servername` is the server's NetBIOS name (which is listed as Computer Name in the General settings for the SMB service settings); `sharename` is the share point; and `usershortname` is the user's short name. An example is:

`\\homeserver\profiles\oduser1`

▶ To use a local profile that stays on the Windows computer, type a drive letter and folder path in UNC format, such as:

`C:\Documents and Settings\oduser1.`

See *Mac OS X Server Windows Services Administration for Version 10.4 or Later* for more information about the login script, but this must be a relative path to a login script in the PDC's /etc/netlogon directory.

5 In the Windows Home Directory section, use the Hard Drive pop-up menu to set a letter for the user's network home folder.

6 Fill in the Path field of the Windows Home Directory section. Your options here are similar to the options for User Profile Path:

▶ To use the same network home directory for Mac OS X as Windows, leave this field blank.

▶ To use a different network share point, type a UNC path to the network share point. The UNC syntax is:

`\\`*servername*`\`*sharename*`\`*usershortname*

where *servername* is the server's NetBIOS name (which is listed as Computer Name in the General settings for the SMB service settings) or FQDN; *sharename* is the share point; and *usershortname* is the user's short name. An example is:

```
\\homeserver\Homes\oduser1
```

You can also take advantage of an SMB server's ability to use "virtual share points" (which makes it appear that each user has their own network share point dedicated to them) and not specify the share point name in the UNC path, as in:

```
\\homeserver\oduser1
```

Mac OS X Server's SMB service has virtual share points enabled by default.

▶   To use a local home directory local to the Windows computer, type a drive letter and folder path in UNC format, such as:

```
C:\Homes\oduser1.
```

7   To create the home directory, click the Create Home Now button, then click Save. Alternately you can simply wait until the user authenticates to the AFP service to create the directory automatically. When you use Workgroup Manager to specify the home directory for an Open Directory user, the home directory is not created until one of these two things happens.

Be sure to create the home directory in advance if the first login by a user will be from Windows, not from Mac OS X, otherwise the home directory will not exist for the Windows user.

Providing a Single Network Home Directory for Windows and Mac OS X Logins

You can provide a single network home folder for Windows and Mac OS X logins, so that no matter which platform a user logs in on, they will have common access to their files. Note that the user should never access the same file using two different file-sharing protocols simultaneously (for example, with AFP on Mac OS X and SMB on Windows simultaneously) otherwise the files may become corrupted.

To configure the Windows computers for access, you need to obtain and install the Poledit.exe Policy Editor tool, create profiles, and distribute them via the /etc/netlogin folder that Windows clients use. Poledit.exe is available only from Microsoft; you can install it from the Windows Server 2000 installation media, or you can extract it from various Microsoft Service Packs. See the site http://www.pcc-services.com/custom_poledit.html for more information about obtaining and using Poledit.exe.

You can use the Microsoft tools to make two common changes so that users see files and folders in similar places when they log in on either Mac OS X or Windows computers:

▶ Redirect Desktop to the network home directory Desktop folder.

▶ Redirect My Documents to the network home directory Documents folder.

The exact steps are outside the scope of this book. There are commercially available products to manage policy for Windows computers in the absence of Active Directory, such as Nitrobit Group Policy, but this too is outside the scope of this book. For more information on providing Windows services, see *Mac OS X Server Essentials, Second Edition*, pages 264-273, and *Mac OS X Server Windows Services Administration for Version 10.4 or Later* for more information.

Managing Data Stored in an Open Directory Master

Workgroup Manager is the main graphical application you use to edit the data stored in the Open Directory master's directories, but Mac OS X Server also offers a series of command-line utilities to help you import and export data.

In this section, you will learn how to use Workgroup Manager to assign limited directory administration privileges to users, as well as explore the DACs that Workgroup Manager creates to enforce these limited administrative privileges. You will learn how to use `ldap*add` to add new entries to the LDAP data store, and contrast `ldap*` tools with such `slap*` tools as `slapadd`. To better determine which is best for your situation, you will compare these tools to `dsimport` (which was introduced in Chapter 1) for adding users to the Open Directory master.

Defining Limited Administrators

One of the new features of an Open Directory master with Mac OS X Server v10.5 is the ability to give very granular administrative privileges to individual users and groups. When you use Workgroup Manager to set the privileges, Workgroup Manager dynamically edits the DACs to make the changes effective immediately. The LDAP service evaluates each LDAP request against the list of DACs to determine the level of authorization that it should extend to the request. If you use Workgroup Manager or the Directory application as a limited administrator and attempt to modify an attribute that you are not authorized to write, you will not be able to complete the modification.

It can be very useful to assign a user to have administrative capabilities for a group, to free some of your time for other tasks. Be careful when assigning capabilities; you may not want to enable a limited administrator to change another user's password, or to change their managed preferences.

Note that a limited administrator in Mac OS X v10.5 is limited in regards to all methods of LDAP access. Previously, in Mac OS X v10.4 and earlier, a limited administrator was limited only when using Workgroup Manager; the standard LDAP tools would allow that limited administrator full control over the entire LDAP database.

To create a limited administrator, do the following:

1   Open Workgroup Manager. Click the Accounts tab in the toolbar, and then select the Users icon in the left column. Authenticate as a directory administrator if necessary.

2   Choose the user to whom you want to extend limited administration privileges.

3   Click the Privileges tab.

4   In the "Administration capabilities" pop-up menu, choose Limited.

5   Click the Add button at the right edge of the Workgroup Manager window to open the drawer for Users and Groups.

6   Click the Groups icon in the drawer, and then drag a group into the "User can administer" field.

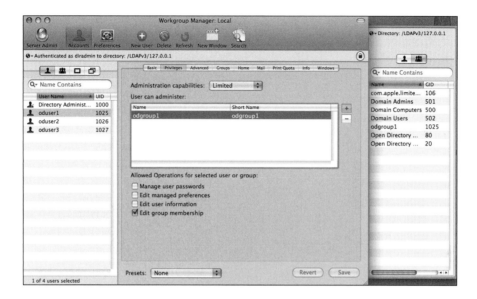

7   Select the group that you just added in the "User can administer" field.

8   Click the appropriate checkboxes in the section "Allowed Operations for selected user or group." By default, all the checkboxes are enabled.

Inspecting the Resulting DACs

A new Open Directory master comes preconfigured with several DAC rules. When you add the ability for one user to edit the group membership for a group, Workgroup Manager creates three new rules granting write access for the user to each of these attributes for the group: `memberUID`, `apple-group-memberguid`, and `apple-group-nestedgroup`. Here is how to use Workgroup Manager to inspect one of the rules:

1   Open Workgroup Manager. Click the Accounts tab in the toolbar, and then select the Users icon in the left column. Authenticate as a directory administrator if necessary.

2   Open Workgroup Manager Preferences and enable the "Show 'all records' tab and inspector."

3   Select the All Records Inspector.

4   Click the pop-up menu and select OLCBDBConfig. (The name comes from "OpenLDAP configuration—Berkeley DB configuration"; Berkeley DB is the data store format.)

5   Select the {1}bdb entry in the left column.

6   In the right column, click the disclosure triangle for dsAttrTypeNative:olcAccess to reveal the full list of DAC rules.

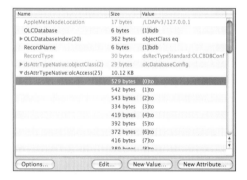

7   Select the first rule, which starts with {0}. Click the Edit button.

The syntax of the OpenLDAP access rule is beyond the scope of this book, but in short, this rule allows oduser1 to write the attribute memberUid of the group odgroup1. The rule permits administrative write access to the selected user and allows everyone else read access.

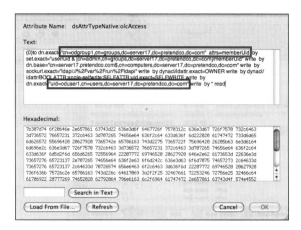

8   Click Cancel to close the Edit window, and then quit Workgroup Manager.

Understanding OpenLDAP Components

Mac OS X Server implements the OpenLDAP project's LDAP service with slapd. To automatically launch and keep slapd running, launchd (the process responsible for managing many processes for Mac OS X and Mac OS X Server) uses the configuration file in /System/Library/LaunchDaemons/org.openldap.slapd.plist. Applications and utilities make calls to DirectoryService, which in turn uses the LDAPv3 plug-in to make requests to slapd (the LDAP service). See *Mac OS X Server Command-Line Administration for Version 10.5 Leopard* for more information on these processes and commands.

This book focuses on the commands that specifically relate to importing users into an Open Directory master.

Using ldapadd to Add Records to the Directory

When you need to create only a few users, Workgroup Manager is an acceptable tool. When you have many users or other records to create, however, using ldapadd, slapadd, and dsimport may be more convenient ways to add new entries to your LDAP database.

Because all the ldap* commands (ldapadd, ldapmodify, and so on) communicate with slapd, the LDAP service must be available for them to work correctly. The slap* commands (slapadd, for example), however, modify the LDAP database directly and don't require the LDAP service to be running, so slap* commands can work in single-user mode if necessary.

ldap* commands are appropriate for scripting changes, whether for an initial setup or for peri-odically updating your directory to complement your organization's information workflow.

Understanding LDIF Files

To use the ldap* tools, you need to use the LDAP Data Interchange Format (LDIF), which represents LDAP entries and changes records in text form. The man page entry for ldif contains the full documentation, but this is a simple syntax for adding a new record:

```
dn: <distinguished name>
<attrdesc>: <attrvalue>
```

You need to specify a distinguished name (DN) for the record that you want to add, fol-lowed by one or more sets of attributes and values. To specify multiple records, separate the records with a blank line. You can wrap the line by typing a return in the middle of the value, then starting the next line with a single space character before continuing with the value. The wrapping is illustrated in the last two attributes in the example LDIF file below (userforldapmodify.ldif). Note that each attribute/value pair here has its own line:

```
dn: uid=userforldapmodify,cn=users,dc=server17,dc=pretendco,dc=com
uid: userforldapmodify
objectClass: inetOrgPerson
objectClass: posixAccount
objectClass: shadowAccount
objectClass: apple-user
objectClass: extensibleObject
objectClass: organizationalPerson
objectClass: top
objectClass: person
sn: 99
cn: User for LDAP modify
uidNumber: 3001
gidNumber: 20
homeDirectory:/Network/Servers/server17.pretendco.com/
 Users/userforldapmodify
apple-user-homeurl: <home_dir><url>afp://server17.pretendco.com/
 Users</url><path>userforldapmodify</path></home_dir>
```

Using ldapmodify to Add New Records with LDIF Files

You can consult the `man` page entry for `ldapadd` and `ldapmodify` for the complete syntax, but a simple syntax to use for `ldapmodify` is:

```
ldapmodify -a -D binddn -w passwd -H ldapuri -x -f file
```

where:

▶ -a specifies *adding* new entries (rather than modifying existing entries)

▶ -D `binddn` -w `passwd` specifies the DN and password with which to bind

▶ -x specifies simple authentication rather than SASL

This example uses the LDIF file userforldapmodify.ldif:

```
server17:~ ladmin$ ldapmodify -a -D uid=diradmin,cn=users,dc=server17,dc=pretendco,
dc=com -w apple -H ldap://server17.pretendco.com -x -f userforldapmodify.ldif
adding new entry "uid=userforldapmodify.ldif,cn=users,dc=server17,dc=pretendco,dc=com"
```

TIP If you use `ldapadd` in a script, and store the DN and password in the script, take precautions to prevent unauthorized users from viewing the contents of the script. Consider using a Service Access Control rule to disable SSH access to the Open Directory master for all users except administrators, disallowing user logins at the console, and setting permissions on the script to withhold access for "others."

Using Kerberos with ldapadd to Add New Records with LDIF Files

`ldapadd` is a symbolic link to `ldapmodify`; when you use `ldapadd` you are actually using `ldapmodify` with the -a option to add records.

Because the LDAP service is Kerberized, you do not need to specify a DN and password if you have a Kerberos TGT for your Open Directory master realm; `ldapadd` uses your TGT to acquire a service-granting ticket for the LDAP service, which authenticates you to the LDAP service so you can complete the write operation. Here's an example of obtaining a TGT and then using `ldapadd` to import a user with the LDIF file userforldapadd.ldif:

```
server17:~ ladmin$ kinit diradmin
Please enter the password for diradmin@SERVER17.PRETENDCO.COM:
```

```
server17:~ ladmin$ ldapadd -H ldap://server17.pretendco.com -f userforldapadd.ldif
SASL/GSSAPI authentication started
SASL username: diradmin@SERVER17.PRETENDCO.COM
SASL SSL: 56
SASL installing layers
adding new entry "uid=userforldapadd,cn=users,dc=server17,dc=pretendco,dc=com"
```

Understanding the Limitations of ldap* Commands

Like dscl, ldap* commands such as ldapmodify can add users to a running LDAP directory. However, unlike dscl the ldap commands communicate directly with the LDAP service, so they are not mediated by the directory services layer. When you add new users with ldap* commands, DirectoryService does not create a new GeneratedUID attribute for the user if you do not specify one, nor does it create an entry for the Password Server or a Kerberos principal.

Without a GeneratedUID, a user cannot take advantage of such features as file system access control lists (ACLs). If you are programmatically converting information from other sources into an LDIF file, you could use the uuidgen command for each new user to generate a random value for the GeneratedUID attribute.

If you create a user without a password, it is impossible to authenticate as that user with just a password; however, you can always use su to switch to another user's identity if you have root credentials. You can specify an encrypted password for the userPassword attribute in the LDIF file. If you do not prefix the encrypted password with the encryption method surrounded by braces, as in {CRYPT}, the LDAP service assumes that the password is encrypted with the crypt method, so it is not possible to import a user with a clear text password.

> **NOTE ▸** It is not recommended to store the user password as part of the user record. This book includes these examples in case you want to specify a temporary password for a user record, especially if you also configure the user record to require users to change their password at the next login.

After you create the user with ladpadd, you could use Workgroup Manager to set or change a user's password, which sets up the Password Server entry and Kerberos principal for the user.

The ldapadd command is most useful if you have an LDIF file that contains all the required attributes for a full user experience. One source for such an LDIF file is the output from a slapcat dump of all the users in an existing Open Directory master data store.

Understanding the slap* Commands

slap* commands such as slapadd and slapcat operate directly on the LDAP data store. To prevent your LDAP data store from becoming out of sync, you should stop the LDAP service before using a slap* command like slapadd. For example, when you set up an Open Directory replica, slapconfig stops slapd, initiates slapcat to generate an LDIF file of the data store, and then starts slapd after completing various other intermediate processes.

> **NOTE** ▶ Changes you make with the slap* commands do not get replicated to existing Open Directory replicas.

Using dsimport to Create New Open Directory Users

The dsimport command is a tool for importing records in Open Directory, regardless of the directory node. The basic syntax for dsimport is:

```
dsimport <-a|-g|-s|-x> filePath DSNodePath <O/M/A/I/N> -u username [-p passwd]
```

See "Creating a Local User Record with dsimport" in Chapter 1 for more details on using dsimport.

One of the helpful things about dsimport is that when you specify the password for the new user in the file, dsimport converts it to a shadow password. In contrast, with ldapmodify or ldapadd you can specify an encrypted password for a user, but that password remains in the directory until a directory administrator or the user changes the password, which converts the password from crypt to shadow.

dsimport can use a delimited file or an XML file that is either exported from Apple's AppleShare IP (which predated Mac OS X Server) or from a very early version of Mac OS X Server (version 10.1.x). An XML file doesn't need a header line to describe the delimiters (characters that you use to separate records, fields, values, and other delimiting characters) and the type of records and attributes that the file contains; an XML file defines the data as part of the file contents.

You can use Workgroup Manager to export user and group records, creating delimited files appropriate for dsimport. See "Exporting and Importing Directory Information Using Workgroup Manager," later in this chapter, for details. Because user passwords must be kept private, you cannot use Workgroup Manager to export user passwords. You can use Workgroup Manager and dsimport to import a delimited file that contains user passwords, but the user record will contain the encrypted password until the user or an administrator changes the password. Storing an encrypted password as part of a user record is a security risk.

TIP MacInMind's Passenger is a popular commercially available application that you can use to edit and create files to import with Workgroup Manager and `dsimport`.

Each time you import records with Workgroup Manager or `dsimport`, a new log file is created in your directory ~/Library/Logs/ImportExport/.

Using Server Admin to Archive Your Directory Information

Before making any drastic changes to your Open Directory master, you should make an *archive*, or backup, of your directory data. Before you make an archive, keep in mind that the archive process stops the services of the Open Directory master to ensure a solid backup. If you have Open Directory replicas, however, they will continue to provide identification and authentication services to bound computers; see Chapter 6 for instructions on configuring Open Directory replicas.

Follow these steps to create an archive of your directory data:

1   Open Server Admin, select the Open Directory service in the left column, and then click Archive in the toolbar.

2   Click the "Archive in" field's Choose button, and then navigate to a directory in which to store the archive.

3 Click the Archive button.

The archive name and password dialog appears.

4 Type a meaningful name for the archive.

5 Type a password. Be very careful because there is no password verification, and you cannot see if you mistyped the password.

This password is used to encrypt the disk image that contains the archive. You can leave the password blank, but note that this archive contains extremely sensitive authentication information. Also keep in mind that this archive is useless to you if you cannot remember the password required to open it.

6 Click OK.

Server Admin displays the progress of creating the archive, as shown in this figure:

7 Use the Console application in /Applications/Utilities to inspect /Library/Logs/ slapconfig.log.

Note that the archive process uses `slapcat`, `mkpassdb`, `kdb5_util`, and `sso_util`, among other commands, to back up the data and configuration files relating to your Open Directory master.

Exporting Directory Information Using serveradmin

You can programmatically script the archive process, but the command requires the password for the archive to be stored in the script or be otherwise accessible to the script.

The following transcript illustrates the command file to feed to the `serveradmin` command. You must specify an `archivePassword`, as shown here, but you can use two double-quote characters (`""`) to specify no password:

```
server17:~ ladmin$ cat archiveODM.commands
dirserv:backupArchiveParams:archivePassword = notsosecure
dirserv:backupArchiveParams:archivePath = /Volumes/BU/ODMarchive
dirserv:command = backupArchive
server17:~ ladmin$ cat archiveODM.sh
#!/bin/sh
/usr/sbin/serveradmin command < /Users/ladmin/archiveODM.commands
server17:~ ladmin$ sudo sh /Users/ladmin/archiveODM.sh
dirserv:readStatus = 0
```

After running the script, check /Library/Logs/slapconfig.log to monitor the progress of the archive. See *Mac OS X Server Command-Line Administration version 10.5* for more information on using `serveradmin`.

Exporting and Importing Directory Information Using Workgroup Manager

You can use Workgroup Manager to export and import user, group, computer, and computer list information from any directory node.

In the following sections you will export a user record and inspect the resulting export file, then import user records. Because Workgroup Manager does not export any sort of authentication information, you should not rely on a Workgroup Manager export as a backup or to move users from one node to another if you need to preserve existing user passwords. Instead, use an Open Directory replica as a backup and use a Server Admin archive of your directory to move users from one server to another.

Exporting User Information Using Workgroup Manager

You can use Workgroup Manager to export user and group records, but the resulting delimited file does not preserve user passwords or `AuthenticationAuthority` values. The resulting file is a colon-delimited file appropriate for importing with `dsimport` or Workgroup Manager; see "Specifying the Record Description in the Input File" in Chapter 1 for a review of the delimited file format.

Follow these steps to create a new user, export it, and then inspect the resulting text file:

1 Open Workgroup Manager, select Accounts in the toolbar, and then click the Users icon in the left column.

2 Click the globe in the upper-left corner and confirm that you are editing your Open Directory shared domain, /LDAPv3/127.0.0.1 or /LDAPv3/server17.pretendco.com. If necessary, click the lock in the upper-right corner and authenticate as a directory administrator.

3 Click New User in the toolbar to create a new user. For Name and Short Name type `tempuser`, assign the password `temppass`, and then click Save.

4 To verify that you do not need administrator rights to export directory information, click the lock in the upper-right corner to deauthenticate as the directory administrator.

5 Select the user tempuser in the left column.

6 From the Server menu, choose Export.

7 Choose your Documents folder, specify the filename ExportFromWorkgroupManager, and then click Export.

8   Open Terminal and view the contents of the export file to confirm that it contains the data for the user.

The first line defines the data contained in the file, and the second line contains the data for a user record. Note that the header line states that 40 attributes exported, including dsAttrTypeStandard:Password as the third element, but the third element in the tempuser entry (the user record) is empty: the two colons between the user GUID and the text isDisabled=0.The export file contents are shown here:

```
server17:~ ladmin$ cat Documents/ExportFromWorkgroupManager
0x0A 0x5C 0x3A 0x2C dsRecTypeStandard:Users 40 dsAttrTypeStandard:RecordName
dsAttrTypeStandard:GeneratedUID dsAttrTypeStandard:Password dsAttrTypeStandard:
PasswordPolicyOptions dsAttrTypeStandard:UniqueID dsAttrTypeStandard:
PrimaryGroupID dsAttrTypeStandard:Comment dsAttrTypeStandard:
Expire dsAttrTypeStandard:Change dsAttrTypeStandard:RealName dsAttrTypeStandard:
NFSHomeDirectory dsAttrTypeStandard:HomeDirectoryQuota dsAttrTypeStandard:
UserShell dsAttrTypeStandard:PrintServiceUserData dsAttrTypeStandard:
HomeDirectory dsAttrTypeStandard:MailAttribute dsAttrTypeStandard:
MCXSettings dsAttrTypeStandard:Keywords dsAttrTypeStandard:Picture
dsAttrTypeStandard:MCXFlags dsAttrTypeStandard:SMBHome dsAttrTypeStandard:
SMBHomeDrive dsAttrTypeStandard:SMBProfilePath dsAttrTypeStandard:
SMBScriptPath dsAttrTypeStandard:FirstName dsAttrTypeStandard:
LastName dsAttrTypeStandard:Street dsAttrTypeStandard:City dsAttrTypeStandard:
State dsAttrTypeStandard:PostalCode dsAttrTypeStandard:Country dsAttrTypeStandard:
WeblogURI dsAttrTypeStandard:EMailAddress dsAttrTypeStandard:
PhoneNumber dsAttrTypeStandard:MobileNumber dsAttrTypeStandard:
FAXNumber dsAttrTypeStandard:PagerNumber dsAttrTypeStandard:
IMHandle dsAttrTypeStandard:ServicesLocator dsAttrTypeStandard:URL
tempuser:184F2EAA-7A35-4EE5-BD6D-5C8F69FE3081::isDisabled=0 isAdminUser=0
newPasswordRequired=0 usingHistory=0 canModifyPasswordforSelf=1
usingExpirationDate=0 usingHardExpirationDate=0 requiresAlpha=0
requiresNumeric=0 expirationDateGMT=4294967295 hardExpireDateGMT=4294967295
maxMinutesUntilChangePassword=0 maxMinutesUntilDisabled=0 maxMinutesOfNonUse=0
maxFailedLoginAttempts=0 minChars=0 maxChars=0 passwordCannotBeName=0
requiresMixedCase=0 requiresSymbol=0 notGuessablePattern=0 isSessionKeyAgent=0
isComputerAccount=0 adminClass=0 adminNoChangePasswords=0 adminNoSetPolicies=0
adminNoCreate=0 adminNoDelete=0 adminNoClearState=0 adminNoPromoteAdmins=
0:1075:20::::tempuser:99::/bin/bash:::::::<?xml version="1.0" encoding="UTF-8"?>\
```

```
<!DOCTYPE plist PUBLIC "-//Apple//DTD PLIST 1.0//EN" "http\://www.apple.com/DTDs/
PropertyList-1.0.dtd">\
<plist version="1.0">\
<dict>\
    <key>simultaneous_login_enabled</key>\
    <true/>\
</dict>\
</plist>\
::::::tempuser:::::::::::::::
```

Importing Directory Information Using Workgroup Manager

You can use Workgroup Manager or `dsimport` to import the file that you exported in the previous section.

After you import this user into an Open Directory server domain, you can assign a new password with Workgroup Manager or use `dscl` to set the user's password. This will create a new Password Server slot and Kerberos principal for the user, and update the user record with new `AuthenticationAuthority` attributes. The following steps illustrate both methods:

1 Open Workgroup Manager, select Accounts in the toolbar, and select the Users icon in the left column.

2 Click the globe in the upper-left corner and confirm that you are editing your Open Directory shared domain, /LDAPv3/127.0.0.1 or /LDAPv3/server17.pretendco.com.

3 If necessary, click the lock in the upper-right corner to authenticate as a directory administrator.

   You do need to be authenticated in order to create new records in your shared domain.

4 Select tempuser from the list of users in the left column, and then click Delete in the toolbar.

5 From the Server menu, choose Import.

6 To avoid overwriting any existing user records, confirm that the setting for Duplicate Handling is "Ignore new record." Select the ExportFromWorkgroupManager file and click Import.

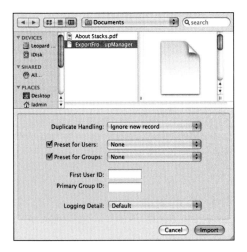

7   Type tempuser in the user search field in the upper-left corner to make it easy to find the user. Select tempuser in the left column, and then click the Inspector tab. Note that this user has no AuthenticationAuthority attribute.

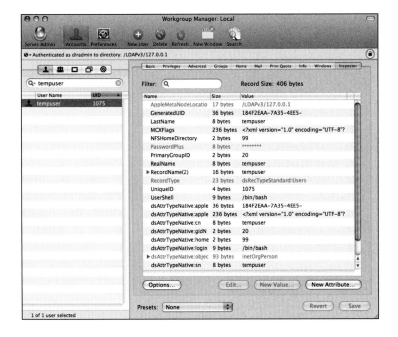

8   At this point you could use the Workgroup Manager to set the user's password, but for illustration, open Terminal and use the `dscl` command to change the user's password.

This has the same effect as changing the password with Workgroup Manager. You could use this in a script if you need to import users on a periodic basis.

The syntax for using `dscl` to change a password is:

```
dscl -u diradmin -P diradmin-password node passwd path-to-user newpassword-for-user
```

The `-u` and `-P` options allow you authenticate as a directory administrator.

Use `dscl` to change the password for tempuser to `newpass`:

```
server17:~ ladmin$ dscl -u diradmin -P apple /LDAPv3/127.0.0.1 passwd
/Users/tempuser newpass
```

9   In Workgroup Manager, click Refresh to refresh the view of the `oduser1` record. Note that the user now has two values for `AuthenticationAuthority`; one for Password Server and one for Kerberos.

Troubleshooting Issues Promoting Mac OS X Server to an Open Directory Master

If your Mac OS X Server computer has forward and reverse DNS records available, you should be able to promote it to Open Directory master.

In this section you will learn techniques for changing your IP address or host name if necessary, promoting to Open Directory master at the command line, and viewing the main log file created during the promotion process. You will also learn how to review the files created or modified during the promotion process, troubleshoot basic LDAP connectivity, and change the logging characteristics of the LDAP service.

Using changeip to Change IP Address and Host Name of Mac OS X Server

You *must* have access to forward and reverse DNS records for Mac OS X Server to promote to Open Directory master. Even though you can add an entry for your host in /etc/hosts that is immediately available for tools that use directory services such as Server Admin and Workgroup Manager, that workaround for the lack of DNS records will not suffice to allow you to promote your OS X Server computer to Open Directory master.

You learned to use `changeip -checkhostname` to confirm forward and reverse DNS records in the section "Using changeip to Confirm Your DNS Records" at the beginning of this chapter. You can also use `changeip` to change the IP address and host name of your Mac OS X Server computer. If you ever need to change the IP address or the host name (the FQDN) for Mac OS X Server, use the `changeip` command before you make the change in the Network pane of System Preferences. This is especially important if you have already promoted to Open Directory master, because many pieces of data in your Open Directory master contain the IP address or FQDN. The syntax for `changeip` is:

```
changeip <directory node path> <oldIP> <newIP> <oldFQDN> <newFQDN>
```

You must supply all the arguments above. The `<directory node path>` is /LDAPv3/127.0.0.1 if you are changing an Open Directory master or a dash (-) if you are changing a standalone server. If you are not changing the IP address, but changing the host name only, you must provide your IP address twice, once for the old IP address and again for the new IP address. Similarly, if you are changing your IP address only, you must still provide your host name twice.

> **TIP** If you need to change the IP address or host name for an Open Directory replica, then it is best to make that server standalone, run `changeip`, and then bind again, because `changeip` does not update the computer record and replication information in the shared directory.

In this scenario, you need to move your Open Directory master to a different network topology and change its name:

1   Use `changeip` to change the IP address from `10.1.17.1` to `192.168.40.1` and the FDQN from `server17.pretendco.com` to `newserver.pretendco.internal`:

`server17:~ ladmin$` `sudo changeip /LDAPv3/127.0.01 10.1.17.1 192.168.40.1 server17.`
`pretendco.com newserver.pretendco.internal.`

2   Use the Network pane of System Preferences to change the IP address to `192.168.40.1`.

3   Use the Sharing pane of System Preferences to change the computer name to `newserver`.

Changing the computer name should automatically change the Bonjour name to `newserver.local`.

The search base and Kerberos realm reflect their original values, but they are still valid. End users rarely notice the search base, but they may see a Kerberos authentication dialog and notice that the Kerberos realm reflects the original name.

Using slapconfig to Promote to Open Directory Master

As an alternative to using Server Admin, you can use the `slapconfig` command, alone or in a script, to promote a standalone Mac OS X Server to Open Directory master. The general syntax for `slapconfig` is:

`slapconfig` *command* `[command-options] [-q]`

The syntax to create an Open Directory master is:

`slapconfig -createldapmasterandadmin [--allow_local_realm] <new-admin> <new-fullname>`
`<new-uid> [<search base suffix> [<realm>]]`

If your host name ends in `.local`, `slapconfig` will not set up a Kerberos realm. The `--allow_local_realm` option forces the creation of a Kerberos realm, and you must provide a search base suffix and a Kerberos realm name.

To set up an Open Directory master, you must specify the information for a new user to be created in the new shared directory. The password that you specify interactively will be used to set up the password of the root user in the LDAP directory. The LDAP root user is different than the Mac OS X Server root user; for more details about the LDAP root user see "Managing Data Stored in an Open Directory Master," earlier in this chapter. The following command sets up a fully functioning Open Directory master:

```
server17:~ ladmin$ sudo slapconfig -createldapmasterandadmin diradmin "Directory
Administrator" 1000
password: [type the password for ldamin here, for sudo; this is hidden]
diradmin's password: [specify the new password here; this is hidden]
```

The rest of the output is not included here, but it contains the details of setting up the Password Server, the LDAP server, and the Kerberos realm.

If you want to completely script this process, you can use the -q option to suppress the command from prompting you for the password, and then pipe the password to the slapconfig command. Using a pipe (|) or a redirect (<, >, and >>) with sudo is a little tricky, so you need to encapsulate the entire command with quote characters.

> **TIP** The character for the pipe symbol is above the Return key on many keyboards.

The following command is one line, and it uses the output of the echo command as the input to the to the slapconfig command. In this command, you create a new Open Directory master and specify that the new password for the directory administrator (and for the LDAP root user too) is newpass:

```
server17:~ ladmin$ sudo sh -c '/bin/echo "newpass" | /usr/sbin/slapconfig
-createldapmasterandadmin diradmin "Directory Administrator" 1000 -q'
```

Note in the output from the previous command that slapconfig -createldapmasterandadmin initiates various commands, including slapconfig, mkpassdb, ldapadd, ldapmodify, kerberosautoconfig, kdcsetup, and sso_util. This is the same set of commands that Server Admin initiates when you promote to Open Directory master.

Viewing the slapconfig.log Generated from Promoting to Open Directory Master
You can use the Console application or the command tail -f /Library/Logs/slapconfig.log to watch the logs in real time while promoting (press Control-C to stop tail -f). There are around 100 log lines generated when you use Server Admin to promote to Open Directory master, and many more when you use slapconfig to promote manually. Unfortunately, the logging output does not contain all the details for the commands that are used.

You can safely ignore some warning messages that reflect the fact that there is no Kerberos password policy. Messages like this are normal:

```
WARNING: no policy specified for principal; defaulting to no policy
```

The last line in the `slapconfig.log` file related to promoting to Open Directory master is shown below. Once you see this, you can be sure the promotion process has completed:

```
command: /usr/bin/ldapmodify -c -x -H ldap://%2Fvar%2Frun%2Fldapi
```

Understanding the Files Modified or Created when Promoting to Open Directory Master
The following files are modified or created when you promote a standalone Mac OS X Server computer to Open Directory master. Not every file listed below is changed, but the promotion process at least touches the file's timestamp. This list gives you an idea of the number of files possibly involved. You can also use this list as a starting point to explore the contents of various log and configuration files:

▶ /Library/Logs/PasswordService/ApplePasswordServer.Replication.log

▶ /Library/Logs/PasswordService/ApplePasswordServer.Server.log

▶ /Library/Logs/DirectoryService/DirectoryService.error.log

▶ /Library/Logs/DirectoryService/DirectoryService.server.log

▶ /Library/Logs/SingleSignOnTools.log

▶ /Library/Logs/slapconfig.log

▶ /Library/Preferences/DirectoryService/ContactsNodeConfig.plist

▶ /Library/Preferences/DirectoryService/ContactsNodeConfigBackup.list

▶ /Library/Preferences/DirectoryService/DSLDAPv3PlugInConfig.plist

▶ /Library/Preferences/DirectoryService/PasswordServerPluginPrefs.plist

▶ /Library/Preferences/DirectoryService/SearchNodeConfig.plist

▶ /Library/Preferences/DirectoryService/SearchNodeConfigBackup.plist

▶ /Library/Preferences/SystemConfiguration/com.apple.RemoteAccessServers.plist

▶ /Library/Preferences/SystemConfiguration/com.apple.smb.server.plist

▶ /Library/Preferences/SystemConfiguration/preferences.plist

▶ /Library/Preferences/.GlobalPreferences.plist

▶ /Library/Preferences/com.apple.loginwindow.plist

- ▶ /Library/Preferences/com.apple.openldap.plist
- ▶ /Library/Preferences/com.apple.passwordserver.plist
- ▶ /Library/Preferences/com.apple.security.systemidentities.plist
- ▶ /Library/Preferences/com.apple.server_info.plist
- ▶ /Library/Keychains/.fl947E1BDB
- ▶ /Library/Keychains/System.keychain
- ▶ /private/var/db/smb.conf
- ▶ /private/var/db/samba/secrets.tdb
- ▶ /private/var/run/.DSRunningSP3
- ▶ /private/var/run/DirectoryService.ldap-replicas.plist
- ▶ /private/var/run/ldapi
- ▶ /private/var/run/passwordserver
- ▶ /private/var/run/slapd.args
- ▶ /private/var/run/slapd.pid
- ▶ /private/var/servermgrd/[*several services*].lock
- ▶ /private/var/log/slapd.log
- ▶ /private/var/log/system.log
- ▶ /private/etc/asl.conf
- ▶ /private/etc/auto_master
- ▶ /private/etc/autofs.conf
- ▶ /private/etc/hosts
- ▶ /private/etc/krb5.keytab
- ▶ /private/etc/MailServicesOther.plist
- ▶ /private/etc/ntp.conf
- ▶ /private/etc/smb.conf
- ▶ /private/etc/syslog.conf
- ▶ /private/etc/openldap/ldap.conf
- ▶ /private/etc/openldap/slapd.conf

▶ /private/etc/openldap/slapd_macosxserver.conf

▶ /System/Library/LaunchDaemons/com.apple.FileSyncAgent.sshd.plist

▶ /System/Library/LaunchDaemons/com.apple.PasswordService.plist

▶ /System/Library/LaunchDaemons/org.net-snmp.snmpd.plist

▶ /System/Library/LaunchDaemons/org.ntp.ntpd.plist

▶ /System/Library/LaunchDaemons/org.openldap.slapd.plist

▶ /System/Library/LaunchDaemons/ssh.plist

▶ /System/Library/LaunchDaemons/xftpd.plist

▶ /Users/ladmin/Library/Preferences/com.apple.PubSubAgent.plist

▶ /Users/ladmin/Library/PubSub/Database/Database.sqlite3

Troubleshooting LDAP Connections

As with most Mac OS X Server troubleshooting, begin by consulting the log files—specifically /var/log/system.log and /Library/Logs/DirectoryServices. As always, use tools such as `ping` to check that your underlying network connectivity is good, and tools such as `host` to check DNS service. Use Directory Utility to confirm that the correct directory nodes are listed in the Authentication pane of the Search Policy window.

To confirm that your LDAP service responds to basic LDAP requests, use a simple `ldapsearch` request:

```
server17:~ ladmin$ ldapsearch -LLL -x -H ldap://server17.pretendco.com -b
"dc=server17,dc=pretendco,dc=com"
```

To confirm that `DirectoryService` is using your LDAP service, use `dscl` to check that `DirectoryService` has access to the shared directory from the client and from the server. The command to use from the client is:

```
mac-seventeen:~ cadmin$ dscl /LDAPv3/server17.pretendco.com list /Users
```

The command to use from the server is:

```
server17:~ ladmin$ dscl /LDAPv3/127.0.0.1 list /Users
```

The reply should be a list of the users available in the directory node.

Configuring slapd Logging

By default, `slapd` does not log any debugging information, but you can change this. Edit the log level in `slapd`'s configuration file (specify it after the `-d` program argument), and then stop and start `slapd`. The values for log level are additive. For example, if you want to log for search filter processing *and* access control list processing, add their values (as listed below: 32 and 128) and specify their sum (160). The levels of debugging are listed in Table 5.1.

Table 5.1 slapd Debug Values

Log Level	Description
-1	Enable all debugging
0	No debugging
1	Trace function calls
2	Debug packet handling
4	Heavy trace handling
8	Connection management
16	Print out packets sent and received
32	Search filter processing
64	Configuration file processing
128	Access control list processing
256	Stats logs connections/operations/results
512	Stats log entries sent
1024	Print communications with shell back ends
2048	Entry parsing

By default, the log level is zero, and `slapd` sends all logging information to /var/log/system.log. You can segregate the `slapd` logging output from the rest of the system logging output by specifying the `StandardOutPath` and the `StandardErrorPath` in the `slapd` configuration file. Follow these instructions to change the log level and establish a separate log dedicated to `slapd`:

1   With root privileges, edit the configuration file /System/Library/LaunchDaemons/
     org.openldap.slapd.plist.

The original section of the file looks like this:

```
<key>Program</key>

<string>/usr/libexec/slapd</string>

<key>ProgramArguments</key>

<array>

    <string>/usr/libexec/slapd</string>

    <string>-d</string>

    <string>0</string>
```

Change the zero after the -d option to your desired log level (this example uses the
value of 160, the sum of 32 and 128 from above). Also, insert the extra lines specified
below. This same section of file should look like this:

```
<key>Program</key>

<string>/usr/libexec/slapd</string>

<key>StandardOutPath</key>

<string>/var/log/slapd.log</string>

<key>StandardOutPath</key>

<string>/var/log/slapd.log</string>

<key>ProgramArguments</key>

<array>

    <string>/usr/libexec/slapd</string>

    <string>-d</string>

    <string>160</string>
```

2 Stop and then start the LDAP service:

```
server17:~ ladmin$ sudo launchctl unload /System/Library/LaunchDaemons/org.openldap.
slapd.plist
```

```
server17:~ ladmin$ sudo launchctl load /System/Library/LaunchDaemons/org.openldap.
slapd.plist
```

After you have collected information with the increased debug level, set the log level back to zero, and then stop and restart the LDAP service. This is necessary or you will take up a large amount of disk space with unnecessary log text.

What You've Learned

▶ When you set up Mac OS X Server, you have a choice of Standard, Workgroup, and Advanced configurations. The Standard and Workgroup configurations automatically set up an Open Directory master.

▶ You can upgrade a computer with Mac OS X Server that is an Open Directory master from Mac OS X Server v10.3 or v10.4 to Mac OS X Server v10.5, using the same computer, with minimal disruption. You can migrate data from another Open Directory master, but this is more involved.

▶ You can use an Open Directory master to provide the functionality of a Windows NT PDC, and you can use an Open Directory replica as a BDC. This allows you to log in on Windows computers with Open Directory network user accounts, using a roaming profile and network home folder that are stored on Mac OS X Server. You can access the same network home folder from Mac OS X and from Windows.

▶ You can control access to the data in the directory data with DACs, which can be specified in `slapd` configuration files or stored in the directory itself.

▶ You can use Workgroup Manager to grant to a user the ability to administer directory information for a list of users and groups that you specify. You can enable full administration or enable editing of any of the following: user passwords, managed preferences, user information, and group membership. Workgroup Manager automatically creates the necessary DACs to enable the limited administrator access that you specify.

▶ You can use commands that start with `ldap*` (like `ldapadd` and `ldapmodify`) to make requests through the LDAP service to add and modify information in the LDAP database. You can also use commands that start with `slap*` (like `slapadd` and `slapcat`) to modify information in the LDAP database without going through the `slapd` LDAP daemon. You should stop the LDAP service before directly modifying the data store.

▶ You can import users with the `dsimport` command, which works through `DirectoryService`. `dsimport` automatically generates necessary attributes like `GeneratedUID`, which is required for the user to be able to use file system ACLs, among other services.

▶ You can use `launchctl` to stop and start the LDAP service.

▶ You can edit the `org.openldap.slapd.plist` configuration file to change where and how much logging information `slapd` generates. `slapd` doesn't pay attention to changes you make to the `slapd.conf` and `slapd_macosxserver.conf` files, unless you use `slaptest` to regenerate the `slad.d` configuration directory.

▶ /Library/Logs/slapconfig.log is a good source to use when investigating problems with promoting to Open Directory master.

References

Documentation

▶ Mac OS X Server Command-Line Administration for Version 10.5 Leopard
http://images.apple.com/server/macosx/docs/Command_Line_Admin_v10.5.pdf

▶ Mac OS X Server Open Directory Administration for Version 10.5 Leopard, Second Edition
http://images.apple.com/server/macosx/docs/Open_Directory_Admin_v10.5.pdf

▶ Mac OS X Server Upgrading and Migrating for Version 10.5 Leopard
http://images.apple.com/server/macosx/docs/Upgrading_and_Migrating_v10.5.pdf

▶ Mac OS X Server Windows Services Administration for Version 10.4 or Later
http://manuals.info.apple.com/en/Windows_Services_v10.4.pdf

Apple Knowledge Base Documents

▶ Mac OS X Server version 10.5: Custom LDAP Search Policy must be manually reset after upgrade
http://docs.info.apple.com/article.html?artnum=306740

▶ Mac OS X Server: Admin tools compatibility information
http://docs.info.apple.com/article.html?artnum=301590

Websites

▶ OpenLDAP Software 2.4 Administrator's Guide
http://www.openldap.org/doc/admin24

▶ Migrating LDAP Users and Passwords to a Clean 10.4 Server
http://www.afp548.com/article.php?story=20050615173039158

▶ Securing LDAP with DACs
http://www.afp548.com/article.php?story=20050813102154695

▶ SSL and LDAP in Leopard
http://www.afp548.com/article.php?story=20071203011158936

▶ The Great Big Panther SSL article
http://www.afp548.com/article.php?story=20071203011158936

▶ Open Directory Recipe for 10.4 to 10.5 Migration, Keeping Your SID Intact
http://www.afp548.com/article.php?story=20080403185017651

▶ Converting from `slapd.conf` to `cn=config`
http://www.zytrax.com/books/ldap/ch6/slapd-config.html

▶ Samba documentation
http://www.samba.org/samba/docs/

▶ Implementing User & Computer Policies with Samba
http://www.pcc-services.com/custom_poledit.html

▶ OpenLDAP FAQ-O-Matic: How do I Determine the proper BDB/HDB database cache size?
http://www.openldap.org/faq/data/cache/1075.html

▶ How to Implement system policies for Windows XP-based, Windows 2000-based, and Windows Server 2003-based client computers in non-Active Directory environments
http://support.microsoft.com/kb/910203

▶ Implementing system policies with Samba
http://wiki.samba.org/index.php/Implementing_System_Policies_with_Samba

▶ Samba and Windows Profiles
http://wiki.samba.org/index.php/Samba_%26_Windows_Profiles

▶ MacInMind Software Inc. (for Passenger)
http://www.macinmind.com

Review Quiz

1. Do you need DNS forward and reverse entries to promote Mac OS X Server to Open Directory master, or can you just add an entry for server in /etc/hosts?

2. What command-line tool can you use to promote to Open Directory master?

3. What log file should you check if you experience a problem promoting to Open Directory master?

4. If you are migrating to new computer hardware, which Server Admin feature should you use to migrate the data in your Open Directory master to a new installation of Mac OS X Server?

5. What is the requirement for Mac OS X Server v10.5 to act as a PDC for Windows clients?

6. Why should you stop the LDAP service before using a `slap*` tool such as `slapadd`?

7. Which tool would you use to enable a user to control the membership of a group?

8. Can you export user authentication information with Workgroup Manager?

Answers

1. You do need DNS forward and reverse entries in order to promote to Open Directory master.

2. You can use `slapconfig` to promote to Open Directory master.

3. You should check /Library/Logs/slapconfig.log for information about the process of promoting to Open Directory master.

4. You should archive your directory, copy it to the new Mac OS X Server computer, promote it to Open Directory master, and then restore the archive.

5. You need to have an Open Directory master before you can provide PDC services.

6. The `slap*` commands operate directly on the LDAP data store, rather than working through the LDAP service. You could get unreliable results or even corrupt your data store if the LDAP service and the `slap*` command edit the data store simultaneously.

7. You can use Workgroup Manager to grant the user full or limited directory administration privileges.

8. No, you cannot export user authentication information of any kind with Workgroup Manager.

6

Time	This chapter takes approximately 1 hour to complete.
Goals	Configure Mac OS X Server as an Open Directory replica
	Troubleshoot Open Directory replication

Chapter 6
Configuring Open Directory Replicas

Because an Open Directory master provides services that are critical to the operation of your Mac OS X computers, you may want to set up more than one Open Directory server, to provide redundancy and improve performance.

An Open Directory replica offers the same identification and authentication services as the Open Directory master: LDAP, Password Server, and Kerberos Key Distribution Center (KDC). Those services are synchronized with the master's services.

In this chapter you will learn how Open Directory replication works so that you can effectively plan, configure, and troubleshoot an Open Directory replication deployment.

Configuring Mac OS X Server as an Open Directory Replica

Before you set up an Open Directory replica, you need to figure out how many replicas you should set up and where. In this section you will learn information that will help you plan your deployment, such as the number of records and simultaneous connections that an Open Directory server can handle, as well as the possible topologies.

Understanding the Load on an Open Directory Server

LDAP uses the Berkeley DB database, which the *Mac OS X Server Open Directory Administration for Leopard Version 10.5, Second Edition,* guide states is efficient up to 200,000 records. Each Open Directory server, whether a master or a replica, requires enough hard drive space to handle the entire LDAP database. An Open Directory server can handle up to 1000 simultaneous client connections. Connections for the Password Server service and the KDC service are quick and short-lived, but a client can keep an LDAP connection open for up to 2 minutes.

It can be difficult to determine how many simultaneous connections your computers will demand from the Open Directory system, but the more often your users log in and log out, the greater the load will be on your Open Directory servers. You don't want to create too many replicas, however, because replication consumes some network bandwidth and server resources. By default, an Open Directory server replicates any shared directory data change as soon as the change occurs. The load from replication is determined by how often you create and update records (such as user, computer, computer group, and workgroup records), as well as how often users change their passwords. You may find that you and your users primarily use your Open Directory system to *read* information, not to *write* information to the shared directory, so there is not that much replication activity.

> **NOTE ▶** Do not use load balancing hardware with an Open Directory master or Open Directory replicas, as it can compete with Open Directory's built-in redundancy and cause problems for the client systems.

Securing Your Open Directory Server

Because Open Directory servers contain sensitive information (particularly, hashes of all your user passwords in the shared domain), take precautions to secure the computer. Limit physical access to your Open Directory servers, and set up service access controls with Server Admin to prevent users from using Secure Shell protocol (SSH) to connect to and gain shell access on your Open Directory servers. However, during the process of establishing a replica, you need to ensure that port 22 for the SSH service is not blocked by any firewall, and that the SSH service is available for the root user on the remote server. After you have completed the promotion to replica, you can establish SSH restrictions or disable the service. You may want to use servers with redundant power supplies and also use uninterruptible power supplies to help maintain uptime.

As of the current writing, there is no graphical interface to enable Transport Layer Security/ Secure Sockets Layer (TLS/SSL) for the LDAP services of a replica (which is not a supported configuration, and is outside the scope of this book). See "Securing LDAP Connections" in Chapter 5 for more information about the files that you would need to configure on your replica, and how to configure your Mac OS X clients to trust certificates.

Understanding Open Directory Replication Topology

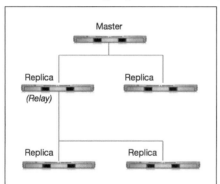

A new feature of Mac OS X Server v10.5 is *cascading replication*, in which each master can have up to 32 *Tier 1 replicas* (a replica of the master), and each Tier 1 replica can in turn have 32 *Tier 2 replicas* (a replica of a replica). A server that is a replica of an Open Directory master *and* has a Tier 2 replica is also called a *relay*.

Cascading replication makes it possible for you to have up to 1057 possible sources of Open Directory services, yet not place too heavy a burden on any one particular server (the number 1057 is the sum of 1 master, 32 Tier 1 replicas, and 1024 [32*32] Tier 2 replicas).

If you provide Open Directory services to clients in more than one subnet or physical location and you have a large amount of clients or replication traffic, you may decide to place a Tier 1 replica and one or more Tier 2 replicas in each subnet or physical location. This way the Tier 2 replicas provide services to clients at each subnet or location, and you dedicate the Tier 1 relays to replication traffic with the Open Directory master and with the Tier 2 replicas. If your client computers have less than a 100 megabits per second (Mb/s) connection to an Open Directory server, you may want to install a replica close to the client computers. If your remote site has only a few client computers, a single Tier 1 replica can probably handle the load.

Setting How Often Replication Occurs

By default, an Open Directory system replicates whenever there is a change in the LDAP data store. You can use Server Admin to set how often the directory replicates. You may want to set the interval before you start adding replicas, in order to establish the interval and prevent immediate replication traffic after establishing replicas.

Follow these steps to change the replication interval to 8 hours (480 minutes):

1 Open Server Admin, select the Open Directory service in the left column, and then click Settings in the toolbar.

2 Click the General tab.

3 In the "Replicate to clients" area, click the radio button for "Every *0* minutes/days."

4 Click the pop-up menu and choose "minutes," as shown in the figure below.

5 Type the number of minutes for the replication interval as shown here, and then click Save.

Once a server has a replica, you can click the Replicate Now button or use the `slapconfig -replicatenow` command to initiate an immediate replication.

Binding to an Open Directory Server

When you bind Mac OS X versions 10.3 and later, as a client to an Open Directory server, the client builds a list of Open Directory servers for LDAP and for Kerberos services, and after the first authentication, builds a list of Password Servers. The client builds the lists using information from the Open Directory server's LDAP configuration branch at `cn=config,`*searchbase*, and uses the lists in the event that an Open Directory service becomes unavailable.

For a list of LDAP services, Mac OS X uses the `dsAttrTypeStandard:LDAPReadReplicas` attribute (which maps to `dsAttrTypeNative:apple-ldap-replica`) of the `ldapreplicas` record (in `cn=config,`*yoursearchbase*). Mac OS X stores this list of replicas in /Library/Preferences/ DirectoryServices/DSLDAPv3PlugInconfig.plist, in the key `Replica Hostname List`. The `LDAPReadReplicas` is a list of all the IP addresses of Open Directory servers, in the chronological order of when you created the replicas. This is the list of LDAP services that your Mac OS X client will attempt to contact and use in the event an LDAP service becomes unavailable.

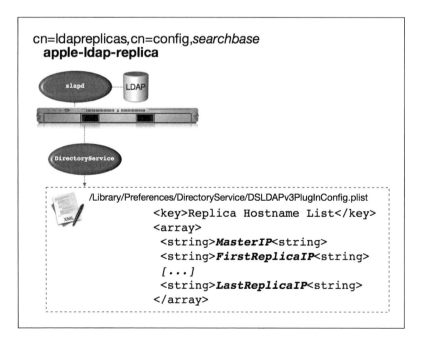

For a list of Kerberos KDCs, Mac OS X has two processes, DirectoryService and kerberosautoconfig, which update the Kerberos configuration files to contain a list of all the KDCs in the Open Directory system's Kerberos realm. One location for Kerberos configuration is /Library/Preferences/edu.mit.Kerberos. An additional location for Kerberos configuration as of Mac OS X v10.5 is /var/db/dslocal/nodes/Default/config/Kerberos:*REALM*.plist, where *REALM* is the name of your Kerberos realm. DirectoryService and kerberosautoconfig use the attribute dsAttrTypeStandard:XMLPlist (which maps to dsAttrTypeNative:apple-xmlplist) of the KerberosClient record (in cn=config,*searchbase*) to get the list of KDCs. The Open Directory master is listed first in the list, followed by each Open Directory replica in the order in which you created them. There is only one admin_server listed, which is the server that handles Kerberos password changes. For client computers, the admin_server is the Open Directory master, so you can initiate a Kerberos password change only if you can reach the KDC on the Open Directory master.

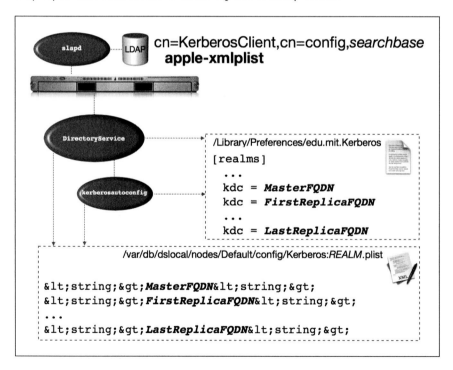

After Mac OS X authenticates a user against an Open Directory node, it updates the list of Password Servers available in that node. DirectoryService searches for the passwordserver_ PasswordServerID record in cn=config,*searchbase*, where *PasswordServerID* uniquely identifies a Password Server. The list is stored in /var/db/authserver/authserverreplicas.local, in base64 encoding. The list of Password Servers starts with the Open Directory master and continues with all the replicas in the order that you created them.

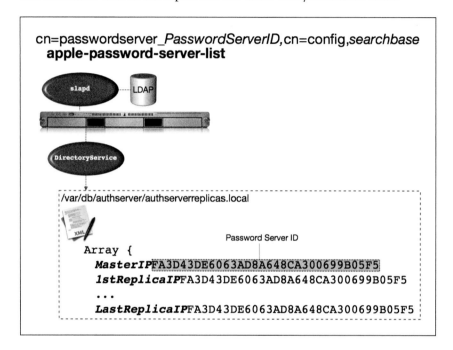

Choosing an Open Directory Server for Binding

Bind Mac OS X to the Open Directory server that you want it to use. When you bind Mac OS X to an Open Directory server, it uses that Open Directory server until one of the services (LDAP, Password Server, or KDC) becomes unavailable.

You may not be able to predict which Open Directory server your client will use if one of the services becomes unavailable. Your client will quickly send requests to many servers, and then use the first responder. This should result in your computer using the "closest" server (in terms of your network topology); but if there is a temporary problem with a close Open Directory server, and the client computer receives a reply from a "distant" server first, it will use that server. Because the Open Directory master is listed first in the LDAPReadReplicas list, it is likely that most clients will use the Open Directory master instead of any replicas in the event of an LDAP service failure. The client will stick with the server it chooses until another failure occurs, you kill DirectoryService, or you reboot the client.

Controlling to Which Open Directory Server a Client Binds

In general, you want to keep clients away from the Open Directory master and Tier 1 replicas, so that you can dedicate them to replication tasks. In order of preference, you should bind each Mac OS X client to only one of the following:

▶   Its closest Tier 2 replica

▶   A Tier 1 replica

▶   The Open Directory master

> **NOTE ▶** Bind Mac OS X to only one Open Directory server per Open Directory domain.

If you have many client computers at one location, you need to manually distribute the Tier 2 replicas to which you bind your clients in order to equalize their loads.

In the figure below, you have many client computers at Location A but many fewer at Location B. At Location A, rather than binding all the clients to the Open Directory master or to a Tier 1 replica, you should bind the clients to Tier 2 replicas, and you should distribute the clients among the available Tier 2 replicas. Contrast this with Location B, which has only a few client computers. You would bind these few client computers to a Tier 1 replica, which should be able to handle the load.

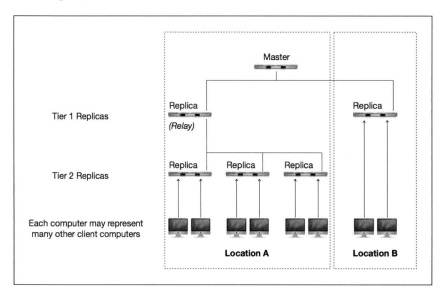

Do not use hardware load balancers with any Open Directory server, or your Open Directory system will fail.

It is possible, but outside the scope of this book, to use firewall rules to allow only certain computers to bind to certain Open Directory servers. In order to keep the Open Directory master dedicated to communicating with its replicas, you may want to set up firewall rules to delay or prevent clients from connecting to the Open Directory master for Open Directory services. The ports associated with Open Directory services are:

▸ `ldap`—port 389 for LDAP and port 686 for secure LDAP

▸ `apple-sasl`—ports 106 and 3659

▸ `kdc`—port 88

If you use Server Admin to configure the Mac OS X Server firewall, there is no default rule for enabling the `kpasswd` service (port 464). On the Open Directory master, you need to keep port 464 open to all clients to allow users to change their passwords with the Kerberos application.

It is also possible to manually modify your `LDAPReadReplicas` so that it contains DNS names that resolve to more than one IP address. Rather than listing `10.1.16.1` and `10.1.15.1`, you could list `tier2.pretendco.com`, which your DNS service resolves to `10.1.16.1` or `10.1.15.1` in a round-robin method. This is a highly specialized solution and may need to be modified if you add another replica later. See *DNS and BIND, Fifth Edition* for more information on configuring round-robin DNS.

Promoting to Open Directory Replica

You can use Server Admin or `slapconfig` to promote your Mac OS X Server computer to an Open Directory replica, with these requirements: You need to specify information for either an Open Directory master or a Tier 1 replica; and you cannot set the computer to become a replica of a Tier 2 replica. Check the log /Library/Logs/slapconfig.log for results of the promotion process.

When you create an Open Directory replica, the creation process temporarily stops services in order to ensure a clean copy of the various data stores. The Open Directory server that you make a replica of cannot process identification and authentication requests until the replication is complete.

Promoting Mac OS X Server to Open Directory Replica with Server Admin

Follow these steps to use Server Admin to promote to an Open Directory replica:

1   Open Server Admin, select the Open Directory service in the left column, and then click Settings in the toolbar.

2   Click the General tab, and then click the Change button.

3   Choose Open Directory Replica and click Continue.

4   In the first field, type the IP address or DNS name of the Open Directory master or a Tier 1 replica.

     Note that the window does not indicate that you can specify a Tier 1 replica, even though you can.

5   Type the password for root account on the computer that you specified in step 4.

6   Type the directory administrator's short name in "Domain administrator's short name" field if it is not already provided.

7   Type the password for the directory administrator in the "Domain administrator's password" field.

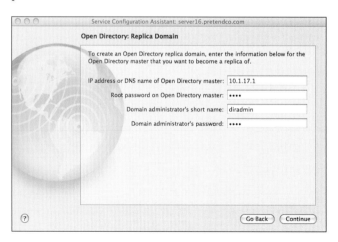

8   Click Continue.

9   Click Continue at the Confirm Settings window, shown below.

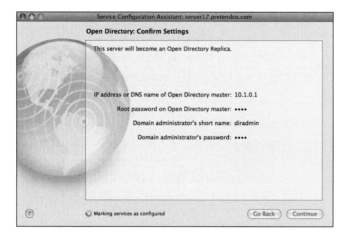

10   Wait while the various data stores are copied from the other server to your new replica.

You can open the Console application and navigate to /Library/Logs/slapconfig.log to see detailed information on progress of the replication process. The Server Admin window displays the general progress of the replication process, as shown in this figure:

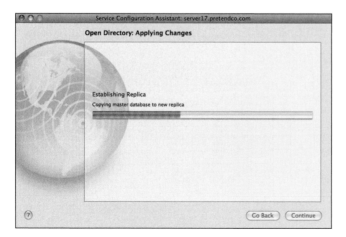

11 At the Service Configuration Complete window, click Close.

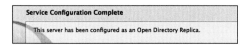

Promoting Mac OS X Server to Open Directory Replica with slapconfig

Instead of using Server Admin, you can create an Open Directory replica from the command line with `slapconfig`. If you use this command, more information is recorded in /Library/Logs/slapconfig.log.

If you have not already used Server Admin to promote your Mac OS X Server computer to an Open Directory replica, use `slapconfig` with the `-createreplica` option, specify the IP address—not the Fully Qualified Domain Name (FQDN)—of the Open Directory server that you want to replicate, and use the short name for the directory administrator. For example:

```
server16:~ ladmin$ sudo slapconfig -createreplica 10.1.17.1 diradmin
Root Password For Master LDAP Server:
diradmin's Password:
```

You need to provide the root password for the computer you are replicating (the challenge says "`Root Password For Master LDAP Server:`" but this is not necessarily the password for the root user of the Open Directory master), and then provide the directory administrator password. The progress is logged to the screen in standard output and similar information is logged to /Library/Logs/slapconfig.log.

Monitoring the Status of the Replication System

You can use Server Admin to check the status of the replication system. The Replica Status pane displays a list of the Open Directory server's direct replicas only, while the Replica Tree pane shows all the replicas in the system. The Result column displays "OK" if the last replication occurred with no problem. If the replica is unavailable or there was a problem with replicating to it, the Result column displays an error.

The Replica Status pane for an Open Directory master shows Tier 1 replicas, not any of the Tier 2 replicas. Likewise, the Replica Status pane for an Open Directory relay shows the Tier 2 replicas. The figure below shows the Replica Status pane for an Open Directory master at 10.1.17.1 with two Tier 1 replicas (10.1.16.1 and 10.1.15.1). Each of the replicas has a Tier 2 replica, but these do not appear in the pane.

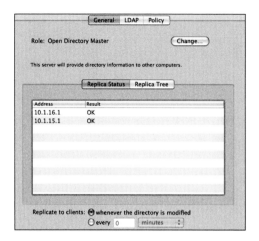

The Replica Tree pane shows the complete replication tree, with disclosure triangles to expand and collapse portions of the tree, as shown in the figure below. Server16 and server15 are Tier 1 replicas. Server14 is a replica of server16, and server13 is a replica of server15.

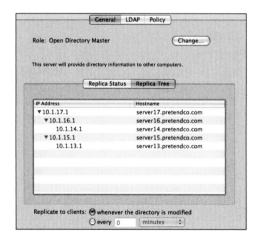

Promoting a Replica to Permanently Replace a Master

If your Open Directory master becomes permanently unavailable, you can promote a replica to become the new master. The replica already contains all the information that the master includes; however, Mac OS X Server versions earlier than 10.5.3 do not include some information, such as Directory Access controls. After promoting the replica to be the new master, you must make all the other relays and replicas standalone and then rebind them to the new master.

The LDAP search domain and the Kerberos realm remain as they were before, most likely containing the default values that are based on the DNS name of the original Open Directory master. Although users are generally not aware of the LDAP search base, it is possible for them to see the Kerberos realm name, which may be confusing.

If you want to create a new Open Directory master at the original IP address of the first Open Directory master, you could configure a new Mac OS X Server computer with the old Open Directory master's IP address, and then do either of the following:

▶   Promote it to Open Directory master and then restore from an Open Directory archive.

▶   Make it a replica of the new Open Directory master, and then promote it to be the newest Open Directory master.

After taking either of these actions, you need to make all the replicas standalone, and then make each one a relay or replica of the new Open Directory master.

Promoting a Replica to Master with Server Admin

You can use either Server Admin or the command line to promote a replica to replace a master. Here is the procedure to follow with Server Admin:

> **NOTE ▶** It is always a good idea to make sure you have a reliable backup of your server before making major changes.

1   Open Server Admin, select the Open Directory service in the left column, and then click Settings in the toolbar.

2   Click the General tab, and then click the Change button.

3   Choose Open Directory Master and click Continue.

4   Even though the next window prompts you to create a new Open Directory master, provide the information for the existing directory administrator, and then click Continue.

5   As the Confirm Settings window shown below states, make sure the computer that is the master for this Open Directory replica is offline. Click Continue at the Confirm Settings window.

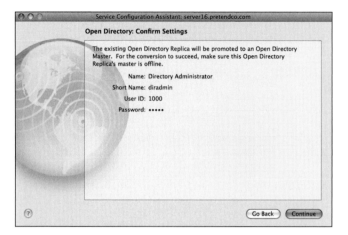

6   Click Close at the Service Configuration Complete window.

7   Make the other Open Directory servers standalone, and then reconfigure them as relays or replicas.

Promoting a Replica to Master with slapconfig

As an alternative to using Server Admin, you can use slapconfig with the -promotereplica option. As with the Server Admin method, ensure that the old Open Directory server that is the master for this replica is offline. Provide the short name of the directory administrator. You will be prompted for the directory administrator's password. The progress will be sent to the screen in standard output; similar information is logged to /Library/Logs/slapconfig.log.

In the transcript below, the old Open Directory master is at server17, and the command makes the Tier 1 replica at server15 the new Open Directory master:

```
server15:~ ladmin$ sudo slapconfig -promotereplica diradmin
Password: [enter the password for the sudo]
diradmin's Password: [enter the diradmin password]
Warning: An error occurred while disabling GSSAPI binding.
command: /usr/bin/ldapmodify -c -x -H ldapi://%2Fvar%2Frun%2Fldapi
modifying entry "olcDatabase={1}bdb,cn=config"
modifying entry "olcDatabase={1}bdb,cn=config"
command: /usr/bin/ldapmodify -c -x -H ldapi://%2Fvar%2Frun%2Fldapi
modifying entry "cn=ldapreplicas,cn=config,dc=server17,dc=pretendco,dc=com"
Stopping LDAP server (slapd)
Starting LDAP server (slapd)
Updating all Password server records
Promoting replica Password server to Master
command: /usr/sbin/kdcsetup -f /LDAPv3/127.0.0.1 -w -x -a diradmin -p **** -v 1
SERVER17.PRETENDCO.COM
kdcsetup command output:
Contacting the Directory Server
Authenticating to the Directory Server
Preparing to promote a replica to a master
Checking existing config
Updating the KerberosClient record
Adding kadmind to launchd~
Finished
command: /sbin/kerberosautoconfig -u -v 1
```

```
Updating the directory records
Replica promoted to master
```

After the process is complete, configure the other Open Directory servers to be stand-alone, and then reconfigure them as relays or replicas.

Troubleshooting Open Directory Replication

Understanding the processes, files, and logs involved in replication can help you trouble-shoot replication problems. After completing this section, you will have the knowledge necessary to inspect the log files and use tools to resolve replication issues.

Understanding the Processes Responsible for Replicating

On the Open Directory master, the `slurpd` process (Standalone LDAP Update Replication Daemon) pushes changes to the LDAP data store to the Tier 1 replicas. If the Tier 1 rep-lica is also a relay, the relay's `slurpd` pushes these changes out to its Tier 2 replicas.

Each server's `slurpd` keeps track of which data was successfully replicated; if a replica becomes unavailable, `slurpd` is able to queue the changes and push them to the replica once it becomes available again. Each server that runs `slurpd` stores LDAP replication information in /var/db/openldap/openldap-slurp.

The figure below traces the events that occur when you use Workgroup Manager to update information in the LDAP data store. Note that whenever you use Workgroup Manager to edit LDAP data in an Open Directory node, you actually edit the data in the Open Directory master, regardless of which server you're connected to. Here is the general process:

1. Workgroup Manager requests an update to LDAP data.

2. The LDAP service on the Open Directory master, `slapd`, makes the change in the LDAP data store.

3. The LDAP replication service on the Open Directory master, `slurpd`, sends the change out to the Tier 1 replicas. `slapd` handles the change on the Tier 1 replicas.

4. The LDAP replication service on any relays—in this case, `slurpd` on the Location A relay—sends the change to any Tier 2 replicas that are replicas of the relay. `slapd` han-dles the change on the Tier 2 replicas.

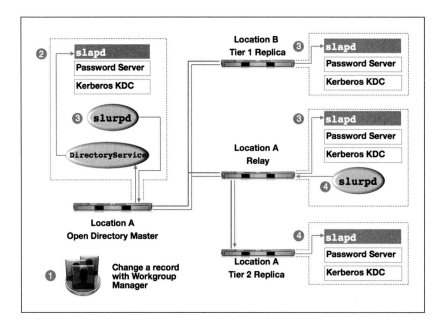

On all the Open Directory servers (the master and all the replicas), the Password Server process is *multimaster*, which means that a password change on one Open Directory server is replicated to the other Open Directory servers' Password Service. Each server that runs PasswordService stores Password Server information in /var/db/authserver and keeps log files in /Library/Logs/PasswordService.

The figure below traces the events that occur when users change their password from a Mac OS X computer bound to the Tier 2 replica at Location A. The general process follows:

1. A user uses the Accounts preference to change the password. PasswordService on the Location A Tier 2 replica to which the Mac OS X computer is bound handles the password change.

2. The Location A Tier 2 replica PasswordService daemon that handled the password change sends the change to its local kadmind to update the local KDC.

3. The Location A Tier 2 replica PasswordService daemon sends the change to the PasswordService daemon on its parent, the Location A Tier 1 replica. Although the figure does not show this, PasswordService would also send the change to any other Tier 2 replicas of the parent Tier 1 replica.

4. `PasswordService` at the Location A relay notifies its local `kadmind` of the change to update its local KDC.

5. `PasswordService` at the Location A relay sends the password change to all Tier 1 replicas and to the Open Directory master.

6. Each `PasswordService` daemon that received the change notifies its local `kadmind` daemon of the change.

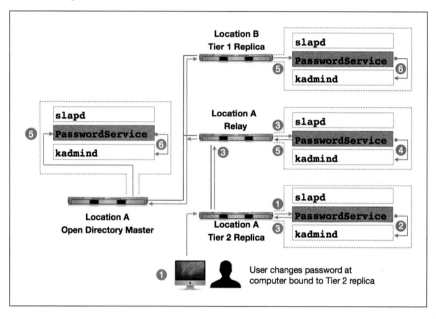

A server's KDC service (`kadmind`) does not replicate changes directly to other KDCs; instead, `kadmind` sends any changes to the local PasswordService, which then communicates the change to the other Password Servers. The `PasswordService` process sends changes to its local `kadmind`. Each Open Directory server stores Kerberos information in /var/db/krb5kdc.

The figure below traces events that occur when users change their password using the Kerberos application on a Mac OS X computer bound to *any* Open Directory server in the figure. The general process is as follows:

1. A user uses the Kerberos application in /System/Library/CoreServices to change the password. `kadmind` on the Open Directory master handles the password change.

2. `kadmind` on the Open Directory master sends the change to its local `PasswordService`.

3. `PasswordService` replicates the change to all the Tier 1 replicas.

4. `PasswordService` on each of the Tier 1 replicas sends the password change to its local `kadmind` to update its local KDC.

5. `PasswordService` on the Open Directory relay replicates the password change to any replicas of the relay; in the figure below, only one is shown.

6. `PasswordService` on the Location A Tier 2 replica sends the password change to its local `kadmind` to update its local KDC.

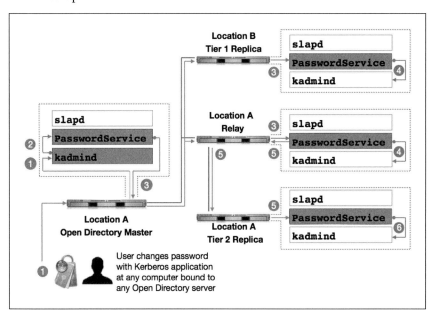

Ensuring SSH Is Available When You Create a Replica

You must be able to open an SSH connection to the remote Open Directory server and authenticate as the root user with a password. Any of the following could cause the SSH connection to fail:

▶ Port 22 is blocked by any firewall in the network path.

▶ The SSH service is not running on the remote server.

▶ A service access control list prevents root access to the SSH service.

▶ A bad RSA key for the remote server exists in /etc/ssh_known_hosts.

▶ Password authentication is disabled in favor of identity key pair authentication.

Understanding the Replica Creation Process

`slapconfig` initiates the series of processes that are necessary to create an Open Directory master or an Open Directory replica. On the server that you make the new replica, look at /Library/Logs/slapconfig.log to get a broad overview of the processes that take place. You will investigate each step after a quick overview.

> **NOTE** ▶ The word *master* can refer to either the Open Directory master (as in step 1 below) or the Open Directory server that you are replicating (as in all the other steps below).

On the new replica, /Library/Logs/slapconfig contains this information from a successful replica creation process:

```
1   Updating master's configuration
2   Stopping master LDAP server
3   Restarting master LDAP server
4   Updating local replica configuration
5   Copying master database to new replica
6   Starting new replica
7   Starting replicator on master server
8   Enabling password server replication
9   Enabling local Kerberos server
```

Before performing any of the actions above, the first thing the replication process does is open an SSH connection on the remote Open Directory server to run `slapconfig -checkmaster` on the remote server, with this command:

```
ssh root@remoteip slapconfig -checkmaster diradmin 0 4 4
```

The command runs on the remote server to confirm that these conditions are met:

▶   It is a master or a replica.

▶   It is not a Tier 2 replica.

▶   It is not configured with a Workgroup configuration.

▶   It has not already reached its maximum number of replicas.

▶   The software versions between the server and the prospective replica match.

You can safely ignore the message "`Warning: An error occurred while disabling GSSAPI binding.`"

Each step from /Library/Logs/slapconfig.log is explained below. While you could issue the commands contained in a verbose log of the replication process, there are a few commands that are not logged, so it is best to use Server Admin or `slapconfig -createreplica` to initiate the process of promoting to replica.

1. `Updating master's configuration`

    Use SSH to run the following command on the remote Open Directory server:

    `ssh root@remoteip /usr/sbin/slapconfig -addreplica youripaddress`

    where *remoteip* is the IP address of the server of which you are trying to become a replica, and *youripaddress* is the IP address of the server you are promoting to replica. If *youripaddress* is behind a Network Address Translation device and the Open Directory server cannot reach your potential replica at *youripaddress*, the replication process fails at this point.

    This `slapconfig -addreplica` command initiates a few other commands. One is an `ldapmodify` command that is logged only on the remote server, as the partial command. It shows up in the remote server's /Library/Logs/slapconfig.log as:

    `command: /usr/bin/ldapmodify -c -x -H ldapi://%2Fvar%2Frun%2Fldapi`

    The above command adds a new value for your new replica to the Native `olcReplica` attribute of the record in the record `OLCDatabase={1}bdb,cn=config`. In the new value, *n* = (the number of replicas already listed in the attribute) +1:

    `{n}uri=ldap://youripaddress:389 startls=no bindmethod=sasl credentials=updaterstring1`
    `saslmech=CRAM-MD5 authcid=updaterstring2`

This `olcReplica` value is not automatically removed if you later make your replica a standalone.

You can view this object with Workgroup Manager by clicking the All Records tab, then choosing OLCBDBConfig from the pop-up menu.

The `slapconfig -addreplica` command also appends a line (similar to the modification to the record above) to /etc/openldap/slapd_macosxserver.conf:

```
replica host=youripaddress:389 bindmethod=sasl credentials=updaterstring1
saslmech=CRAM-MD5 authcId=updaterstring2
```

2. Stopping master LDAP server

    Stop the `slapd` and `surpd` services on the remote Open Directory server in order to make a backup of the LDAP data store with the command:

    ```
    ssh root@remoteip /usr/sbin/slapconfig -stopldapserver
    ```

    ```
    Stopping LDAP server (slapd)
    ```

    ```
    Stopping LDAP replicator (slurpd)
    ```

    Run db_recover to restore the database to a consistent state. Use `slapcat` to create an LDIF file (`backup.ldif`) of the contents of the LDAP data store:

    ```
    ssh root@remoteip /usr/bin/db_recover -h /var/db/openldap/openldap-data;
    /usr/sbin/slapcat -l /var/db/openldap/openldap-data/backup.ldif
    ```

    You can safely ignore the warnings:

    ```
    overlay_config(): warning, overlay "dynid" already in list
    ```

3. Restarting master LDAP server

    Start the LDAP service on the remote Open Directory server:

    ```
    ssh root@remoteip /usr/sbin/slapconfig -startldapserver
    ```

    ```
    Starting LDAP server (slapd)
    ```

4. Updating local replica configuration

    Make a backup of /etc/openldap/slapd.conf on the computer of which you are becoming a replica. The log does not reflect the changes that occur on the remote server, but if this is the first replica of the remote server, the remote server's slapd.conf file gets updated to include references to the replication daemon, `slurpd`.

    ```
    ssh root@remoteip cp /etc/openldap/slapd.conf /etc/openldap/slapd.conf.backup
    ```

5. `Copying master database to new replica`

    There shouldn't be a local LDAP data store on the server you are promoting to replica, but remove the local LDAP data store if one exists.

    `/bin/rm -R /var/db/openldap/openldap-data`

    Use `scp` to copy the following files or directories to the local computer: the entire /etc/openldap/schema directory, the complete LDAP data store LDIF created in step 2 (backup.ldif), and the file rootDSE.ldif, which contains the DNS host name and the LDAP Kerberos principal:

    `scp root@`*`remoteip`*`:/var/db/openldap/openldap-data/backup.ldif /var/db/openldap/`
    `openldap-data`

    `scp root@`*`remoteip`*`:/etc/openldap/schema /etc/openldap/`

    `scp root@`*`remoteip`*`:/etc/openldap/rootDSE.ldif /etc/openldap/rootDSE.ldif`

    Use `slapadd` to load the contents of backup.ldif into the local LDAP data store. Remember that `slapadd` should not be used when `slapd` is running, to prevent data store corruption:

    `/usr/sbin/slapadd -c -l /var/db/openldap/openldap-data/backup.ldif`

6. `Starting new replica`

    Start the local LDAP replica.

    `Starting LDAP server (slapd)`

    Use `slaptest` to generate the `slapd.d` configuration directory from the `slapd.conf` and `slapd_macosxserver.conf` configuration files. Finally, modify the `cn=config` entry of the local LDAP data store:

    `/usr/sbin/slaptest -f /etc/openldap/slapd.conf -F /etc/openldap/slapd.d`

    `slaptest command output:`

    `config file testing succeeded`

    Use `scp` to copy the customSchema.ldif file (which may not exist):

    `scp root@`*`remoteip`*`:/etc/openldap/slapd.d/cn=config/cn=schema/cn={9}customSchema.ldif`
    `/etc/openldap/slapd.d/cn=config/cn=schema/cn={9}customSchema.ldif`

The commands are not logged, but the outputs are logged: stop the local LDAP server, then start it again to activate any configuration changes from the previous step.

```
Stopping the LDAP server (slapd)
```

```
Starting the LDAP server (slapd)
```

The following command and output is logged in the local server's slapconfig.log:

```
/usr/bin/ldapmodify -x -c -H ldap://%2Fvar%2Frun%2Fldapi
```

```
modifying entry "cn=config"
```

The above command modifies or updates several objects in the shared LDAP data store: the computer record for the remote server, the computer record for the local server, and the list of Open Directory servers (`cn=com.apple.opendirectory.` `master,cn=computer_groups,`*`yoursearchbase`*).

7. ```
   Starting replicator on master server
   ```

   Start the `slurpd` (Standalone LDAP Udate Replication Daemon) on the remote server. The `-startreplicator` option is undocumented, but it starts `slurpd` if it is not already running.

   ```
   ssh root@remoteip /usr/bin/slapconfig -startreplicator
   ```

   ```
   Starting LDAP recplication (slurpd)
   ```

   The command is not logged, but the output is:

   ```
   kerberosautoconfig -r REALM -m remoteip
   ```

   ```
   Configuring Kerberos server, realm is REALM
   ```

   The next several steps prepare the Kerberos database on the local server, preserving the LKDC (local KDC) configuration. For example, the /var/db/krb5kdc/kdc.conf file on two different Open Directory servers will share elements in common, but each will also refer to its own LKDC.

   Copy the "key stash file" that holds the key that is used to encrypt the Kerberos data store:

   ```
   scp root@remoteip:/var/db/krb5kdc/.k5.REALM /var/db/krb5kdc/
   ```

   Copy the access control list for `kadmind`, which specifies principals and the administrative functions they are allowed to perform:

   ```
   scp root@remoteip:/var/db/krb5kdc/kadm5.acl /var/db/krb5kdc/kadm5.acl.REALM
   ```
   ```

Copy the keytab file that contains the keys that allow `kadmind` to administer the Kerberos database:

```
scp root@remoteip:/var/db/krb5kdc/kadm5.keytab /var/db/krb5kdc/kadm5.keytab.REALM
```

Copy the Kerberos KDC configuration file:

```
scp root@remoteip:/var/db/krb5kdc/kdc.conf /var/db/krb5kdc/kdc.conf.REALM
```

Create a temporary directory on the remote server:

```
ssh root@remoteip /bin/mkdir /var/run/slapconfig_string
```

Use `kdb5_util` on the remote server to dump the Kerberos data store to the file initial.dump, and store it in the temporary directory:

```
ssh root@remoteip "/usr/sbin/kdb5_util -r REALM dump > /var/run/slapconfig_string"
```

Copy the file initial.dump to the local server:

```
scp root@remoteip:/var/run/slapconfig_string/initial.dump /var/db/krb5kdc/initial.dump
```

Remove the temporary directory that contains the initial.dump file on the remote server:

```
ssh root@remoteip rm -r /var/run/slapconfig_string
```

8. `Enabling password server replication`

Use `mkpassdb` on the remote server to create a compressed copy of the password server data store. This creates the file /var/db/authservermain/authservermain.initial.gz:

```
ssh root@remoteip /usr/sbin/mkpassdb -copy -gzip
```

Copy the zipped file to the local server:

```
scp root@remoteip:/var/db/authserver/authservermain.initial.gz /var/db/authserver/
authservermain.initial.gz
```

Remove the zipped file on the remote server:

```
ssh root@remoteip /bin/rm /var/db/authserver/authservermain.initial.gz
```

Unzip the local copy of the Password Server data store:

```
/usr/bin/gunzip /var/db/authserver/authservermain.initial.gz
```

Use `mkpassdb` (with undocumented options) to create the local Password Server. The values of `X` and `Y` in `ReplicaX.Y` below vary.

```
/usr/sbin/mkpassdb -zoq -s 521 -e 1021 -n ReplicaX.Y
```

Set the replication interval, represented by ₙ below. The default replication interval is 300 seconds (5 minutes). If you have changed this on the master, it will be reflected in the value below.

```
/usr/sbin/mkpassdb -setreplicationinterval n
```

```
/usr/sbin/mkpassdb -setrealm realm
```

```
/usr/sbin/mkpassdb -key
```

Although not noted in any logs, during this step, some records in the shared LDAP data store are created or updated.

If this is the first replica of the Open Directory master, create a new record, `cn=passworserver_32characterstring,cn=config,yoursearchbase`, where the 32 character string is the ID of the Open Directory master's Password Server.

Add information about your replica to the attribute `apple-password-server-list` of the records `cn=passwordserver` and `cn=passworserver_32characterstring`. This attribute stores an XML value that contains information about each replica.

Append the IP address of your server to the attribute `apple-ldap-replica` of the record `cn=ldapreplicas,cn=config,yoursearchbase`.

9. `Enabling local Kerberos server`

    Set up the local Kerberos server with `kdcsetup`.

    ```
    /usr/sbin/kdcsetup -c /LDAPv3/127.0.0.1 -a diradmin -p obscuredpassword -v 1 REALM
    ```

    This forces an update to /Library/Preferences/edu.mit.Kerberos.

    ```
    kdcsetup command output:
    ```

    ```
    Contacting the Directory Server
    ```

    ```
    Authenticating to the Directory Server
    ```

    ```
    Creating Kerberos directory
    ```

    ```
    Adding the new KDC into the KerberosClient config record
    ```

    ```
    Finished
    ```

    Use `kdb5_util` to load information from the initial.dump file from the previous step into the *REALM*.

    ```
    /usr/sbin/kdb5_util -r REALM load /var/db/krb5kdc/initial.dump
    ```

Clean up some of the files. The commands are not logged, but their output is.

```
Removed file at path /var/db/krb5kdc/initial.dump.
```

```
Removed file at path var/db/krb5kdc/kdc.conf.REALM.
```

```
Removed file at path /var/db/krb5kdc/kadm5.keytab.REALM.
```

Use `kdcsetup -e` to enable `kdcmond` and `kadmind` in the configuration for `launchd`:

```
/usr/sbin/kdcsetup -e
```

```
kdcsetup command output:
```

```
com.apple.kdcmond: Already loaded
```

```
kdcsetup: command failed with status 3
```

Use `sso_util` to create service principals for all the services that this server offers. There will be several "no policy specified" warnings, but you can ignore these.

```
/usr/sbin/sso_util configure -x -r REALM -f /LDAP/127.0.0.1 -a diradmin -p
hidden-password -v 1 all
```

```
sso_util command output:
```

```
Contacting the directory server
```

```
Creating the service list
```

```
Creating the service principals
```

There are many warnings about "`defaulting to no policy;`" you can ignore these.

```
Creating the keytab file
```

You can ignore the messages about "`No entry for principal`" existing.

```
Configuring services
```

```
WriteSetupFile: setup file path = /temp.randomstring/setup
```

Force an update of the /Library/Preferences/edu.mit.Kerberos configuration file:

```
/sbin/kerberosautoconfig -u -v 1
```

Finally, add a new *keyagent* user to the shared directory in case you ever want to use this server as a VPN server:

```
/usr/sbin/vpnaddkeyagentuser -q /LDAP/127.0.0.1
```

This is not logged, but this step also adds your server to the attribute `apple-xmlplist` of the record `cn=KerberosClient,cn=config,`*searchbase*. Mac OS X clients use this record to create their /Library/Preferences/edu.mit.Kerberos configuration file.

This step also updates various service configuration files, to make the services aware of the realm and the service principals.

It is remarkable that all of the above activity takes place within a few minutes, and that you need only provide the host name or IP address and password of the root account of the remote server, and the directory administrator's short name and password. If the process fails somewhere in the middle, it may be difficult to recover because some of the commands are not meant to be issued interactively. However, when you understand the processes that normally take place when making a replica, you have a better understanding of how to recover if there is a problem.

What You've Learned

▶ You can use Open Directory replicas to provide redundancy and increase availability to your directory.

▶ Replication does not provide load balancing, but you can manually distribute the servers to which you bind your Mac OS X computers.

▶ You should not use a hardware load balancer with an Open Directory master or replica.

▶ Each Open Directory master or replica supports up to 1000 simultaneous client computer connections.

▶ In order to make a Mac OS X Server computer into a replica, you need to ensure that on the remote server the SSH service is running and enabled for the root user, and there is no firewall blocking the SSH port (port 22).

▶ /Library/Logs/slapconfig.log contains detailed information about the processes of becoming a replica.

▶ An Open Directory master can have 32 Open Directory replicas. Each of these replicas can have 32 replicas.

▶ A Tier 1 replica is a direct replica of the Open Directory master, and a Tier 2 replica is a replica of a Tier 1 replica.

▶ A relay is a replica that has at least one replica.

▶ If you have many clients in your Open Directory system, you should bind your Mac OS X computers to Tier 2 replicas, to keep the master and Tier 1 replicas available for replication communications.

▶ Do not bind Mac OS X to multiple Open Directory servers in the same Open Directory domain; Mac OS X automatically maintains a list of all the servers that offer Open Directory services in the domain.

▶ In the event that that the Open Directory server that you bind Mac OS X to becomes unavailable, Mac OS X automatically attempts to bind to another Open Directory server. It uses the list in the Replica Hostname List, located in the configuration file DSLDAPv3PlugInConfig.plist, which is found in /Library/Preferences/DirectoryService/.

References

Documentation

▶ Command-Line Administration for Version 10.5 Leopard
http://images.apple.com/server/macosx/docs/Command_Line_Admin_v10.5.pdf

▶ Open Directory Administration for Version 10.5 Leopard, Second Edition
http://images.apple.com/server/macosx/docs/Open_Directory_Admin_v10.5.pdf

Apple Knowledge Base Documents

▶ Mac OS X Server: Admin tools compatibility information
http://docs.info.apple.com/article.html?artnum=301590

▶ If Kerberos Is Stopped on an Open Directory Master or Replica
http://docs.info.apple.com/article.html?path=ServerAdmin/10.5/en/c9od2.html

▶ Open Directory Master and Replica Compatibility
http://docs.info.apple.com/article.html?path=ServerAdmin/10.5/en/c3od2.html

Books

▶ Garman, Jason. *Kerberos The Definitive Guide* (O'Reilly & Associates, Inc 2003).

▶ Bartosh, Michael and Faas, Ryan. *Essential Mac OS X Panther Server Administration* (O'Reilly Media, Inc., 2005).

▶ Albitz, Paul and Liu, Cricket. *DNS and BIND, Fifth Edition* (O'Reilly 2006).

Websites

▶ Replication with slurpd
http://www.openldap.org/doc/admin23/replication.html

Review Quiz

1. What is the maximum number of servers that can provide Open Directory services associated with one Open Directory master?

2. What are the two requirements for Mac OS X Server to be considered a relay?

3. Which Open Directory server should you bind your client to?

4. When should you promote a replica to become the new Open Directory master?

5. Why are Open Directory services unavailable to clients during the process of making a replica of an Open Directory master or relay?

6. Which port needs to be available in order to make a replica of an Open Directory master or replica?

7. What changes cannot be made if the Open Directory master is unavailable?

8. Where can you find log files relating to replication?

Answers

1. You can have up to 1057 Open Directory servers for a single shared domain: 1 master, 32 relays, and 1024 replicas of those relays.

2. A Mac OS X Server computer that is a replica of an Open Directory master and has at least one replica of its services is referred to as a relay.

3. You should bind your clients to the closest replica. Avoid binding a client to a relay; you want to free up resources on the relay to enable it to communicate with its replicas.

4. You should promote a replica to a master only if the original master has become permanently unavailable.

5. The services are stopped in order to make a copy of the services' databases. As soon as the databases are copied to the new replica, the service should start again and be available to clients.

6. Port 22 needs to be available, and the SSH service needs to be running and available to the root user. Once the replication process has completed, you can block port 22 or use a service access control to limit the users that have access to the SSH service.

7. If the Open Directory master is unavailable, you cannot make changes to the LDAP directory and you cannot make Kerberos password changes.

8. You can find logs relating to replication in /Library/Logs/PasswordServer/ and /var/db/openldap/openldap-slurp/.

7

Time

Goals

This chapter takes approximately 4 hours to complete.

Configure a Mac OS X Server computer to connect to an existing
Open Directory master

Configure a service to use Open Directory network users and groups

Troubleshoot binding issues

Troubleshoot authentication issues

Chapter 7

Connecting Mac OS X Server to Open Directory

In the last chapter you learned how to set up Open Directory replicas in order to provide high availability for identification and authentication services.

In this chapter you will learn how to bind a Mac OS X Server computer to your Open Directory system and configure it to offer services to Open Directory network users. You will learn how to configure file system access control lists (ACLs) and service access control lists (SACLs) to authorize network users and groups to have varying levels of access to the files and services that your Mac OS X Server computer offers. You will build on your knowledge of the Password Server and the Kerberos service, and how these services work and interact, so that you can troubleshoot problems if they occur.

Configuring a Mac OS X Server to Connect to an Existing Open Directory Master

In order for Mac OS X Server to use the identification and authentication services of an Open Directory shared domain, you must bind the server to the shared domain, then confirm that the shared domain was added to the authentication search path. Your Mac OS X Server computer can then provide services to Open Directory network users, even though your server does not store any identification or authentication information for these users in any of its data stores. When an Open Directory network user attempts to access a service that your server offers, your server sends identification and authentication requests to the Open Directory replica or Open Directory master to which it is bound.

You can take this one step further and provide single sign-on to network users by joining the shared domain's Kerberos realm and Kerberizing your server's services. Users who have a valid Kerberos ticket-granting ticket (TGT) in the shared domain's Kerberos realm now can use your server without providing their credentials again.

Configuring Mac OS X Server with authenticated directory binding to an Open Directory server automatically joins your server to the shared domain's Kerberos realm as well, and Kerberizes the services on Mac OS X Server.

Joining Kerberos with Server Admin

Another way to join the Kerberos realm is to click the Join Kerberos button in Server Admin. Follow these instructions on a computer running Mac OS X Server that is not yet bound to any shared domain to bind it to the shared domain and Kerberize its services in the shared domain's Kerberos realm:

1   Open Server Admin, choose the Open Directory service in the left column, and then click Settings in the toolbar.

2   Click the General tab.

3   The action that you take here depends on your setup:

   ▶   If your server is an Open Directory master or Open Directory replica, see Chapter 8.

   ▶   If your server is already bound to an Open Directory server, skip ahead to step 9.

▶   If you set up authenticated directory binding, you do not need to use the steps in this section, but you should review the contents to be familiar with this method of joining Kerberos.

▶   If none of these three conditions apply, click the Change button.

4   Click "Connected to a directory server" and then click Continue.

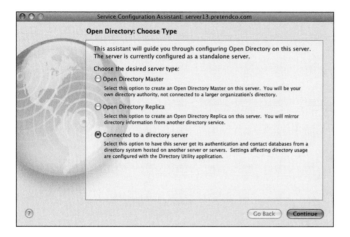

5   Click Continue at the Confirm Settings window.

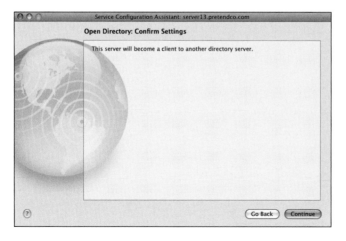

6 Click Close at the Service Configuration Complete window.

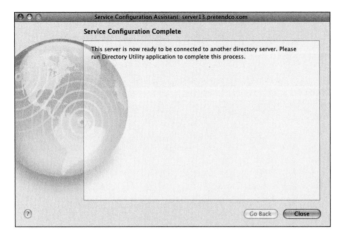

Server Admin now displays "Connected to a Directory System" for Role. Also notice the two buttons: Open Directory Utility and Join Kerberos.

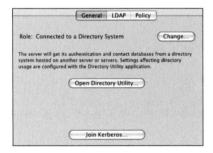

7 Click the Open Directory Utility button, which opens the Directory Utility application (and keeps Server Admin open). Bind to an Open Directory replica or an Open Directory master, just as you would with Mac OS X (see Chapter 2).

Depending on your Open Directory master policy, you may or may not need to provide credentials and set up Trusted Binding.

8 Quit Directory Utility after you successfully bind to an Open Directory server.

9 Return to Server Admin, which still displays the Open Directory Utility button, and from the View menu, select Refresh (or press Command-R).

If the Join Kerberos button is no longer displayed, you may have previously joined the Kerberos domain, or you may have set up authenticated directory binding. Either way, you can skip the rest of these steps.

Click the Join Kerberos button if it is still displayed.

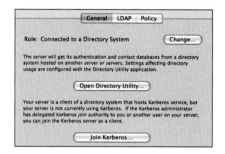

10 Find the Realm pop-up menu in the Join Kerberos Realm dialog, shown in the figure below. (This menu displays your server's local Kerberos Key Distribution Center, or KDC, by default.) Choose the shared Open Directory realm; if you select the local KDC realm, nothing will happen.

In certain circumstances, Server Admin may show an unexpected choice or status. After binding to a different Open Directory master, if you click Join Kerberos, you may see a dialog that looks like the following figure. If this happens, go to Server Admin's View menu, select Refresh, and then try the operation again.

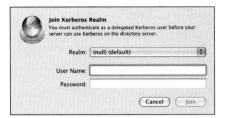

If you have not bound to a directory node, your Join Kerberos Realm window may look like the figure below, with four empty fields. If this is the case, click Cancel, use Directory Utility to bind to the Open Directory's shared domain, confirm it is in the authentication search path, and then try step 9 again.

11 Provide credentials for a network administrator who has the ability to join a computer to the Kerberos realm. The directory administrator is a good choice for this example. Click OK to continue.

12 At this point, Server Admin should display "Connected to a Directory System" for Role, but the Join Kerberos button should not appear. If you still see the button, choose Refresh from the View menu to refresh the view. The dialog should now look like the figure at the top of the next page.

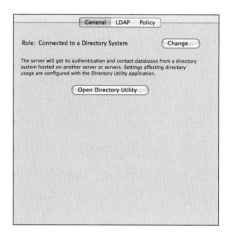

NOTE ▶ Sometimes Server Admin displays the Join Kerberos button even though it shouldn't. If your server is successfully joined to the Kerberos realm, ignore the fact that you can still see the button.

The services running on your server are now available to Open Directory network users. You can quit Server Admin, or keep it open and use it to enable and configure services. You now can access any Kerberized service on your server from another computer, as long as the user has a valid TGT, the service is running on your server, and there are no firewall rules or SACLs that prevent access.

This process of joining the shared domain's Kerberos realm preserves your existing local KDC information, so that if you later unbind your local KDC will still be intact.

Joining Kerberos at the Command Line

A recurring theme in this book is to enable you to script procedures when possible. Instead of using Server Admin, you can also use command-line tools to bind to an Open Directory server and join its Kerberos realm.

In Chapter 2 you learned how to use `defaults`, `dsconfigldap`, and `dscl` to enable the LDAPv3 plug-in, bind to an Open Directory server, and update the authentication search path. These steps work for Mac OS X Server as well as Mac OS X, but there is the additional step of joining Mac OS X Server to a Kerberos realm.

This additional step for Mac OS X Server follows. You can use `sso_util` (single *sign*-on utility) to join a Kerberos realm. This sets up shared secrets between your server and the shared domain's KDC, for all the standard services that can be Kerberized on Mac OS X Server. The options in the following example are:

▶   `configure` configures Kerberized services on the local machine for the given realm.

▶   `-r` specifies the Kerberos realm to join.

▶   `-a` specifies an administrator authorized to make changes in the Kerberos database.

▶   `-p` specifies the password for that user.

▶   `-f` specifies the shared domain node path.

▶   `-v 1` specifies the level of verbosity for the output. The log level corresponds to `syslog` *priority* (level); see the `man` page for `syslog` for an explanation of the log level priority. 1 is basic level, and 7 is the highest level of verbosity.

▶   `all` specifies to Kerberize *all* possible services, so you need to run this command only one time.

The command takes the form:

```
server12:~ ladmin$ sudo /usr/sbin/sso_util configure -r SERVER17.PRETENDCO.COM -a
diradmin -p apple -f /LDAPv3/server17.pretendco.com -v 1 all
```

The following figure illustrates the basic output of the `sso_util` command. Although you'll notice several warnings about "`no policy specified`" and "`defaulting to no policy`," you can safely ignore these messages.

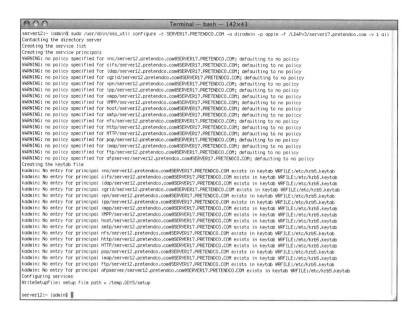

There is more information about `sso_util` in the section "Troubleshooting Binding Issues," later in this chapter.

Scripting the Entire Binding Process

The following code brings together the commands necessary to bind to an Open Directory domain and join its Kerberos realm. In this example, server17.pretendco.com is the Open Directory master, and SERVER17.PRETENDCO.COM is the realm name:

```
sudo dscl /Search create / SearchPolicy CSPSearchPath
sudo defaults write /Library/Preferences/DirectoryService/DirectoryService LDAPv3 Active
sudo killall DirectorySerivce
sudo dsconfigldap -v -a server17.pretendco.com -n server17 -u diradmin -p apple -l admin
-q apple
sudo dscl /Search append / CSPSearchPath /LDAPv3/server17.pretendco.com
sudo /usr/sbin/sso_util configure -r SERVER17.PRETENDCO.COM -a diradmin -p apple -f
/LDAPv3/server17.pretendco.com -v 1 all
```

Configuring a Service to Use an Open Directory Network User or Group Record

In the previous section you learned how to configure your server to fully participate in the Open Directory shared domain. In this section you will learn how to authorize network users and groups to access services on your server. There are two broad categories of access: service access and file access. For the big picture on how to configure file system ACLs and SACLs, see pages 136–170 of *Mac OS X Server Essentials, Second Edition*. In this section you will learn how to configure access to files and services for network users and groups.

Using Workgroup Manager to View Users and Groups in the Shared Domain

Even though you may not have administrative access to change records in the Open Directory shared domain, you can use Workgroup Manager on your Mac OS X Server computer to view the Open Directory user and group records.

Workgroup Manager displays one directory node per window. When you want to add users to groups, or groups to users, you can use Workgroup Manager's drawer, which can display users and groups from a different node. The steps are as follows:

1   Open Workgroup Manager, connect to your Mac OS X Server, and then authenticate with local administrator credentials.

2   From the Workgroup Manager menu, select Preferences.

3   Ensure "Show 'All Records' tab and inspector" checkbox is selected, and then click OK.

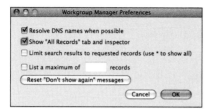

4   Click the Globe icon in the upper-left corner of Workgroup Manager and select your shared domain. If no entry for your shared domain appears in the list, select Other and navigate through LDAPv3 to the server for your shared domain, then click OK.

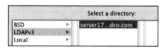

5   Verify that the Globe icon in the left-upper corner indicates that you are viewing the shared directory, and you are not authenticated as a directory administrator.

> ▼ **Viewing directory: /LDAPv3/server17.pretendco.com. Not authenticated**

6   It is possible that you have previously stored directory administrator credentials in your keychain and are authenticated as a directory administrator. If this is the case, click the Lock icon in the upper-right corner of Workgroup Manager to deauthen-ticate as a directory administrator and use Workgroup Manager without directory administrator access.

7   Click the Accounts button in the toolbar.

8   Click the User Accounts icon in the left column.

9   Choose an Open Directory user account in the list of users.

10 Click the Inspector tab in the right column. Note that you cannot make any changes because you have not authenticated as a directory administrator. You can view the various `dsAttrTypeNative` and `dsAttrTypeStandard` attributes, but some attribute names and values are not displayed fully, and you cannot resize columns or select an attri-bute to inspect its full value. However, in this figure, you can see at least the beginning value of the `GeneratedUID` for the selected user.

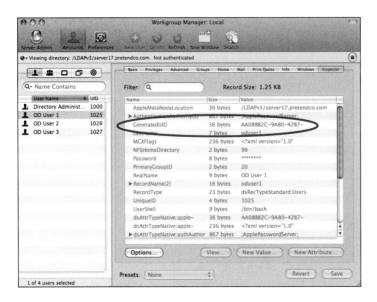

Configuring Service Authorization for Network User and Group Records

If you start a service on Mac OS X Server, your server authorizes any authenticated network user to use that service, unless you set up a SACL.

NOTE ▶ The Secure Shell (SSH) service is automatically started by default on Mac OS X Server.

In previous versions of Mac OS X Server, you had to use Workgroup Manager to edit file system ACLs. In Mac OS X Server v10.5, you use Server Admin to set both SACLs and ACLs.

Follow these steps to limit access to the SSH service to the local administrator, an Open Directory network user, and the members of an Open Directory network group:

1   Open Server Admin.

2   In the left column, labeled Servers, select your server (as opposed to one of the services that it offers).

3   In the toolbar, select Settings.

4   Click the Access tab.

The Services tab should be selected by default. Network users can gain access to all of the services listed below, provided the service is running and the user authenticates successfully.

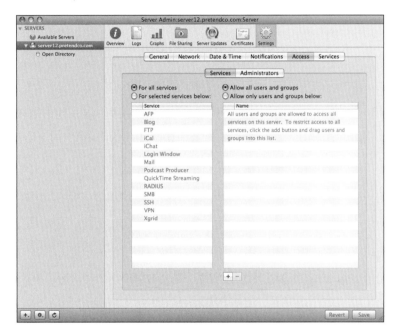

5   Click "For selected services below."

6   In the left column (Service), choose the SSH service.

By default, your server allows all users in its authentication search path to use SSH.

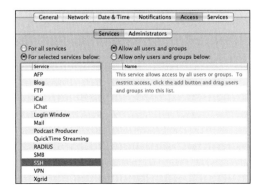

7 Above the right column (Name), click "Allow only users and groups below."

8 Click the Add (+) button at the bottom center of the Server Admin window. This is one of the ways to display the Users and Groups window; you will learn more about this window later in this chapter. Drag the local administrator and an Open Directory user into the right column of Server Admin to add them to the list of allowed users and groups for the SSH service.

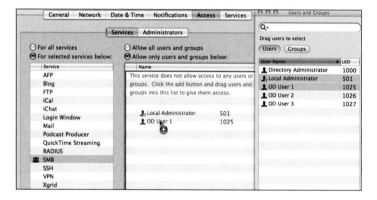

9 Click Save in the lower-right corner of Server Admin.

10 In the Users and Groups window, click Groups.

11 Drag an Open Directory group into the right column of Server Admin to add it to the list of allowed users and groups for the SSH service.

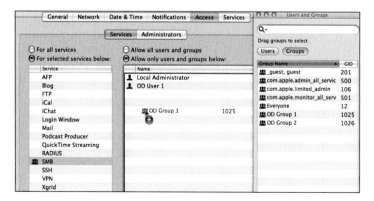

You have configured the SSH service on your server to allow only the local administrator, one specific Open Directory network user, and any member of a specific Open Directory network group to have access to the service. It is possible for other users to authenticate, but you have configured the SSH service to not allow any user account except those you specified in the SACL to access the SSH service. In the figure below, notice that there is an icon to the left of the SSH service in the Service column; this indicates that access to the service is restricted.

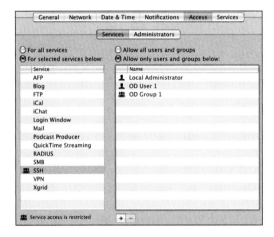

NOTE ▶ To remove this restriction, see step 5 of "Understanding How ACLs and File System ACLs Use a Record's UUID," later in this chapter. If you do not remove the restriction, keep in mind that you have this SACL in place for the SSH service as you work through the rest of this book.

Configuring File System Authorization for Network User and Group Records

Configuring file system ACLs for network users and groups is similar to the process for local users and groups.

Follow these steps to add a network user and a network group to your server's Public folder ACL:

1   Open Server Admin and connect to your local Mac OS X Server computer.

2   Choose your server in the left column.

3   Click the File Sharing button in the toolbar.

4   Click the Share Points and List buttons under the toolbar.

5   Select the Public share point.

6   Click the Permissions tab.

7   If the "Users and Groups" window is not displayed, click the Add (+) button in the lower portion of Server Admin to display it. Click the Users button in the "Users and Groups" window.

8   Drag a network user from the "Users and Groups" window into the ACL portion of the Permissions view.

     You just created an access control entry (ACE) for that folder's ACL.

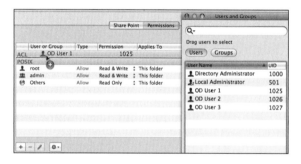

9   Click the ACE's Read Only pop-up menu in the Permission column and choose Full Control. Click Save.

10   Click Groups in the "Users and Groups" window.

11   Drag a network group into the ACL portion of the Permissions view.

12 In the ACE for the network group, click the Read Only pop-up menu in the Permission column and choose Full Control. Click Save.

Understanding How SACLs and File System ACLs Use a Record's UUID

When you add an Open Directory network user or group to either a SACL or file system ACL, the operating system uses the Universally Unique ID (`dsAttrTypeStandard:GeneratedUID` attribute, referred to as GUID or UUID) in addition to or instead of the record's names. If Mac OS X Server's connection to its Open Directory system is interrupted, you will see this 128-bit unique identifier listed instead of the record name. In the figure below, the `GeneratedUID` of the network user record and of the network group record are listed, because the connection to the Open Directory service is not available.

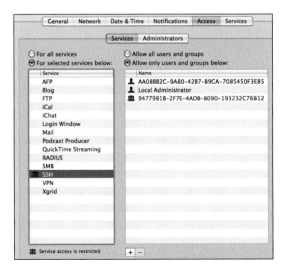

When you set the SACL for SSH in the previous steps, this resulted in a group that you can examine and find user and group UUIDs. Follow these steps to inspect the group with dscl:

1 Open Terminal.

2 Use dscl to view the local group com.apple.access_ssh, which controls access to the SSH service. Note that the GUIDs for the user records in the group are listed in the GroupMembers attribute, and the UUID for the group record in the group is listed in the NestedGroups attribute.

```
server12:~ ladmin$ dscl localhost read /Local/Default/Groups/com.apple.access_ssh

AppleMetaNodeLocation: /Local/Default

GeneratedUID: 16939056-05E7-4BCD-AD78-93F083B3BE19

GroupMembers: C29C3EB8-FF6E-442E-B155-FEFBA2E148A9 AA08BB2C-9A80-42B7-B9CA-7085450F3E85

GroupMembership: ladmin oduser1

NestedGroups: 9477981B-2F7E-4ADB-8090-193232C76812

PrimaryGroupID: 502

RecordName: com.apple.access_ssh

RecordType: dsRecTypeStandard:Groups
```

3 Use dscl to confirm that the GUIDs for ladmin, oduser1, and odgroup1 match the contents of the com.apple.access_ssh group attributes.

```
server12:~ ladmin$ dscl localhost read /Search/Users/oduser1 GeneratedUID

GeneratedUID: AA08BB2C-9A80-42B7-B9CA-7085450F3E85

server12:~ ladmin$ dscl localhost read /Search/Users/ladmin GeneratedUID

GeneratedUID: C29C3EB8-FF6E-442E-B155-FEFBA2E148A9

server12:~ ladmin$ dscl localhost read /Search/Groups/odgroup1 GeneratedUID

GeneratedUID: 9477981B-2F7E-4ADB-8090-193232C76812
```

4   Optional: Attempt to open an SSH connection to your server as a user that you haven't authorized to use the service.

Your server should deny the attempt. The SSH service does not send an error message, it just asks for the password repeatedly.

`server12:~ ladmin$ ssh oduser2@localhost`

`Password:` [type correct password, which is hidden]

`Password:` [press Control-D to exit]

5   Use Server Admin to remove the SACL by clicking "Allow all users and groups" for the SSH service.

Like SACLs, file system ACLs use the user and group record UUIDs. In the previous section, you created ACEs for the Public shared folder. When the shared domain is available, Server Admin displays that folder's ACL with the names of the user records (the group short name oduser1, and the user name OD User 1). When the shared domain is unavailable, however, Server Admin displays each record's 128-bit UUID, as shown in this figure.

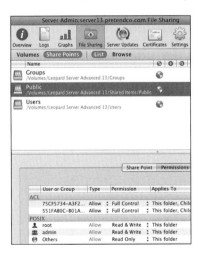

Troubleshooting Binding Issues

In Chapter 2 you learned about binding Mac OS X to an Open Directory server. The same tools, processes, and logs are used for Mac OS X Server, but there is the additional step of joining Mac OS X Server to a Kerberos realm.

This section focuses on troubleshooting binding to the Kerberos realm. It uses a transcript of the sso_util command, the command-line equivalent to Server Admin's Join Kerberos button, with the highest level of verbosity to illustrate the series of processes and actions involved in joining a Kerberos realm.

At its most basic, sso_util initiates the following actions:

1. Contacts each directory node and looks for Kerberos configuration information
2. Creates a list of services
3. Connects to the KDC and has it create or update a principal for each of the services in step 2
4. Creates or populates the local keytab file with the principals created in step 3
5. Configures local services to use Kerberos

In order to understand each of the steps that sso_util initiates to join Mac OS X Server to a Kerberos realm, it helps to understand Kerberos principals, keys, and keytabs, as well as some of the processes that handle these elements of a Kerberos realm. These terms are defined in the next few sections.

Go to the section "Tracing the Steps of sso_util" and follow the series of events presented there to understand what sso_util does to join to a Kerberos realm.

Understanding Kerberos Principals

A Kerberos *principal* is a Kerberos entity. Each principal has a *key* associated with it, which is a secret string of characters. There are two main kinds of Kerberos principals: *service* and *user*. A third category, *host* principal, is actually a type of service principal; the service name is "host."

A service principal's name defines the service type, the server hosting the service, and the Kerberos realm. The name consists of the name of the service, a forward slash, the host name of the server that hosts the service, the @ sign, and the realm. By convention, the realm is in all uppercase characters to prevent confusion with DNS names. An example Kerberos service principal is:

```
afpserver/server13.pretendco.com@SERVER17.PRETENDCO.COM
```

When you join your Mac OS X Server computer to a Kerberos realm, `sso_util` sets up a service principal with randomly generated keys for each of your services that can be Kerberized. Only the newly joined server and the KDC know the randomly generated keys. The KDC stores principals in the principal data store for the realm, located in /var/db/krb5kdc/principal.*REALM,* where *REALM* is the realm name. The newly joined server stores the principals in /etc/krb5.keytab.

The term *keytab* is short for key table, and is a collection of keys—or a collection of principals and their keys. The principal data store and the keytab contain sensitive information (the secret keys), and you should protect these files both on your live systems and on your backup media.

A user principal's name is usually just the user's short name, the @ sign, and the realm, as in this example:

```
oduser1@SERVER17.PRETENDCO.COM
```

When you create a new user in an Open Directory shared domain, using tools that access Directory Services, such as Workgroup Manager and `dscl`, you automatically create a user principal; the key is the user's password. The KDC stores the user principal in its principal data store. The client does not store the user's password; the user must provide it at login or when authenticating for a Kerberized service.

Understanding the Kerberos KDC

Every Mac OS X server runs the KDC service, the `krb5kdc` daemon, to handle requests for at least the local KDC realm. `krb5kdc` can handle multiple realms at once with the `-r` option, which Open Directory masters and replicas use to handle the local Kerberos realm and the Open Directory shared Kerberos realm.

The command `launchd` starts `kdcmond`, which in turn starts `krb5kdc`.

The configuration file for `kdcmond` is /System/Library/LaunchDaemons/com.apple.kdc-mond.plist. The default options in the config file are `-n` (*do not daemonize,* common for launchd-controlled processes) and -a, which causes krb5kdc to use the -a option; this last is quite important because it enables integration between krb5kdc and PasswordService. You can change the configuration file to add the -s option to log debugging information to /var/log/system.log, and the -v option to set the level of debugging information.

Below is a snippet from the default configuration plist for kdcmond:

```
<key>Program Arguments<key>
<array>
    <string>/usr/sbin/kdcmond</string>
    <string>-n<string>
    <string>-a</string>
</array>
```

kdcmond uses the configuration file /var/db/krb5kdc/krb.conf to launch krb5conf with the appropriate options. On an Open Directory master or replica, krbkdc runs with two -r options: one that specifies the local KDC and the other that specifies the shared Kerberos realm.

kdcmond attempts to register Bonjour service records for each realm's KDC. It also monitors krb5kdc and sends a USR1 signal to krb5kdc in the event of a network transition, to notify the KDC to reinitialize its network listeners.

kdcmond starts krb5kdc with the -a option, so that krb5kdc sends all changes to the PasswordService daemon.

krb5kdc uses the principal databases in /var/db/krb5kdc. Each realm that it handles has a data store named principal.*REALM*.

Understanding kadmind

The KADM5 administration server, kadmind, handles requests to manage the information in the Kerberos data stores, such as a request to create or modify a principal or to change a password. Only Open Directory masters and replicas run the kadmind daemon. kadmin, kadmin.local, and kpasswd can send requests to kadmind. The Kerberos configuration files in /var/db/dslocal/nodes/Default and /Library/Preferences/edu.mit.Kerberos configuration file specify which kadmind to use, with the directive admin_server.

If the Open Directory master is server17, for example, then all replicas and all bound computers will have the following lines in their Kerberos configuration file /Library/Preferences/edu.mit.Kerberos:

```
[realms]
    SERVER17.PRETENDCO.COM
            admin_server = server17.pretendco.com
            kdc = server17.pretendco.com
            kdc = replica.pretendco.com (one line per replica)
```

The `admin_server` directive specifies that you must contact the `kadmind` on the Open Directory master if you want to create or modify principals. Consequentially, if the Open Directory master is down, you cannot join a server to the Kerberos realm, nor can you use the `kpasswd` command or the Kerberos application to change the password.

`launchd` starts `kadmind` using the configuration file /System/Library/LaunchDaemons/edu.mit.kadmind.plist. The options in the config file are `-passwordserver` (to send changes to the local system's `PasswordService`) and `-nofork`. When you join a server to the Kerberos realm, `sso_util` uses `kadmind` to create service principals and store them in the Open Directory master's principal database, and also store them in the bound server's keytab file.

Tracing the Steps of sso_util

When you use the highest log levels with `sso_util`, you get a better idea of what `sso_util` is doing when it joins a Kerberos realm. Not all the commands are revealed with extensive logging, but you still get a good sense of most of the things that take place.

If you ever experience problems joining Mac OS X Server to a Kerberos realm, compare the transcript of a successful bind to Kerberos with the transcript of your failing `sso_util`. Your goal is to resolve the problems that prevent `sso_util` from completing the bind. Rather than attempt to replicate each of the individual steps that `sso_util` initiates, focus instead on the individual steps that fail, resolve the issues, and then run `sso_util` again to attempt to initiate a complete bind.

To use `sso_util` with the highest log levels, issue the `sso_util` command with the `-v 7` option, which specifies the highest level of verbosity (the other options are explained earlier in "Configuring a Mac OS X Server to Connect to an Existing Open Directory Master").

```
server13:~ ladmin$ sudo sso_util configure -r SERVER17.PRETENDCO.COM -a diradmin -p
apple -v 7 all
```

Following is an explanation of the actions that the `sso_util configure` command performs:

1. The command contacts the directory server and looks for the realm name, which it finds in the attribute `apple-config-realname` in the record `cn=KerberosKDC,cn=config,`*sea rchbase*. In this example, the realm name is SERVER17.PRETENDCO.COM.

2. The command then creates a list of services to Kerberize. Specifying list `all` includes: `cifs`, `Ldap`, `xgrid`, `vpn`, `ipp`, `xmpp`, `XMPP`, `host`, `smtp`, `nfs`, `http`, `HTTP`, `pop`, `imap`, `ftp`, and `afpserver`.

3. For each service in the previous step, the command creates service principals and keys. It uses `kadmin` to connect to the Open Directory server's KDC and set up the principal: -r specifies the realm; -p and -w specify the directory administrator name and password; -q specifies the command to send; and -s specifies the server that hosts the KDC. The `add_principal` command creates a new principal and -randkey creates a random shared secret to use (rather than specifying a password). The command that accomplishes this is:

   ```
   kadmin -r SERVER17.PRETENDCO.COM -p diradmin -w apple -q "add_principal -randkey
   service/server13.pretendco.com@SERVER17.PRETENDCO.COM" -s server17.pretendco.com
   ```

4. `sso_util configure` uses `kadmin ktremove` to delete all existing and potentially outdated entries for each service in the realm from the local /etc/krb5.keytab with the following command:

   ```
   kadmin -r SERVER17.PRETENDCO.COM -p diradmin -w apple -q "ktremove -k
   /etc/krb5.keytab service/server13.pretendco.com@SERVER17.PRETENDCO.COM all" -s
   server17.pretendco.com
   ```

5. The command then adds the principals that you just generated to the keytab file on the local server (/etc/krb5.keytab), using `kadmin ktadd` to retrieve the service keys for each service from the KDC's principal data store and add them to the local /etc/krb5.keytab. ktaadd adds an entry or entries to a keytab, and -k specifies the keytab file, like so:

   ```
   kadmin -r SERVER17.PRETENDCO.COM -p diradmin -w apple -q "ktadd -k
   /etc/krb5.keytab service/server13.pretendco.com@SERVER17.PRETENDCO.COM"
   ```

6. `sso_util configure` configures services to use the new Kerberos realm with the `krbservicesetup` command. This service-level configuration alerts connecting clients that Kerberos is supported for the service, and that the client should attempt to obtain a service ticket from the KDC if it does not already have one. It also specifies

which Kerberos realm the service should use. `krbservicesetup` uses the temporary configuration file to configure various services to be aware of their new Kerberos realm and principal, as follows:

```
krbservicesetup -r SERVER17.PRETENDCO.COM -a diradmin -p apple -t /etc/krb5.keytab
-f /temp.RANDOM/setup
```

`krbservicesetup` updates the configuration files for these services:

VPN:

▶ /Library/Preferences/SystemConfiguration/com.apple.RemoteAccesServers.plist

CIFS:

▶ /System/Library/LaunchDaemons/nmdb.plist

▶ /System/Library/LaunchDaemons/smbd.plist

▶ /System/Library/LaunchDaemons/org.samba.winbindd.plist

▶ /etc/smb.conf

▶ /Library/Preferences/SystemConfiguration/com.apple.smb.server.plist

▶ /var/db/smb.conf

FTP:

▶ /Library/FTPServer/Configuration/ftpaccess

▶ /System/Library/LaunchDaemons/xftpd.plist

Xgrid:

▶ /etc/xgrid/controller/service-principal

IMAP, POP, and SMTP:

▶ /etc/MailServicesOther.plist

Apple Filing Protocol (AFP):

▶ /Library/Preferences/com.apple.AppleFileServer.plist

7. `sso_util configure` uses `kerberosautoconfig` to update or create the Kerberos configuration files in/Library/Preferences/edu.mit.Kerberos and the DSLocal node /var/db/dslocal/nodes/Default/config/Kerberos:*REALM*.plist

Viewing Log Files Created in the Binding Process

Using Server Admin's Join Kerberos button logs basic information to /Library/Logs/SingleSignOnTools.log and stores more detailed information in /Library/Logs/slapconfig.log.

Inspect the log of a Mac OS X Server computer that has successfully joined a Kerberos realm so that you know what a successful event looks like. You may want to archive the log so that you can go back and compare the known-good log to the log of a server on which you experience problems joining a Kerberos realm.

Reverting a Server to a Prejoin State

If you need to revert your Mac OS X Server to being a standalone server—for example, if you need to bind to a different Kerberos realm—you can use Server Admin. Keep in mind, however, that doing so has these consequences:

▶ Your authentication search path is reset to "Local directory."

▶ /Library/Preferences/edu.mit.Kerberos is updated or removed.

Changing your server back to standalone does not do any of the following:

▶ Remove the principals for the shared Kerberos realm from /etc/krb5.keytab.

▶ Reconfigure your services' configuration files.

▶ Disable the LDAPv3 plug-in or remove the node from the list of bound nodes.

▶ Remove the Kerberos configuration file Kerberos:*REALM*.plist in /var/db/dslocal/nodes/Default/config.

To use Server Admin to change your server back to standalone status, follow these steps:

1 Open Server Admin. Select Open Directory from the list of services in the left column, click Settings in the toolbar, and then click the General tab.

2   Click the Change button.

3   In the Open Directory: Choose Type window, select Standalone and click Continue.

4   In the Confirm Settings window, click Continue.

5   In the Server Configuration Complete window, click Close.

To connect your server to a directory system again, follow these steps:

1   Open the Directory Utility application.

2   Click the Show Advanced Settings button if necessary.

3   Click the lock and authenticate if necessary.

4   Click Search Policy in the toolbar, and then click the Authentication tab.

5   Change the search path from "Local directory" to "Custom path" and click Apply.

6   Click Apply, then quit Directory Utility.

7   If Server Admin is not already open, open Server Admin (or bring it to the foreground).

8   Select Open Directory from the list of services in the left column, click Settings in the toolbar, and then click the General tab.

Server Admin should again list "Connected to a Directory System" for Role. It should also display the Join Kerberos button, even though your principals and keytabs are already created and stored in /etc/krb5.keytab, and your services are still configured to accept Kerberos authentication.

If you want to rejoin the same Kerberos realm, you must change your authentication search path from "Local directory" to "Custom" and confirm that your Open Directory shared domain is listed, in order to kick off `kerberosautoconfig` and prepare your server to be part of the Kerberos realm again.

Troubleshooting Authentication Issues

When troubleshooting authentication issues, begin by isolating the problem.

When a Mac OS X Server computer receives a request for one of its services, it must identify, authenticate, and authorize the user that made the request. You can use the same identification and authentication troubleshooting techniques you have already mastered, such as first using dscl or id, then moving on to su and possibly dirt.

One of the most common authentication problems is that the system clocks are not synchronized between all players. If this is the case, users do not get a Kerberos TGT when they log in, and they get an authentication dialog when they attempt to access a network service. To resolve the issue, configure all of your computers to use the same Network Time Protocol (NTP) time service and confirm that each computer's time zone is configured correctly. If you do not have access to a public NTP server, see "Synchronizing the Date and Time with a Local NTP Service," below.

Another common issue stems from problems with DNS. If you rely on DNS to locate authentication services and DNS is not available, you will not be able to authenticate. Use tools such as ping and host to ensure that your computers can resolve the host names and IP addresses for all computers involved in offering services and authentication services.

As in Mac OS X, Mac OS X Server sends authentication requests to the Open Directory master or the Open Directory replica to which your computer is bound with Directory Utility. You can therefore check the logs associated with Kerberos and Password Server on the Open Directory server that accepts authentication requests. Unfortunately, if you have a complicated replication system, you may not know for certain which Open Directory server your server will use for LDAP, Password Server, and Kerberos requests in the event that one of the services fails or otherwise becomes unavailable.

To assist in troubleshooting, you can inspect the logs on the Open Directory server that performs authentication to confirm that it is receiving authentication requests, and verify it responds appropriately to the requests. See "Using the Authentication Log Files," later in this chapter, for troubleshooting techniques using the authentication logs.

Synchronizing the Date and Time with a Local NTP Service

If the system clocks are more than 5 minutes apart, after considering time zones, you cannot authenticate using Kerberos. You should use NTP to synchronize the clocks of all your computers. If you cannot access a public NTP server such as time.apple.com, you can use one of your Mac OS X Server computers as an NTP server, like so:

1 Open Server Admin and select your server in the left column.

2 Click Settings in the toolbar.

3 Click the General tab.

4 Confirm that the Network Time Server (NTP) checkbox is enabled. Click Save in the lower-right corner if you make a change to the setting.

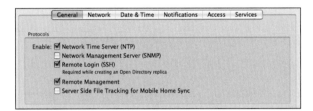

5 Click the Date & Time tab, as shown below.

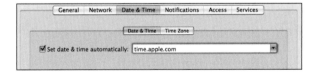

6 On the server that you want to make your local NTP server, change time.apple.com to 127.127.1.0. This forces the NTP service to use the local clock.

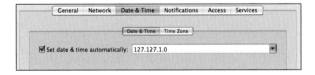

7 Click Save in the lower-right corner.

8 For your bound servers, change time.apple.com to the IP address or host name of your local time server.

9 For your Mac OS X client computers, use the Date & Time Preference pane to specify the IP address or host name of your local time server.

Understanding the Processes That Handle Authentication

There are two main systems that handle authentication: the Password Server and Kerberos. This next several sections contain information that will help you understand and troubleshoot Password Server and Kerberos.

Understanding the Password Server

PasswordService is the daemon that handles Password Server authentication requests. Apple's Password Server offers Simple Authentication and Security Layer (SASL) authentication protocols, including APOP, CRAM-MD5, DHX, Digest-MD5, MS-CHAPv2, NTMLv2 (also referred to as Windows NT or SMB-NT), LAN Manager (LM), and WebDAV-Digest.

Only Open Directory masters and replicas run PasswordService. Mac OS X and Mac OS X Server use the Password Server of the Open Directory server to which they are bound to authenticate any user with an AuthenticationAuthority attribute that contains ;PasswordService;.

PasswordService stores authentication information for each user in /var/db/authserver/authservermain; this file contains various hashes of each user's password, so protect this file not only on disk but also on backup media. The authservermain file also contains information for each user about password policy and last login time. The Password Server associates each user with a 128-bit slot-ID.

launchd uses the configuration file /System/Library/LaunchDaemons/com.apple.PasswordService.plist to start PasswordService.

`PasswordService` sends the changes it receives for a user's password and policy to its local `kadmin.local`, so that these changes are updated for the Kerberos principal as well.

You can use the `mkpassdb -dump` to get a list of the Password Server's users and compare this against the list of users in your Open Directory data store. You may find the `mkpassdb -dump` *slot-ID* form useful to get information about a specific user's slot-ID. You will want to familiarize yourself with what a functional Password Server dump looks like for the list of users as well as for an individual slot-ID's characteristics, so you can compare good information with data that you gather when troubleshooting a problem.

The following steps show you the results of `mkpassdb -dump`, a dump for a particular user, and output from `dscl` to confirm that the user's `AuthenticationAuthority` matches the Password Server slot-ID:

1 Use `dscl` to find the `AuthenticationAuthority` for a user—in this case, oduser4.

```
server17:~ ladmin$ dscl /Search read /Users/oduser4 AuthenticationAuthority

AuthenticationAuthority:

 ;ApplePasswordServer;0x4853762772a815630000000a0000000a, 1024 35 14184265464727470215
865335857371642784001379304088184487081094769303649801997264232092096409299480361064704
534845391879903851323416966975006014407492014227657146045656372745326916156858635878462
696200421543508410547253027062382551405522335643535651774972135955884145283418476236773
033571484392112863841196048 9 root@server17.pretendco.com:10.1.17.1

;Kerberosv5;0x4853762772a815630000000a0000000a; oduser4@SERVER17.PRETENDCO.
COM;SERVER17.PRETENDCO.COM;1024 35 14184265464727470215865335857371642784001379304
088184487081094769303649801997264232092096409299480361064704534845391879903851323
416966975006014407492014227657146045656372745326916156858635878462696200421543508 41
0547253027062382551405522335643535651774972135955884145283418476236773033571484392 1
128638411960489 root@server17.pretendco.com:10.1.17.1
```

2 On your Open Directory master, use `mkpassdb` to get a list of all the users.

In this example, server17 has been recently re-created so it has no replicas and has only a few users. Note that the slot-ID of oduser4 is `0x4853762772a815630000000a0000000 a`, which matches the value in the user's `AuthenticationAuthority` from step 1.

```
server17:~ ladmin$ sudo mkpassdb -dump

signature: pwfi

version: 1

entrySize: 4360

sequenceNumber: 10

numberOfSlotsCurrentlyInFile: 512

deepestSlotUsed: 10

deepestSlotUsedByThisServer: 10

Shutdown State: 0

Access Features:

usingHistory=0 canModifyPasswordforSelf=1 usingExpirationDate=0
usingHardExpirationDate=0 requiresAlpha=0 requiresNumeric=0
expirationDateGMT=4294967295 hardExpireDateGMT=4294967295
maxMinutesUntilChangePassword=0 maxMinutesUntilDisabled=0
maxMinutesOfNonUse=0 maxFailedLoginAttempts=0 minChars=0 maxChars=0
passwordCannotBeName=0 requiresMixedCase=0 requiresSymbol=0
newPasswordRequired=0 minutesUntilFailedLoginReset=0 notGuessablePattern=0

last modified: 06/14/2008 01:36:05

Weak Authentication Methods:

SMB-NT

SMB-LAN-MANAGER

CRYPT

APOP
```

Public Key: 1024 35 141842654647274702158653358573716427840013793040881844870810947693
036498019972642320920964092994803610647045348453918799038513234169669750060144074920 14
227657146045656372745326916156858635878462696200421543508410547253027062382551 40552233
564353565177497213595588414528341847623677303357148439211286384119604 89 root@server17.
pretendco.com

Replica Name: (Parent)

slot 0001: 0x00000000000000000000000000000001 disabled-slot-0x1   06/14/2008
01:51:10 AM

slot 0002: 0x48536a506b8b45670000000200000002 diradmin   06/14/2008
02:41:27 AM

slot 0003: 0x48536a516b8b45670000000300000003 root   06/14/2008
01:51:10 AM

slot 0004: 0x48536a516b8b45670000000400000004 server17.pretendco.com$ 06/14/2008
01:51:10 AM

slot 0005: 0x48536a5f3256576f0000000500000005 vpn_ebe783d34076   06/14/2008
01:51:11 AM

slot 0006: 0x4853751028e2a5ee0000000600000006   06/14/2008
02:41:04 AM

slot 0007: 0x4853761618064f0f0000000700000007 oduser1   06/14/2008
02:41:11 AM

slot 0008: 0x4853761c5340f29a0000000800000008 oduser2   06/14/2008
02:41:16 AM

slot 0009: 0x48537623730069590000000900000009 oduser3   06/14/2008
02:41:23 AM

slot 0010: 0x4853762772a815630000000a0000000a oduser4   06/14/2008
02:41:27 AM

3 Use `mkpassdb` with one of the slot-IDs to gather information about that user's password policy, including the last login time, stored hashes, and more. Use the last user's slot-ID just as an example.

```
server17:~ ladmin$ sudo mkpassdb -dump 0x4853762772a815630000000a0000000a

slot 0010: 0x4853762772a815630000000a0000000a      oduser406/14/2008 02:41:27 AM

Last password change: 06/14/2008 02:41:27 AM

Last login:            06/14/2008 02:41:27 AM

Failed login count:  0

Disable reason:            none

Hash-only bit:             0

Last Transaction ID:  668

Transaction requires kerberos: 1

Record is dead: 0

Record is not to be replicated: 0

Access Features:

isDisabled=0 isAdminUser=0 newPasswordRequired=0 usingHistory=0
canModifyPasswordforSelf=1 usingExpirationDate=0 usingHardExpirationDate=0
requiresAlpha=0 requiresNumeric=0 expirationDateGMT=4294967295
hardExpireDateGMT=4294967295 maxMinutesUntilChangePassword=0
maxMinutesUntilDisabled=0 maxMinutesOfNonUse=0 maxFailedLoginAttempts=0
minChars=0 maxChars=0 passwordCannotBeName=0 requiresMixedCase=0 requiresSymbol=0
notGuessablePattern=0 isSessionKeyAgent=0 isComputerAccount=0 adminClass=0
adminNoChangePasswords=0 adminNoSetPolicies=0 adminNoCreate=0 adminNoDelete=0
adminNoClearState=0 adminNoPromoteAdmins=0

Group(s) for Administration: unrestricted

digest 0:    method: *cmusaslsecretSMBNT
```

```
                 digest length: 16

                 digest: 5EBE7DFA074DA8EE8AEF1FAA2BBDE876

digest 1:        method: *cmusaslsecretSMBLM

                 digest length: 16

                 digest: E79E56A8E5C6F8FEAAD3B435B51404EE

digest 2:        method: *cmusaslsecretDIGEST

                 digest length: 16

                 digest: 6E442BFE2B960D94F42E08FA27992255

digest 3:        method: *cmusaslsecretCRAM-M

                 digest length: 32

                 digest: B5907A57ED8E72BB6A14E343F88BBC0888CA1B5B5BEFBF20A031C12B6459A6AC

digest 4:        method: KerberosRealmName

                 digest: SERVER17.PRETENDCO.COM

digest 5:        method: KerberosPrincName

                 digest: oduser4

digest 6:        method: *cmusaslsecretPPS

                 digest length: 24

                 digest: A70BFD58A53925321333651975598EE6AE9B406E3C9AE7D9

digest 7:        <empty>

digest 8:        <empty>

digest 9:        <empty>

slot checksum:       48B3E9F7CF40C2D06A913B26695A03DE
```

Using Statistics from the Password Server

The `mkpassdb -getstats` command shows statistics for the Password Server over 1-minute intervals. You can use this to find patterns of successful and failed authentication. In the following example, the output shows several successful and failed authentication attempts. This information isn't helpful when you need to determine why one particular user is having problems, but it is useful in trying to figure out trends or where failed attempts may be coming from.

```
server17:~ ladmin$ sudo mkpassdb -getstats
results for the interval from 11:26:57 AM - 11:27:57 AM
(statistics are delayed up to one minute)
connection count: 266
good authentications: 99
 breakdown by type:
 apop               0          0 percent
 cram-md5           0          0 percent
 digest-md5         94         94 percent
 mschap-v2          0          0 percent
 smb-lm             0          0 percent
 smb-nt             5          5 percent
 smb-ntlm-v2        0          0 percent
 webdav-digest-md5  0          0 percent
 other              0          0 percent
bad authentications:  165
 breakdown by type:
 apop               0          0 percent
 cram-md5           0          0 percent
 digest-md5         110        66 percent
 mschap-v2          0          0 percent
 smb-lm             0          0 percent
 smb-nt             55         33 percent
 smb-ntlm-v2        0          0 percent
 webdav-digest-md5  0          0 percent
 other              0          0 percent
percent of replicator capacity used:
 incoming: 0%
```

```
outgoing: 0%
high watermark (tid): 1009
```

Understanding How the Password Server and Kerberos Service Interact

For the most part, the Password Servers for each Open Directory server effectively synchronize password changes to their local KDCs. However, in the event that user password information gets out of sync, you can use your knowledge of how the Password Server and the KDC interact to solve any underlying problems.

Every Open Directory master and replica runs a Password Server (the `PasswordService` daemon). These Password Servers are multimaster, which means that a change to one Password Server gets replicated to the other Password Servers in the shared domain.

If you make a change with `PasswordService`, the `PasswordService` daemon initiates a `kadmin.local` command to update its own KDC for the shared domain, which in turn communicates with the local `kadmind` to update the principal database.

If you make a change with the `kpasswd` command or with the Kerberos application, this initiates a `mkpassdb` command to change the password for the Password Server, which in turn gets replicated to the other Password Servers in the shared domain; then each `PasswordService` daemon on each Open Directory server uses `kadmin.local` to update its own KDC for the shared domain.

In order to make a password change with Kerberos, port 464 on the Open Directory master must be available.

Understanding the Process of Kerberos Authentication

Understanding the process of authenticating to a Kerberized service can help you troubleshoot Kerberos issues. You can use the Kerberos application, Kerberos log files, or even a protocol analyzer such as `tcpdump` to verify that each of the steps along the way is occurring. To authenticate to a Kerberized service, a client must:

1   Obtain a ticket-granting ticket (TGT) from the KDC.

2   Obtain a service ticket for the service, also from the KDC.

3   Authenticate itself to the Kerberized service using the service ticket.

The next three sections illustrate each step.

> **NOTE ▸** Keep in mind that Kerberos is just an authentication mechanism; once the user proves authentication, there's no guarantee that the user has authorization to use the service.

Obtaining a TGT

The first step in the process of using Kerberos to provide authentication to a Kerberized service is to obtain a TGT. Mac OS X performs this step for you automatically and transparently when you log in to a Mac OS X computer that is bound to a Kerberos realm; you should not have to do anything other than log in. The process is as follows:

1. The client sends the KDC a Kerberos authentication service request (`KRB_AS_REQ`). This request includes the user principal, the service name (`krbtgt`), the requested time constraints on the ticket, and possible encryption types.

2. The KDC rejects the request, with `ERR_PREAUTH_REQUIRED`.

3. The client generates preauthentication data in the form of a timestamp, encrypted with the user's password. This helps to prevent packet replay—and demonstrates how important it is for the participants in a Kerberos realm to have synchronized system clocks.

    The client sends sends another `KRB_AS_REQ` to the KDC, this time with preauthentication data included in the `KRB_AS_REQ`.

    The KDC, which knows the user principal's password (it is stored in /var/db/krb5kdc/principal), attempts to decrypt the preauthentication data. If this is successful, the KDC considers the user to be authenticated and continues.

    The KDC generates a *session key* to encrypt communications between the client and the KDC. The key is a shared secret used to encrypt and decrypt data; the session key will be shared by the client and the KDC. The trick is how to get this session key to the client, using a network that may be unsecure.

    The KDC generates a TGT, which it will send to the user. From the client's point of view, the TGT is just a blob of data that it cannot decrypt. The TGT contains the KDC's copy of the session key, the client's principal name, the ticket time constraints, a timestamp, and the client's IP address (optional). The KDC encrypts all of this with a private key that only the KDC knows.

4. The KDC sends a Kerberos authentication service reply (KRB-AS-REP) to the client. This contains the session key, encrypted with the user's password, and the TGT. If anyone captures this packet, the encrypted session key will be useless without the user's password. An attacker would find the TGT useless as well.

    The client saves the TGT and the session key in the client's credentials cache. Mac OS X does not store these on disk, only in RAM. This makes it difficult for attackers on the client's local system to obtain the TGT or session key.

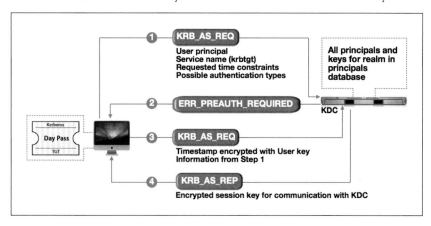

To verify that you have a TGT, run the command klist or open the Kerberos application in /System/Library/CoreServices, which displays any Kerberos tickets you may have. If you do not have a TGT, run the command knit or press the New Ticket button in the Kerberos application, and then use any error messages you receive to resolve the problem.

Obtaining a Service Ticket

Once a user has a TGT, any time the user attempts to access a Kerberized service, Mac OS X automatically attempts to obtain a service ticket for the user. Note that this happens transparently to the user. Here are the steps involved:

1. The client decrypts the session key using its password. Now it can use this session key to encrypt the data that it sends to the KDC. The client then sends the KDC a Kerberos ticket-granting service request (KRB_TGS_REQ). The request includes the TGT, the realm, the principal name for the requested service (like afp/server13.pretendco.com), the requested ticket lifetime, and supported encryption types. The request also includes preauthentication information: a timestamp encrypted with the session key (only the

client and the KDC know the session key). Note that this request does not contain any information about the user principal; that information is encrypted within the TGT.

The KDC decrypts the preauthentication information (using the session key) and the TGT (using the private key only the KDC knows) in the `KBB_TGB_REQ`. Because the KDC succeeds in decrypting the preauthentication information as well as the TGT, it authenticates the user.

The KDC generates a random *service session key* that the client and the service will use to communicate with each other.

The KDC prepares a service ticket that contains the service session key and the user principal. The KDC encrypts the service ticket with the service's key, which was set up back when you joined the server to the Kerberos realm. The client cannot see inside the service ticket; only the service or the KDC can decrypt the service ticket.

2.   The KDC prepares a Kerberos ticket-granting service reply (`KRB_TGS_REP`) and sends it to the client. This `KRB_TGS_REP` contains the new service session key (encrypted with the user's password) and the service ticket (which is encrypted with the service's key).

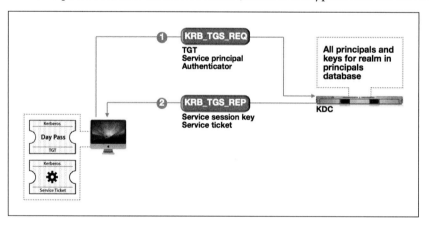

To verify that you have a service ticket, run the `klist` command or use the Kerberos application. If you have a valid TGT in the realm, but do not get a service ticket when you attempt to access a Kerberized service, there are several possibilities:

▶   The service you are attempting to access is not running. Start the service.

▶   The DNS records for the server hosting the service are not available. Use tools such as `host` to confirm DNS records.

▶ The server hosting the Kerberized service is not set to a time within 5 minutes of the other participants in the Kerberos realm. Confirm that the server is using the same NTP service and has the appropriate time zone set.

▶ The server hosting the Kerberized service does not have the node that hosts the Kerberos realm in its authentication search path. Use `dscl` or Directory Utility to check the authentication search path.

▶ The server hosting the Kerberized service is not joined to the same Kerberos realm. Use `sso_util` to join the appropriate Kerberos realm.

▶ The service is not configured to use the Kerberos realm. Use `PlistBuddy` or `defaults` to inspect the service's configuration files.

▶ The server hosting the Kerberized service is using a different set of principals. See the section "Confirming Your Keytab," later in this chapter.

▶ Your client software is not Kerberized. For example, the Finder is not a Kerberized FTP client. You must use a third-party software package such as Fetch for Kerberized FTP access.

▶ The port associated with the service is blocked by a firewall. Use commands such as `telnet`, `nc`, and `openssl s_connect` to confirm your ability to reach that port.

Authenticating to a Kerberized Service

Now that the user has a service ticket, Mac OS X presents the service ticket to the Kerberized service. Again, this happens transparently to the user, as described below:

1. The client generates an authenticator, a timestamp encrypted with the service session key.

   The client sends a Kerberos application request (`KRB_AP_REQ`) to the server hosting the service that the client wants to use. The `KRB_AP_REQ` includes the service ticket and the authenticator.

   Or

   The client makes a request for service with the service ticket embedded in the request. The methods for providing the service ticket vary from service to service.

2.   The server that hosts the desired service attempts to decrypt the service ticket and the authenticator. It uses its service key, which is stored in its /etc/krb5.keytab file, to decrypt the service ticket. Inside the service ticket is the service session key, which the server uses to decrypt the authenticator. If the server succeeds in these tasks, it has authenticated the user, without ever knowing the user's password.

Typically, the client's request includes both the authentication information and the service request itself, and the server doesn't need to send a Kerberos application reply (KRB_AP_REP) to the client.

NOTE ▸ Only the server and the KDC know the service key, which was randomly generated when you joined the server to the Kerberos realm.

Once the server authenticates the user, the service checks to see if the user is authorized to use the service. The server then attempts to carry out the request for service.

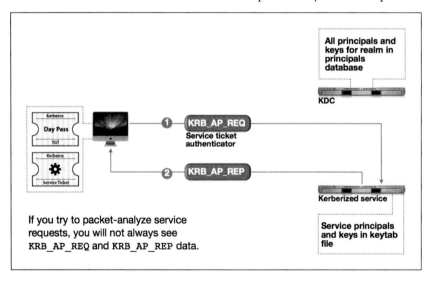

If you are trying to track down a problem and use tcpdump with a protocol analyzer to trace requests for service, you may not see KRB_AP_REQ and KRB_AP_REP packets. For example:

▸   For Kerberized AFP, the client first sends a FPLoginExt request packet that contains the user principal name and the realm, then sends a FPLoginCont packet that contains the service ticket.

▶ For Kerberized NFS, the protocol analyzer may show a `V3 NULL Call` packet, which actually contains the service ticket and the authenticator.

▶ For Kerberized XMPP (iChat service), the client sends a packet with XML data including the text `mechanism=GSSAPI` and the ticket.

If you *do* get a valid service ticket but are still challenged to authenticate for the service, or are denied access, there are a couple of possibilities:

▶ The server hosting the Kerberized service does not have the node that hosts the Kerberos realm in its authentication search path. Use `dscl` or Directory Utility to check the authentication search path.

▶ There is a SACL that does not allow access to the service for the user whom you authenticated. Check the SACL.

Confirming Your Keytab

In order for a Kerberized service to participate in a Kerberos realm, it must be able to use a Kerberos principal and its associated keys. If you understand your server's keytab, you can use this information to verify that its contents match the KDC's data store of principals. You can use the command `klist -k` to check that the principal keys were created on the bound server, then compare the list of principals to the list in the next section, "Confirming Your KDC Principals."

The keys for your server's service principals are stored in /etc/krb5.keytab. You can view these keys with the `klist` command, which you must run with root privileges. Some useful options for `klist` include:

▶ `-k`—List all the keys in a keytab file.

▶ `-e`—Show the encryption type for each key. Each service usually has three keys, one for each of the following encryption types: Triple DES sbs mode with HMAC/sha1, ArcFour with HMAC/md5, and DES cbc mode with CRC-32.

▶ `-K`—Display the value of each encryption key, which contains very sensitive information.

▶ `-t`—List the time entry timestamp.

klist with the -k option also shows the name of the keytab file (/etc/krb5.keytab by default). For each key, klist -k shows the KVNO (Kerberos version number) and the service principal name. The KVNO is incremented each time the key is updated. Each service key in your keytab should match the service key stored in the KDC's principal database, including the KVNO. If the KVNO differs between the server hosting the Kerberized service and the KDC, the principals almost certainly have different keys.

The figure below shows the output from klist -ke on server12 that has joined the Kerberos realm for server17. It also shows that the keytab contains service keys for all possible services on host server12, in server17's Kerberos realm. Due to space constraints, the entire list is not displayed. The first few lines are from the local KDC realm, and the rest are from server17's realm. Each service principal has three keys, because there are three different default encryption types.

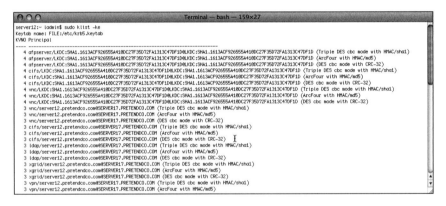

Confirming Your KDC Principals

Compare the principal information from klist -k in the previous section with information from the KDC's principal data store.

Each KDC stores service keys for principals in /var/db/krb5kdc/principal.*REALM*. Mac OS X Server v10.5 has a principal data store for the local KDC, and Open Directory masters and Open Directory replicas have an additional file for the principals of the shared domain's Kerberos realm.

kadmin and `kadmin.local` are command-line tools for the Kerberos administration system (kadmind). Use `kadmin` to interact with a local or a remote `kadmind`. Use `kadmin.local` to interact directly with the local Kerberos data as root; this does not require Kerberos authentication. You can use `kadmin` and `kadmin.local` interactively, or you can use the `-q` option to send a command, which is useful for scripting. (The `man` page entry indicates that `q` stands for query, but it is more of a command than a query.) You can specify the realm, principal with which to authenticate, and password with the flags `-r realm -p principal -w password`.

Some useful commands to use with `kadmind` for troubleshooting are:

- ▶ `list_principals`—List the principals.

- ▶ `get_principal principal`—Get details about a principal.

- ▶ `add_principal`—Create a new principal.

- ▶ `ktadd`—Add a key from the principal data store to a keytab, re-randomizing the key.

- ▶ `ktremove`—Remove a key from a keytab.

Follow these steps to compare the KVNO of the keys associated with the principal afpserver/server12.pretendco.com@SERVER17.PRETENDCO.COM on the member server and the KDC:

1 Open Terminal on the Mac OS X Server computer that you joined to the Kerberos realm.

2 Use `klist -ke` to get a list of all the principals in the default keytab.

-e includes the encryption types. `grep` shows only the entries that contain the string afpserver. grep
-v `LKDC` filters out any entries that contain the string LKDC. The first character in the output of each line is KVNO.

```
server12:~ ladmin$ sudo klist -ke | grep afpserver | grep -v LKDC

  3 afpserver/server12.pretendco.com@SERVER17.PRETENDCO.COM (Triple DES cbc mode with
HMAC/sha1)

  3 afpserver/server12.pretendco.com@SERVER17.PRETENDCO.COM (ArcFour with HMAC/md5)

  3 afpserver/server12.pretendco.com@SERVER17.PRETENDCO.COM (DES cbc mode with
CRC-32)
```

3   Use kadmin to connect to the remote KDC and get information about the principal.

The -r specifies the realm, -p and -w specify the credentials of the user to authenticate as, and -q specifies the command to send to kadmind. The command get_principal *principal* displays information about the principal. Note that the KVNO and encryption types match the KVNO and encryption types from step 2.

```
server12:~ ladmin$ sudo kadmin -r SERVER17.PRETENDCO.COM -p diradmin -w apple -q
"get_principal afpserver/server12.pretendco.com@SERVER17.PRETENDCO.COM"

Authenticating as principal diradmin with password.

Principal: afpserver/server12.pretendco.com@SERVER17.PRETENDCO.COM

Expiration date: [never]

Last password change: Sat Jun 14 01:55:08 CDT 2008

Password expiration date: [none]

Maximum ticket life: 0 days 10:00:00

Maximum renewable life: 7 days 00:00:00

Last modified: Sat Jun 14 01:55:08 CDT 2008 (diradmin@SERVER17.PRETENDCO.COM)

Last successful authentication: [never]

Last failed authentication: [never]

Failed password attempts: 0

Number of keys: 3

Key: vno 3, Triple DES cbc mode with HMAC/sha1, no salt

Key: vno 3, ArcFour with HMAC/md5, no salt

Key: vno 3, DES cbc mode with CRC-32, no salt

Attributes:

Policy: [none]
```

4   In this case the KVNOs match, so there should be no problem. If the KVNOs do not match (perhaps because you restored a member server from a backup that was made before a change was made to the Kerberos principal keys) the fix is quite simple: Run the `sso_util configure` command again. Running `sso_util configure` is not destructive; it updates the principal at the KDC and at the local server so both servers have the same principals and keys.

```
server12:~ ladmin$ sudo /usr/sbin/sso_util configure -r SERVER17.PRETENDCO.COM -a
diradmin -p apple -f /LDAPv3/server17.pretendco.com -v 1 all
```

Using the Authentication Log Files

There are three main authentication service logs: Password Server, KDC, and kadmin. It is a good idea to become familiar with their contents before you run into problems. This makes it easier for you to use the logs to track down authentication problems if they do occur. The following sections contain sample log entries for both successful and unsuccessful authentication events.

Using the Password Server Log

The Password Server logs to /Library/Logs/PasswordService. The ApplePasswordServer. Server.log contains Kerberos-related messages, usually in this form:

```
KERBEROS-LOGIN-CHECK: user {passwordserverid, principal} result
```

The *passwordserverid* is the Password Server ID of the user, and `principal` is the name portion of the user principal.

Below are sample messages in ApplePasswordServer.Server.log after you use the Kerberos application to obtain a ticket for oduser1 and enter a bad password:

```
May 2 2008 11:52:15 KERBEROS-LOGIN-CHECK: user {0x481a90792309abc70000000600000006
oduser1} authentication failed
```

Log entries after using Kerberos to obtain a ticket with a correct password:

```
May 2 2008 11:52:42 KERBEROS-LOGIN-CHECK: user {0x481a90792309abc70000000600000006
oduser1} is in good standing
May 2 2008 11:52:42 KERBEROS-LOGIN-CHECK: user {0x481a90792309abc70000000600000006
oduser1} authentication succeeded
```

Log entries after using Kerberos application to change a Kerberos password:

```
May 2 2008 11:53:04 KERBEROS-LOGIN-CHECK: user {0x481a90792309abc70000000600000006
oduser1} is in good standing
May 2 2008 11:53:04 KERBEROS-LOGIN-CHECK: user {0x481a90792309abc70000000600000006
oduser1} authentication succeeded
May 2 2008 11:53:04 KERBEROS-LOGIN-CHECK: password changed for principal oduser1@
SERVER17.PRETENDCO.COM
```

When you create a new Open Directory network user with Workgroup Manager, the log will contain messages like the ones below. DIGEST-MD5 authentication is for changing the short name from the generic untitled_1 to the new short name, and the DHX authentication enables changing the password. The change is logged twice, once for the Password Server, and once for the KDC, as you see here:

```
timestamp NEWUSER: {diradminPWSid, diradmin} created new user {passwordserverid,
untitled_1}
timestamp RSAVALIDATE: success.
timestamp AUTH2: {diradminPWSid, diradmin} DIGEST-MD5 authentication succeeded.
timestamp SETUSERNAME: short name changed for user {passwordserverid, untitled_1} to
oduser10.
timestamp AUTH2: {diradminPWSid, diradmin} DHX authentication succeeded.
timestamp CHANGEPASS: {diradminPWSid, diradmin} changed password for user
{passwordserverid, oduser10}
timestamp CHANGEPASS: {diradminPWSid, diradmin} changed password for user
{passwordserverid, oduser10}
```

Using the KDC Log

The KDC process, krb5kdc, is responsible for handing out TGTs and service tickets. krb5kdc logs to/var/log/krb5kdc/kdc.log, where you can see evidence of KRB_AS_REQ , KRB_AS_REP, and KRB_TGS_REQ packets.

An attempt to get a TGT with a known-bad password results in at least six log messages. Two of the key entries are shown below. verify failure and the PREAUTH_FAILED indicate that the KDC could not decrypt the timestamp with the user's password, so the KDC could not authenticate the user and did not issue a TGT:

```
timestamp server17.pretendco.com krb5kdc[pid](info): preauth (timestamp) verify
failure: Decrypt integrity check failed.
timestamp server17.pretendco.com krb5kdc[pid](info): AS_REQ ( encryptioninfo)
10.1.16.1: PREAUTH_FAILED: oduser1@REALM for krbtgt/REALM@REALM, decrypt integrity
check failed.
```

A successful attempt to get a TGT results in at least eight log messages to the /var/log/krb5kdc/kdc.log. Three are most important: The first log message is that pre-authentication is needed. The second message is about decrypting the preauthentication information. The third message indicates that the krb5kdc process issued a Kerberos ticket. Here are those messages, with portions highlighted:

```
timestamp server17.pretendco.com krb5kdc[pid](info): AS_REQ ( encryptioninfo)
10.1.16.1: NEEDED_PREAUTH: oduser1@REALM for krbtgt/REALM@REALM, Additional
pre-authentication required
timestamp server17.pretendco.com krb5kdc[pid](debug): handling authdata
timestamp server17.pretendco.com krb5kdc[pid](info): AS_REQ ( encryptioninfo)
10.1.16.1: ISSUE: authtime timestamp, encryptioninfo, oduser1@REALM for krbtgt/REALM@
REALM
```

A successful attempt to get a service ticket, in this case from a client on 10.1.15.1, for AFP service on server12.pretendco.com, logs two entries like this:

```
timestamp server17.pretendco.com krb5kdc[pid](info): TGS_REQ (encryptioninfo)
10.1.15.1: ISSUE: authtime timestamp, encryptioninfo, oduser1@REALM for afpserver/
server12.pretendco.com@SERVER17.PRETENDCO.COM
```

Using the kadmin Log
kadmind is the daemon responsible for managing the principals in the keytabs, and it logs to /var/log/krb5kdc/kadmin.log. When you create a new principal (a service, host, or user principal), you may see a warning in the following format:

```
timestamp server17.pretendco.com kadmin.local[pid](info): No dictionary file specified,
continuing without one.
```

This indicates that `kadmin.local` will not check the proposed shared key for the principal against a dictionary, in order to prevent dictionary-based passwords. You can safely ignore these warnings.

When you join a server to your Open Directory server's Kerberos realm, you'll see log entries in /var/log/krb5kdc/kadmin.log like the following. These are the highlights from server12 joining server17's Kerberos realm. For each principal that you create, you'll see two of each of the following requests handled by `kadmin`: `kadm5_get_policy`, `kadm5_create_principal`, `kadm5_randkey_principal`, and `kadm5_modify_principal`. The messages will be similar to these examples:

```
timestamp server17.pretendco.com kadmin[pid](Notice): Request: kadm5_init,
diradmin@SERVER17.PRETENDCO.COM, success, client=diradmin@SERVER17.PRETENDCO.COM,
service=kadmin/admin@SERVER17.PRETENDCO.COM, addr=10.1.0.1, flavor=300001
timestamp server17.pretendco.com kadmin[pid](Notice): Request: kadm5_get_policy,
default, policy does not exist, client=diradmin@SERVER17.PRETENDCO.COM,
service=kadmin/admin@SERVER17.PRETENDCO.COM, addr=10.1.12.1
timestamp server17.pretendco.com kadmin[pid](Notice): Request: kadm5_create_principal,
cifs/server12.pretendco.com@SERVER17.PRETENDCO.COM, success, client=diradmin@SERVER17.
PRETENDCO.COM, service=kadmin/admin@SERVER17.PRETENDCO.COM, addr=10.1.12.1
timestamp server17.pretendco.com kadmin[pid](Notice): Request: kadm5_randkey_principal,
cifs/server12.pretendco.com@SERVER17.PRETENDCO.COM, success, client=diradmin@SERVER17.
PRETENDCO.COM, service=kadmin/admin@SERVER17.PRETENDCO.COM, addr=10.1.12.1
timestamp server17.pretendco.com kadmin[pid](Notice): Request: kadm5_modify_principal,
cifs/server12.pretendco.com@SERVER17.PRETENDCO.COM, service=kadmin/admin@SERVER17.
PRETENDCO.COM, addr=10.1.12.1
```

If you create a principal manually and don't use `-randkey` to generate a random key, you will not see `kadm5_randkey_principal` and `kadm5_modify_principal` requests.

If you use `kpasswd` or the Kerberos application to change a password, you will see log entries like the following:

```
timestamp server17.pretendco.com kadmd[pid](Notice): chpw request from clientip for
shortname@REALM: success
```

If the proposed new password does not meet the policy, the entry will be similar to this:

```
timestamp server17.pretendco.com kadmd[pid](Notice): chpw request from clientip for
shortname@REALM: KDC policy rejects request
```

When you use `kpasswd` or the Kerberos application to change a password, `kpasswd` or the Kerberos application searches in the Kerberos configuration files; the first preference is an entry for `KADM_List` in /var/db/dslocal/nodes/Default/config/Kerberos:*REALM*.plist, but it will fall back to an entry for `kpasswd_server` or `admin_server` in /Library/Preferences/edu.mit. Kerberos. By default, the `KADM_List` and `admin_server` entries list the Open Directory master.

What You've Learned

▶ You can use Directory Utility (or a series of command-line tools) to bind Mac OS X Server to an Open Directory master or replica, so that your server can identify and authenticate Open Directory network users.

▶ As long as an Open Directory master or replica is in Mac OS X Server's authentication search path, your server can provide services to the Open Directory users in the shared domain.

▶ You can create service access control lists (SACLs) for your server's services using users and groups from the shared domain. You may want to set up a SACL to prevent SSH access to your server.

▶ You can create access control lists (ACLs) for the files on your server's local file system, using users and groups from the shared domain.

▶ File system ACLs use the user's Globally Unique ID (GUID, also known as Generated UID, also known as Universally Unique ID or UUID) rather than the user's short name to determine whether to apply an access control entry (ACE) applies to that user. SACLs use either the short name or the GUID to determine whether to apply a SACL rule to a user.

▶ You can use Workgroup Manager on your server to view remote shared directory domains and to edit remote domains if you have directory administrator credentials.

▶ If you do not bind your server to an Open Directory master or replica with authenticated directory binding, you must take the extra step of using Server Admin's Join Kerberos button (or use `sso_util configure`) to Kerberize your server's services.

▶ A Kerberos principal is an entity in a Kerberos realm and has encryption keys associated with it. A service principal takes the form of *service/servername@REALM*, and a user principal looks like *usershortname@REALM*, where *REALM* is the name of the realm. Kerberos realms are typically in all uppercase characters to distinguish them from DNS realms.

▶ When you join your Mac OS X Server computer to an Open Directory server's Kerberos realm, you create a service principal for each of the services that can be Kerberized on your server. You also generate three keys with different encryption types for that principal. These keys are stored on your local server in /etc/keytab and on the Open Directory servers in /var/db/krb5kdc/principal.*REALM*.

▶ Mac OS X Server's Password Server daemon is `PasswordService` and its Kerberos administration daemon is `kadmind`. The Password Servers are multimaster and they communicate changes to each other. Each Mac OS X Server's Password Service then sends changes to its local Kerberos system by using `kadmin.local` to communicate with `kadmind`.

▶ In order to use `kpasswd` or the Kerberos application to change a password via the Kerberos system, port 464 on the Open Directory master must be open. `kadmind` processes the change and then uses `mkpassdb` to update the Password Server database, which then replicates the change to the other Open Directory servers in the shared domain. Each `PasswordService` then uses `kadmin.local` to communicate with `kadmind` to make the change in the Kerberos system.

▶ You can use `klist -k` to show the contents of your Mac OS X Server's keytab, `kadmin.local -q "list_principals"` on an Open Directory server to show the contents of the Kerberos principal database, and `mkpassdb -dump` to show the contents of the Password Server database.

▶ `PasswordService` logs to three files in /Library/Logs/PasswordService. The KDC process, `krb5kdc`, logs to /var/log/krb5kdc/krb5kdc.log. The Kerberos admin process, `kadmind`, logs to /var/log/krb5kdc/kadmin.log.

References

Documentation

- ▶ Command-Line Administration for Version 10.5 Leopard, Second Edition
  http://images.apple.com/server/macosx/docs/Command_Line_Admin_v10.5.pdf

- ▶ Open Directory Administration for Version 10.5 Leopard, Second Edition
  http://images.apple.com/server/macosx/docs/Open_Directory_Admin_v10.5.pdf

- ▶ User Management for Version 10.5 Leopard
  http://images.apple.com/server/macosx/docs/User_Management_v10.5.mnl.pdf

- ▶ File Services Administration for Version 10.5 Leopard
  http://images.apple.com/server/macosx/docs/File_Services_Admin_v10.5.pdf

Apple Knowledge Base Documents

- ▶ Mac OS X 10.5: Duplicate computer name alert when binding to Open Directory
  http://support.apple.com/kb/TS1245

Books

- ▶ Garman, Jason. *Kerberos The Definitive Guide* (O'Reilly & Associates, Inc., 2003).

- ▶ Bartosh, Michael and Faas, Ryan. *Essential Mac OS X Panther Server Administration* (O'Reilly Media, Inc., 2005).

Websites

- ▶ Kerberos Part 2 - Kerberos on OS X
  http://www.afp548.com/article.php?story=20060714092117916

- ▶ Kerberos Part 3 - Kerberos On Member Servers
  http://www.afp548.com/article.php?story=20060724104018616

- ▶ The Kerberos Network Authentication Service (V5)
  http://www.ietf.org/rfc/rfc1510.txt

▶ Microsoft Windows 2000 Kerberos Change Password and Set Password Protocols
http://www.ietf.org/rfc/rfc3244.txt

▶ Fetch Softworks (Kerberized FTP client)
http://fetchsoftworks.com/

Review Quiz

1. On an Open Directory master, what's the difference between these two commands that display keys for Kerberos service principals: `klist -ke` and `kadmin.local -q listprincs`?

2. If the Open Directory master is unavailable, can you make Kerberos principal changes with the Kerberos application, such as creating new principals or changing passwords?

3. If you add a network group to a SACL, but you temporarily lose access to the directory node that hosts the network group, what does Server Admin display for the group's name in the SACL list of users and groups?

4. Where is the Apple Filing Protocol (AFP) service configuration file that specifies the Kerberos realm in which the AFP service participates?

5. For the realm SERVER17.PRETENDCO.COM, where does the KDC store all the principals it knows about?

6. Where does a Mac OS X Server that has joined a Kerberos realm store its service principals?

7. Where does `PasswordService` log successful authentication events?

8. After you log in to Mac OS X and receive a ticket-granting ticket (TGT), how do you obtain a service ticket in order to authenticate yourself to a given Kerberized service?

Answers

1. `klist -ke` displays the principals for the services offered by the Open Directory master. `kadmin.local -q listprincs` displays all the principals associated with the shared domain's KDC.

2. No. If the Open Directory master is not available, you cannot make Kerberos password changes using `kpasswd` or the Kerberos application.

3. Server Admin displays the GUID of a network user or group from a directory node that is temporarily unavailable.

4. /Library/Preferences/com.apple.AppleFileServer.plist

5. /var/db/krb5kdc/principal.SERVER17.PRETENDCO.COM

6. /etc/krb5.conf

7. /Library/Logs/PasswordService/ApplePasswordServer.server.log

8. Once you have a TGT, attempt to access the Kerberized service using a Kerberized client, and Mac OS X automatically attempts to obtain a service ticket for that Kerberized service. For example, the Finder is a Kerberized AFP client.

8

Time   This lesson takes approximately 2 hours to complete.

Goals   Configure Mac OS X Server to supplement a third-party directory service

        Configure Mac OS X Server to authenticate in a third-party Kerberos realm

        Configure a third-party service to use an Open Directory Key
        Distribution Center

Chapter 8

Integrating Mac OS X Server with Other Systems

Because Mac OS X Server uses industry standards such as LDAP and Kerberos, you can easily integrate Mac OS X Server with other directory services.

In this chapter you will learn how to configure Mac OS X Server to supplement directory data provided by another directory service, use another directory service's Key Distribution Center (KDC), and provide KDC services to other servers.

Configuring Mac OS X Server to Supplement a Third-Party Directory Service

In earlier chapters you learned how to bind Mac OS X to multiple directory systems, including Open Directory, to provide managed preferences and a third-party directory system to provide user identification and authentication.

In this chapter you will learn how to configure Mac OS X Server in a "Magic Triangle" setup with multiple directory systems. You will also learn how to use the new Augmented User Record feature in Mac OS X Server v10.5 to add Mac OS X Server service information to user records that reside in a third-party directory.

Configuring the services on Mac OS X Server to participate in more than one Kerberos realm at a time is beyond the scope of this book. In ordinary configurations with more than one directory node, you need to decide in which realm your services should participate. If you already have a third-party directory service such as Active Directory that provides LDAP and Kerberos services, it is easy to configure Mac OS X Server to use the Active Directory LDAP and Kerberos realms.

> **NOTE ▶** See pages 67–72 of *Open Directory Administration for Version 10.5 Leopard, Second Edition,* for more information about using multiple Kerberos realms.

Preparing Mac OS X Server for the Magic Triangle Configuration

The Magic Triangle configuration is appropriate if you cannot edit user records in a third-party node. You can indirectly manage a user from a third-party node by making it a member of an Open Directory group and configuring managed preferences for that Open Directory group.

In this section you will learn how to set up your Mac OS X server to provide Open Directory information in a situation where a third-party directory service provides the main identification and authentication services.

The recommended procedure is to first bind Mac OS X Server to Active Directory, then promote it to Open Directory master. When you promote to Open Directory master while bound to Active Directory, slapconfig configures an LDAP directory and a Password Server for the new shared domain, but it does not create a Kerberos realm for the Open Directory shared domain. slapconfig logs the following message to /Library/Logs/slapconfig.log:

```
Not configuring Kerberos for this OD master. Remove all nodes on Search Policy except
Local Nodes to kerberize this server
```

NOTE ▶ If you later decide to migrate away from Active Directory and unbind your Open Directory master from Active Directory, you can use `slapconfig` or Server Admin to establish a Kerberos realm for the Open Directory shared domain. After unbinding from Active Directory, Server Admin displays a Kerberize button in the Settings pane for the Open Directory service.

Follow these steps to bind a standalone Mac OS X Server computer to Active Directory, then promote it to an Open Directory master:

1   On your standalone Mac OS X Server computer that will be the Open Directory master, use Directory Utility to bind to the third-party directory service (in the case of a standard LDAP server, see Chapter 3; in the case of Active Directory, see Chapter 4).

2   Use Directory Utility to confirm that the Active Directory server is in the authentication search path, as shown in this figure.

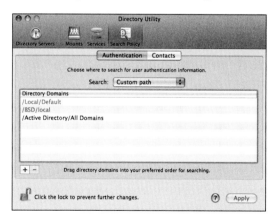

3   Open Server Admin and connect to the Mac OS X Server computer that will be the Open Directory master. Select Open Directory in the left column of servers and services, click Settings in the toolbar, and then click General.

The figure below shows that the Role is "Connected to a Directory System." Click Change to promote to Open Directory master.

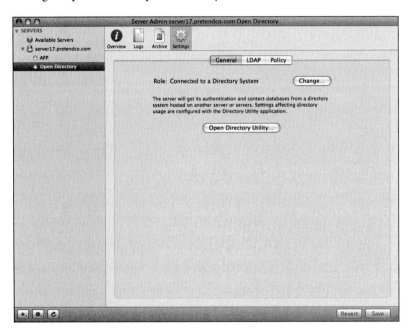

4 At the Choose Type window, choose Open Directory Master and click Continue.

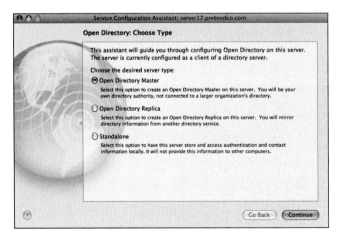

5   At the Master Domain Administrator window, type a password for the new directory administrator and click Continue.

6   At the Confirm Settings window, click Continue.

7   At the Service Configuration Complete window, click Close.

8   Click Overview in the Server Admin toolbar.

Note that the status of Kerberos is Stopped. This is expected, because you will use the third-party directory service's Kerberos realm.

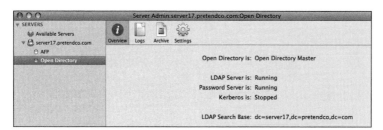

9   Use Server Admin to disable authenticated directory binding, because your Open Directory master does not have its own Kerberos realm and cannot support authenticated directory binding. Click Settings in the toolbar. Click the Policy tab, and within that click the Binding tab. Deselect the "Enable authenticated directory binding" checkbox. Click Save.

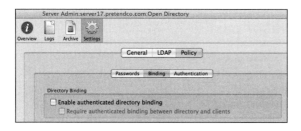

10 Optionally, configure other Mac OS X Server computers to be Open Directory replicas. For each standalone Mac OS X Server, first bind to Active Directory (see Chapter 4), then configure the server to be an Open Directory replica of your Open Directory master (see Chapter 6).

11 Open Directory Utility on your Open Directory master.

The figure below illustrates the display of Directory Utility on an Open Directory master or replica that is also bound to Active Directory. Remember that the order of the nodes in this window is alphabetical and does not indicate the order of the nodes in the authentication search path.

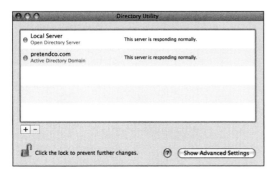

12 If necessary, click Show Advanced Settings to reveal the toolbar, and then click Search Policy in the toolbar.

The order of the nodes is not important, but you should have both directory nodes in the authentication search path.

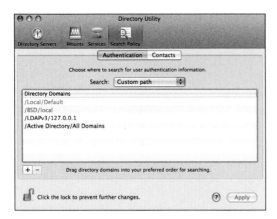

13 Use Terminal or Console (in /Applications/Utilities) to inspect /Library/Logs/ slapconfig.log and look for this text:

```
Not configuring Kerberos for this OD master. Remove all nodes on Search Policy
except Local Nodes to kerberize this server.
```

Preparing Mac OS X for the Magic Triangle Configuration

On your Mac OS X client, first bind to any auxiliary directories, then bind to the primary directory that serves your user records, as described in these steps:

1 Bind your Mac OS X client computer to your Open Directory system (see Chapter 6).

2 Bind your Mac OS X client computer to your third-party directory system (in the case of a standard LDAP server, see Chapter 3; in the case of Active Directory, see Chapter 4).

3 On your Mac OS X computer, open Directory Utility and click Directory Servers in the toolbar to confirm that you are bound to both directory nodes.

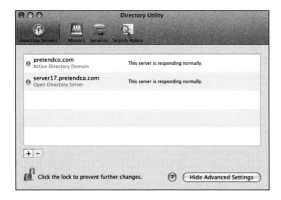

4 Click Search Policy in the toolbar to view the authentication search path. Even though you might not need the Open Directory node for user authentication, DirectoryService uses the authentication search path for other information such as managed preferences and automount records also. Confirm that both directory nodes are in the authentication search path.

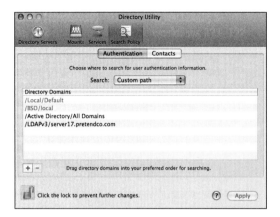

5   On your Mac OS X computer, use `dscl` or `id` to confirm that the system can identify users from the third-party directory service. If there is a problem, use Directory Utility to verify that both directory nodes are listed in the authentication search path.

6   Use `su` or `dirt` to confirm that the system can authenticate users from the third-party directory service (the `dirt` command sends the attempted password in clear text not only to /var/log/system.log, but also to the screen).

7   If you set up the infrastructure to handle network home folders or are simply using local home folders, log out of the client and attempt to log back in as a user defined in the third-party directory system.

Using Workgroup Manager to Provide Managed Preferences in the Magic Triangle Configuration

Even if you may not be able to edit user information in the third-party directory node that stores user records, you can use an Open Directory node to provide managed preferences, also known as Managed Client for X (MCX) settings, to groups and computers. In the following example, you will set up a guest computer record and apply managed preferences for guest computers. A guest computer is any Mac OS X computer that binds to your Open Directory system and does not have a computer record defined in Open Directory. For the guest computers, you will force the Mac OS X login window to display the IP address of the local computer, which is a change that is easy to verify.

NOTE ▸ Update Mac OS X and Mac OS X Server to version 10.5.3 at least before using the guest computer record in the Magic Triangle configuration; you may experience problems with earlier versions.

1 Open Workgroup Manager and connect to your Open Directory master.

2 Click the Globe icon in the upper-left corner of Workgroup Manager to choose the directory node that this window of Workgroup Manager displays.

3 Choose Other.

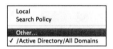

4 Select /LDAPv3 and 127.0.0.1. Click OK.

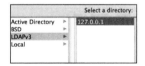

5 If the Lock icon in the upper-right corner of Workgroup Manager is not unlocked, click the icon and authenticate as an Open Directory administrator.

6 Click Preferences in the toolbar.

7 Click the Computers button (to the right of the Groups button).

8 From the Server menu, choose Create Guest Computer.

9 In the list of computers, choose Guest.

10 Click the Login item in the pane of available items for management on the right.

11 Click the Window tab.

12 In the Windows pane, click Always for the Manage setting.

13 Choose IP Address from the Heading pop-up menu.

14 Click Apply Now to apply the settings.

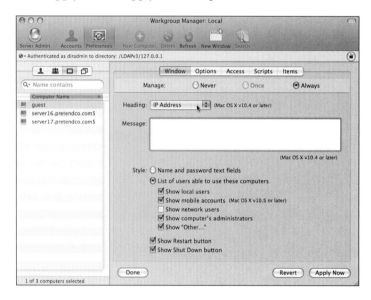

15 The next time a Mac OS X computer (version 10.4 or later) that is bound to both directory nodes displays its login window, it will display its IP address instead of its computer name, as shown in the figure below. Click the heading that displays the IP address in the figure above to cycle through the information that the heading can display: Mac OS X version, build number, serial number, IP address, availability of network accounts, and the full date and time.

Using Workgroup Manager to Add Users from a Third-Party Node to Open Directory Groups

Because it is recommended to avoid using an Open Directory server to manage directory information in a third-party node, instead use Workgroup Manager on a Mac OS X computer that is bound to both nodes.

In this section you will use Workgroup Manager to add users from a third-party node to an Open Directory group, then configure managed preferences for the Open Directory group.

> **NOTE ▶** Do not use Workgroup Manager to create users in a third-party directory domain unless you extend its schema, otherwise Workgroup Manager will attempt to edit attributes that the third-party directory domain cannot handle, causing errors. Workgroup Manager is not supported to use to create Active Directory users.

1 If necessary, install the Server Administration tools on your Mac OS X computer. You can find the Server Administration tools on the Mac OS X Server Installation DVD, or you can download them from Apple at http://www.apple.com/support/downloads/serveradmintools105.html.

2 On the Mac OS X computer, open Workgroup Manager.

3 From the Server menu, choose View Directories.

4 Click OK if you get the message "You are not working in the local configuration database, which is not visible to the network."

5 Click the Globe icon in the upper-left corner of Workgroup Manager to choose the directory node that this window of Workgroup Manager displays.

6 Select Other.

7 Select LDAPv3, then select the Open Directory master.

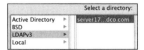

8 If the Lock icon in the upper-right corner of Workgroup Manager is not unlocked, click the icon and authenticate as an Open Directory administrator.

9 Click the Accounts button in the toolbar.

10 Create a new Open Directory group. You will eventually add users from the third-party node to this group and apply managed preferences to the group. Click the Groups button.

11 Click New Group in the toolbar.

12 Name the group Mixed Group 1, with the short name "mixedgroup1." Leave all the other settings at their defaults. Click Save.

The Workgroup Manager window should look like the following figure.

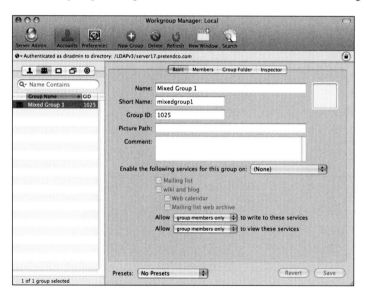

13 Click the Members tab.

14 Click the Add (+) button to display the Users and Groups drawer.

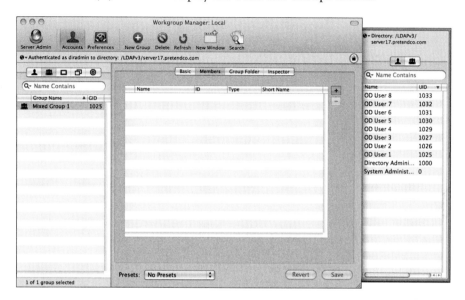

15 The Users and Groups drawer displays the Open Directory node, but you need to drag users from the Active Directory node into the Open Directory group. To change the node that the Users and Groups drawer displays, click the Globe icon at the top of the Users and Groups drawer and choose /Active Directory/All Domains.

16 Drag a user from the list of Active Directory users into the Members pane, as shown in this figure.

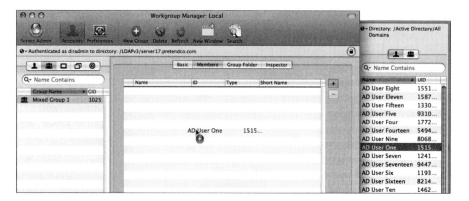

17 Click Save to update the information about the Open Directory group. You did not change the user record from the third-party node, just the list of members of the Open Directory group.

18 Now you will drag an Active Directory group into the list of Open Directory group members. Click the Groups button in the Users and Groups drawer.

19 Expand the drawer by clicking on the right edge and dragging it to the right. You may need to reposition the Workgroup Manager window so you can clearly view the main window and the drawer.

20 Drag an Active Directory group into the Members window for the Open Directory group "Mixed Group 1."

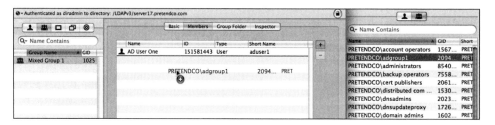

21 Click Save.

22 Click Preferences in the toolbar; you need to configure a managed preference for the Open Directory group.

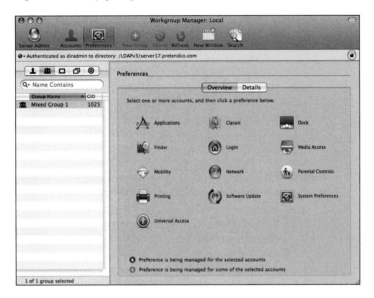

23 Click Dock Items, then select Once to manage the preference for members of the group the next time each one logs in. This will also allow users to change settings after they log in.

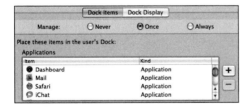

24 To the right of the list of applications to place in the user's Dock, click the Add (+) button.

25 Press Command-Shift-G to bring up the Go To folder dialog. Type /System/Library/ CoreServices to open the folder that contains the Kerberos application. Click Go.

26 Choose the Kerberos application and click Add.

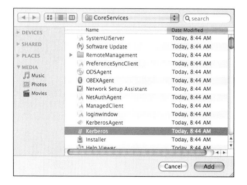

27 Click Apply Now to apply the settings, and then Quit Workgroup Manager.

28 On a Mac OS X computer that is bound to both nodes, log in as an Active Directory user that is a member of the Open Directory group that you just edited.

The Kerberos application is in the Dock for this user. Because you managed the Dock with the Once setting instead of the Always setting, the user can remove the new icon from the Dock if he or she prefers.

Augmenting Third-Party Directory Service User Records with Attributes for Mac OS X Server Services

Some of the services offered by Mac OS X Server, such as Apple Filing Protocol (AFP), don't need any special configuration on a per-user basis; after a user authenticates, the file service presents a list of volumes that the user has authority to read. Other services— such as the iCal calendaring service, the iChat instant message service, and Mail services— require you to configure the user record. If your users are defined in a third-party directory service, but you do not have the ability to save this configuration information in that third-party directory system, you can use the new Augmented User Record feature in Mac OS X Server v10.5 to define service attributes for your users.

Understanding Augments

An augmented user record (or just *augment*) is a record that allows you to add a specific set of extra attributes to an existing record from an external directory. This external directory could be another Open Directory node, an LDAP node, or an Active Directory node.

You cannot use the augment to replace any information that already exists in the user record, and there is no authentication information associated with an augment.

The only time the attributes that you define for the augment get used is when Mac OS X uses the Search node to search for a user record, and DirectoryService composites the original external user record with select attributes defined in the augment.

> **NOTE ▶** Because DirectoryService does not necessarily return all the attributes of an augment, you cannot place standard yet arbitrary attributes, such as apple-keyword, into an augment and expect DirectoryService to return this as a result of a query in the Search node unless you manually edit the augment configuration record.

An Open Directory server stores augments in cn=Augments,*searchbase*. An augmented user record name starts with the string "Users:" and is followed by the name of the original user record name.

If you search for the user record in the usual ways with ldapsearch you will not see the augmented information. You must use DirectoryService to query for the record in the Search node, such as by using dscl /Search. Mac OS X v10.5 searches for augmented user records and combines the original user record with the information it finds in the augment; Mac OS X v10.4 does not search for augments.

Creating an Augment with a Mac OS X Server in Workgroup Configuration

The Workgroup configuration of Mac OS X Server is designed to fit into a larger directory system. Once you bind Mac OS X Server to another directory service, you can use Server Preferences to create augmented user records. Use the following steps to create an augment:

1 Set up a Mac OS X Server computer in Workgroup configuration, but do not bind it to any other directory service yet. Configure the server to host iCal and iChat services.

2   Use Directory Utility to bind to a third-party directory service.

3   Open Server Preferences.

4   Within Preferences, click Users.

5   Click the Add (+) button in the lower-left corner of the Users window and choose
Import User From Directory.

6   View the list of users available in the other directory, as shown in this figure.

7   Select a user and click Import.

This does not import a user record; it creates an augment.

8   Click Done to return to the Users pane in Server Preferences.

Note that the user you selected appears with a small blue icon in the lower-right
corner of its icon. This indicates that it is an augment.

9   Click the Services tab. When you enable services here, the information is stored in the
augment, not the original user record. Select the checkboxes for File Sharing, iCal,
and iChat.

10 Quit Server Preferences.

Inspecting the Augment

When you change attributes for an augment, you change the attributes of the augmented record only, not those of the original user record in the external directory.

To get a better understanding of augmented records, you will use `dscl` to inspect the original record, the augment, and the combined record that `DirectoryService` provides through the search path, and then compare the results. The steps are as follows:

1 Open Terminal.

2 Use `dscl -raw` to view the user record in the original directory.

The `-raw` option instructs `dscl` to not strip the prefix from Standard attribute names.

In this example, the external directory is Active Directory, but the command would also work with an LDAP directory.

```
server15:~ ladmin$ dscl -raw "/Active Directory/All Domains" \

  read /Users/aduser1
```

3 Scroll through the lines of output to view the various Standard and Native attributes and their values. Notice that there is no XML data that defines calendaring or other Mac OS X Server services.

4   Use `dscl` to view the augment. Because the name of the augment contains a colon, which is a special character, use quotes to protect the special character (alternatively, you could use the backslash before the colon):

```
server15:~ ladmin$ dscl -raw /LDAPv3/127.0.0.1 \

 read "/Augments/Users:aduser1"
```

5   Scroll through the lines of output to view the various Standard and Native attributes.

Note that there is a large amount of XML data defined in the attribute `dsAttrTypeStandard:MCXSettings`; `dscl` also displays this information listed for the attribute `dsAttrTypeNative:apple-mcxsettings`. This XML data defines settings for the various Mac OS X Server services that you have defined for the augment.

6   Use `dscl` to view the search results:

```
server15:~ ladmin$ dscl -raw /Search -read /Users/aduser1
```

7   There should be many lines of output, which `DirectoryService` returned as a combination of attributes from the original user record and the augment. Scroll through to view the various Standard and Native attributes. Note that the output contains attributes from the original user record (for example, `dsAttrTypeNative:lastLogon` and `dsAttrTypeNative:userPrincipalName`) as well as attributes from the augment (`dsAttrTypeStandard:MCXSettings`).

NOTE ▶ Even though you saw above that `DirectoryService` returns the MCXSettings attributes, as of this writing, you cannot easily push arbitrary data into an augmented user record's MCXSettings attribute (such as XML that forces the Dock to display on the right side of the desktop) and expect `DirectoryService` to return that data in the results of a query for the record in the Search node in Standard or Workgroup configuration.

Using Workgroup Manager to Inspect an Augment

To illustrate that the augments really are in a separate location and some attributes may be multivalued, use Workgroup Manager to inspect an augmented user record, like so:

1   Open Workgroup Manager and connect to the server that you set up in the Workgroup configuration.

2 Use Workgroup Manager preferences to enable "Show 'All Records' tab and inspector."

3 Click the Globe icon in the upper-left corner of Workgroup Manager and select /LDAPv3/127.0.0.1. If it is not available, select Other, and navigate to LDAPv3 and 127.0.01, and then click OK.

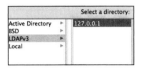

4 Click the All Records inspector next to the Users, Groups, Computers, and Computer Groups buttons.

5 Choose the augmented user record.

6 Scroll through the attributes in the Inspector pane and inspect the available attributes and their values, as shown in the figure below. In the Standard and Workgroup configuration, you won't be able to add arbitrary attributes to the augment.

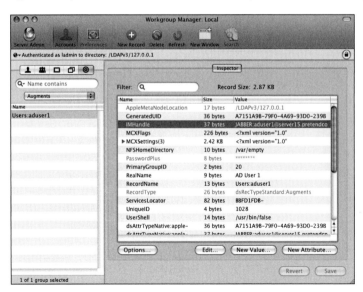

7 Click the disclosure triangle next to the MCXSettings attribute.

This shows that there are several attributes for MCXSettings, as there are settings for more than one service.

8   Select one of the values for MCXSettings and click the Edit button.

9   Scroll through the Text value for the MCXSettings attribute; note that it may contain data for Address book, iChat, iCal, or another service. Do not make any changes; click Cancel to close the window.

10   Quit Workgroup Manager.

Creating Augments on Mac OS X Server in Advanced Configuration with Workgroup Manager

A new feature in Mac OS X Server v10.5.3 is the ability to create augmented user records with Workgroup Manager on Mac OS X Server in Advanced configuration. As of this writing, you can use this feature only to specify the calendar server for a user from a third-party directory service.

Follow these steps to create an augment with Workgroup Manager:

1   Open Workgroup Manager and connect to your Open Directory master.

2   Click the Globe icon in the upper-left corner to specify the /LDAPv3/127.0.0.1 domain.

3   If necessary, click the Lock icon in the upper-right corner to authenticate as a directory administrator.

4   From the Server menu, select New Augmented User Records.

5   Choose a user from the list of users from the third-party node.

6   Click Create and click Done to dismiss the list of users.

7   Choose the newly created augment in Workgroup Manager's list of users. Note that the user has a small blue dot, indicating that it is an augment, not an actual user record.

8   Click the Basic tab.

Notice that you cannot change the value of any of these attributes, even though you authenticated to the node. In this case, User ID is the user ID for the user record that is generated by the Active Directory plug-in.

9   Click the Advanced tab. The only attribute you can modify here is the calendaring server, as shown in this figure.

10   Quit Workgroup Manager.

Understanding How Open Directory Augments a Record

After you create an augmented user record, Open Directory creates a record named `augmentconfiguration` in `cn=config,`*`searchbase`*. This record contains an attribute `dsAttrTypeStandard:XMLPlist` that defines the attributes that `DirectoryService` returns for the augment.

To get a better understanding of how augment records are constructed, look at the `XMLPlist` attribute of the `augmentconfiguration` record. The steps are as follows:

1   Open Workgroup Manager, connect to your Open Directory master, edit the /LDAP/127.0.0.1 node, and ensure the Lock in the upper-right corner is unlocked. If necessary, use Preferences to enable "Show 'All Records' tab and inspector."

2 Click the All Records tab, which looks like a bull's-eye.

3 Click the pop-up menu under the search field and choose Config.

4 Choose the `augmentconfiguration` record.

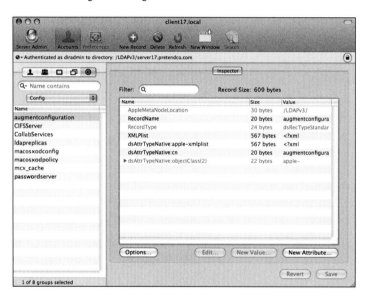

5 Highlight the XMLPlist attribute and click Edit. You should see a window that's similar to the following figure.

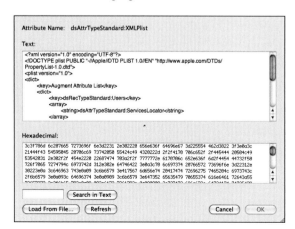

6 Expand the Text field by clicking and holding the dimple that separates the Text field from the Hexadecimal field, and then dragging the separator to the bottom of the pane.

Note that `XMLPlist` contains a list of attributes that Open Directory uses to build the augment (`dsAttrTypeStandard:ServicesLocator`), the node that contains the augment records (/LDAPv3/server17.pretendco.com), and the node that contains the original records (/Active Directory/All Domains), as shown in the figure below.

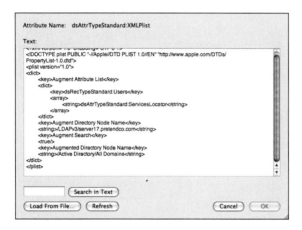

7 Click Cancel to close the Edit pane.

8 Quit Workgroup Manager.

NOTE ▶ Though it is not a supported configuration and is outside the scope of this book, you could edit the `XMLPlist` attribute of the `augmentconfiguration` record to augment with additional attributes, such as `dsAttrTypeStandard:NFSHomeDirectory` and `dsAttrTypeStandard:HomeDirectory`. Be sure to thoroughly test this configuration before deploying it.

Determining Which Directory Will Be Used for Identification and Authentication

When Mac OS X Server is bound to multiple directory nodes, the search path order determines which nodes your system will use to identify and authenticate users.

Recall from Chapter 1 that you cannot remove the /Local/Default or the /BSD/local nodes from the authentication search path, nor can you rearrange their order. On Mac OS X Server in a Workgroup configuration, you cannot move or remove the shared Open Directory node /LDAPv3/127.0.0.1 from the authentication search path. When you attempt to identify a user for authentication using DirectoryService, DirectoryService looks for a matching user record in each node in the authentication search path, and then stops searching with the first match.

The user record's AuthenticationAuthority determines how the system will attempt to authenticate the user. If there is no AuthenticationAuthority attribute, DirectoryService will attempt to guess the user's Kerberos principal based on the local Kerberos configuration and will authenticate with Kerberos. As a last resort, DirectoryService will attempt to authenticate the user via an LDAP bind against the LDAP server that hosts the user record.

Exploring the AuthenticationAuthority Attribute

The AuthenticationAuthority attribute can accept multiple values, as in the case of an Open Directory user that you create on an Open Directory master. Each value takes this form:

```
version; tag; data
```

version and data may be blank, and there may be multiple instances of data separated by a semicolon.

> **NOTE** ▶ See page 254 of *Open Directory Administration for Version 10.5 Leopard, Second Edition,* for full documentation on the AuthenticationAuthority attribute.

Follow these steps to use dscl to inspect the value of AuthenticationAuthority for various users in various nodes:

1   Use dscl to inspect the value of AuthenticationAuthority for an Active Directory user:

```
server15:~ ladmin$ dscl "/Active Directory/All Domains" \

 read /Users/aduser1 AuthenticationAuthority

AuthenticationAuthority: 1.0;KerberosV5;A7151A9B-79F0-4A69-93D0-239B3EF659E4;aduser1@
PRETENDCO.COM;PRETENDCO.COM;
```

In the result, 1.0 is the version; KerberosV5 is the tag. There are several values for data: the user's GUID, Kerberos principal, and Kerberos realm.

2   On a Mac OS X Server in Workgroup configuration, use Server Preferences to create a user with the name "Open Directory Workgroup User 1" and short name "odwguser1."

3   Use dscl to inspect the value of AuthenticationAuthority for the user that you created with Server Preferences:

```
server15:~ ladmin$ dscl /LDAPv3/127.0.0.1 \

 read /Users/odwguser1 AuthenticationAuthority

AuthenticationAuthority:

 ;ApplePasswordServer;0x483d9d5b30a83c0c0000000500000005,1024 35 11775575037207915405
4445756843407711768229934338205932767333447220569892171374911658054366345331715534781
1936443625993640362636856256027964269068042338341012788550257272562320576906143803721
5419843314362006047699700145267375746590397913100471171830381030697154987292203997874
1716082111145620897086287141141351 root@server15.pretendco.com:10.1.15.1
```

In the results there is no version specified; this is permitted. The tag is ApplePasswordServer. The data includes the user's password server slot ID, the RSA public key for the password server, and other password server data. Because the Workgroup configuration is designed to fit into an existing directory system, Mac OS X Server in Workgroup configuration does not run its own shared Kerberos realm, so the user that you created on that server does not get a Kerberos principal.

4   Use `dscl` to inspect the value of `AuthenticationAuthority` for a user that you created on an Open Directory master:

```
server17:~ ladmin$ dscl /LDAPv3/127.0.0.1 \

  read /Users/oduser1 AuthenticationAuthority

AuthenticationAuthority:

 ;ApplePasswordServer;0x00000000000000000000000000000001,1024 35 12060142152503214998
18819788366439536488946251162130702844409490343232853426868472236980205840079800043505
59988348590768862254494741956418607396197924576612832634209510247941429173218033343165
05861531382657215340498057537793039826258469163058017143401175758568927460147132070066
1816266326613886902673233181692557 root@server17.pretendco.com:10.1.17.1

 ;Kerberosv5;0x00000000000000000000000000000001;diradmin@SERVER17.PRETENDCO.
COM;SERVER17.PRETENDCO.COM;1024 35 12060142152503214998188197883664395364889462511
62130702844409490343232853426868472236980205840079800435055998834859076886225449474
41956418607396197924576612832634209510247941429173218033431650586153138265721534040
98057537793039826258469163058017143401175758568927460147132070066181626632661388690
267323318169257 root@server17.pretendco.com:10.1.17.1
```

In the results there is no `version` specified. The first value has a `tag` of `ApplePasswordServer`. The second value has a `tag` of `Kerberosv5`. Both values contain the password server information for `data`, but the second value's `data` also includes the Kerberos principal (`diradmin@SERVER17.PRETENDCO.COM`) and Kerberos realm for the user (`SERVER17.PRETENDCO.COM`).

Configuring Mac OS X Server Services to Authenticate in a Third-Party Kerberos Realm

When you bind Mac OS X Server to an Active Directory domain with Directory Utility's Active Directory plug-in, the plug-in does the following automatically:

▶   Causes Active Directory to set up Kerberos principals for several services that your server may eventually host

▶ Causes Active Directory to generate keytabs for the services

▶ Adds the keytabs to your Mac OS X server's /etc/krb5.keytab file

However, the Active Directory plug-in does not automatically configure the services—that's where you step in.

Configuring Mac OS X Server Services to Use a Third-Party Kerberos Realm

If you are integrating Mac OS X Server to join a Kerberos realm hosted by a server other than an Open Directory or Active Directory server, the following tasks you must perform manually:

1. Create a principal in the third-party Kerberos realm for each Mac OS X Server service.
2. Create a keytab for each Mac OS X Server service (the keytab contains the shared secret between the KDC and the service).
3. Extract the keytabs into a keytab file to be copied to the Mac OS X server.
4. Copy the keytab file to the Mac OS X Server computer.
5. Import the keytab entries into Mac OS X Server's keytab file /etc/krb5.keytab.
6. Configure Mac OS X Server's Kerberos configuration file /Library/Preferences/edu.mit.Kerberos.
7. Configure the services on server for the third-party Kerberos realm.

Here are the specific steps to take on Mac OS X Server:

1   Make a backup of your server's original keytab file. Use this command:

```
server14:~ ladmin$ sudo cp /etc/krb5.keytab /etc/krb5.keytab.backup
```

2   To make sure other users cannot see the contents of this sensitive file, use these commands:

```
server14:~ ladmin$ sudo chgrp _keytabusers /etc/krb5.keytab.backup

server14:~ ladmin$ sudo chmod 640 /etc/krb5.keytab.backup
```

3 Once you generate, extract, and copy the keytabs from the third-party Kerberos system to Mac OS X Server, use the `ktutil` command to import the keytabs into Mac OS X's keytab file /etc/krb5.keytab.

According to the `man` page for `ktutil`, this is the Kerberos keytab file maintenance utility. When you issue `ktutil` with no arguments, you enter an interactive mode, where `ktutil:` is the prompt:

```
server14:~ ladmin$ sudo ktutil
```

4 Use the `read_kt` *keytab* command to read the keytab file `keytab` into the current keylist. The default keytab file for Mac OS X Server is /etc/krb5.keytab, so specify that file:

```
ktutil: read_kt /etc/krb5.keytab
```

5 Use the `list` command to show the contents of the current keylist:

```
ktutil: list
```

The output will be quite long and is not displayed here, but should be similar to the output of the command `klist -k`.

6 Use the `read_kt` command again to read in the keytab that you copied from the third-party Kerberos system:

```
ktutil: read_kt /Users/ladmin/keytabforosxs.keytab
```

7 Use the `list` command to show the contents of the current keylist, which should now contain both the original keytabs from /etc/krb5.keytab as well as the new keytab:

```
ktutil: list
```

8 Use the `write_kt` command to commit this new list of keytabs:

```
ktutil: write_kt /etc/krb5.keytab
```

9 Exit the `ktuil` interactive mode with the `quit` command:

```
ktutil: quit
```

10 Use a text editor to modify your /Library/Preferences/edu.mit.Kerberos file. If the file contains four lines that start with "#WARNING This file is automatically created," remove those lines. See the `man` page entry for krb5.conf or your Kerberos administrator for the settings that you should include in the file.

11 Prepare your Mac OS X Server services to use the new Kerberos realm. There are many ways to accomplish this—such as using `serveradmin`, `defaults`, or a text editor—but follow these directions to use `PlistBuddy` to modify the AFP services configuration file:

```
server14:~ ladmin$ sudo /usr/libexec/PlistBuddy \

-c "Set kerberosPrincipal afpserver/server14.pretendco.com@REALM" \

/Library/Preferences/com.apple.AppleFileServer.plist
```

12 Use `PlistBuddy` again to double-check your work:

```
server14:~ ladmin$ /usr/libexec/PlistBuddy \

-c "Print kerberosPrincipal" \

/Library/Preferences/com.apple.AppleFileServer.plist

afpserver/server14.pretendco.com@REALM
```

NOTE ▶ Other service configuration files include /Library/Preferences/SystemConfiguration/com.apple.smb.server.plist, /etc/MailServicesOther.plist, and /Library/Preferences/SystemConfiguration/com.apple.RemoteAccessServers.plist.

Configuring Mac OS X Server Services to Use an Active Directory Kerberos Realm
The Active Directory plug-in does most of the work to configure your Mac OS X Server services to accept Kerberos tickets from the Active Directory Kerberos realm. The one remaining task is to configure your Mac OS X Server services to use the Active Directory Kerberos realm, as detailed in these steps:

1 Bind a standalone Mac OS X Server computer to Active Directory.

2   Use `klist` `-k` to confirm that Mac OS X Server has keytab entries for its services in the Active Directory Kerberos realm:

```
server14:~ ladmin$ sudo klist -k
```

The full output is not displayed here, but you should see entries in this form:

```
2 vnc/server14.pretendco.com@PRETENDCO.COM
```

This information contains the Kerberos Version Number (KVNO) for that keytab (which increases as you create different versions of the keytab), the service, the server, and the Kerberos realm.

3   Use `PlistBuddy` to confirm that the AFP service is not yet configured for the new Kerberos realm.

The "`Print kerberosPrincipal`" command prints the `kerberosPrincipal` value only, not all the values in the file:

```
server14:~ ladmin$ /usr/libexec/PlistBuddy \

-c "Print kerberosPrincipal" \

/Library/Preferences/com.apple.AppleFileServer.plist

Dict {

    kerberosPrincipal = afpserver/ LKDC:SHA1.07E6D260A31AA81B57CB6F7528D5E1A0AF160BF9@
LKDC:SHA1.07E6D260A31AA81B57CB6F7528D5E1A0AF160BF9
```

The string `LKDC` tells you that the service is still configured for the local KDC.

4   Issue the command `sudo dsconfigad -enableSSO`.

As the `dsconfig` `man` page states, when using Mac OS X Server with Active Directory, the `enablesso` option enables single sign-on for all supported Mac OS X services.

```
server14:~ ladmin$ sudo dsconfigad -enableSSO

Settings changed successfully
```

Alternatively, you could use Server Admin's Join Kerberos button in the settings for the Open Directory service.

5   Use `PlistBuddy` again to confirm that your Mac OS X Server services are configured for the Active Directory Kerberos realm:

```
server14:~ ladmin$ /usr/libexec/PlistBuddy \

-c "Print kerberosPrincipal" \

/Library/Preferences/com.apple.AppleFileServer.plist

Dict {

kerberosPrincipal = afpserver/server14.pretendco.com@PRETENDCO.COM

}
```

That's it—with the `dsconfigad -enablesso` command, you have configured your Mac OS X Server services to use the Active Directory Kerberos realm.

Confirming Your Active Directory Plug-In and the Samba Service Are Using the Same Active Directory Computer Password

The Active Directory plug-in stores the plain-text Active Directory computer password in /var/db/samba/secrets.tdb and also in base64 format in /Library/Preferences/ DirectoryService/ActiveDirectory.plist. You may find that Mac OS X Server is correctly bound to Active Directory, yet the SMB service does not accept authentication for Active Directory users. It could be that the computer password is out of sync. Use the following steps to investigate:

1   Use the `tdbdump` command to inspect the value of the Active Directory computer password in /var/db/samba/secrets.tdb:

```
server14:~ ladmin$ sudo /usr/bin/tdbdump /var/db/samba/secrets.tdb
```

2   In the output from the previous command, look for the key "SECRETS/MACHINE_ PASSWORD/*REALM*".

REALM is the Active Directory Kerberos realm.

In this example, the value is

```
data(15) = "`9bGWotoHGjAtS"
```

3 Use the `PlistBuddy` to display and decode the Active Directory computer password stored in /Library/Preferences/DirectoryService/ActiveDirectory.plist. The `-c` option specifies that you are sending a command, rather than entering an interactive mode. The `Print` command prints the value of an entry, and you will look for the entry `AD Computer Password`:

```
server14:~ ladmin$ sudo /usr/libexec/PlistBuddy \

-c "Print 'AD Computer Password'" \

/Library/Preferences/DirectoryService/ActiveDirectory.plist

`9bGWotoHGjAtS
```

The result shows that the two Active Directory computer passwords from step 2 and step 3 are in sync.

While you could use the `defaults` command to view the value of `AD Computer Password`, you would have to decode it from base64; `PlistBuddy` takes care of that work for you.

4 If the password in /var/db/samba/secrets.tdb is different from the one in /Library/Preferences/DirectoryService/ActiveDirectory.plist, you can use the `net` command with `changesecretpw -f` to update the password in the secrets.tdb file. Copy the exact password from the output of the `PlistBuddy` command and paste that into the Terminal when prompted by the `net` command:

```
server14:~ ladmin$ sudo net changesecretpw -f

Enter machine password: [paste password; press return]

Modified trust account pssword in secrets database
```

As a last resort, you could unbind and rebind to Active Directory to reset the Active Directory computer password.

NOTE ▶ The SMB service of Mac OS X Server will accept only Kerberos tickets that are issued by an Active Directory KDC.

Configuring a Third-Party Server to Use an Open Directory KDC

It is possible for your Open Directory server's KDC to provide Kerberos services for third-party servers. Because the specific requirements of the third-party service may vary, this book provides the general outline of tasks you need to perform on the third-party server, rather than the specific steps.

The general tasks are:

1. Create service principals on Mac OS X Server.

2. Export a keytab from the Mac OS X Server KDC.

3. Copy the keytab to the third-party server.

4. Import the keytabs into the third-party server.

5. Configure the systemwide Kerberos configuration on the third-party server.

6. Configure the services on the third-party server.

Creating Service Principals and Exporting Keytabs

Use the following steps to create a Kerberos service principal for the NFS service on a third-party server, a1.pretendco.com, and to export a keytab to transfer to the third-party server.

You need to know the DNS host name for the third-party server and the Kerberos service name that the service on the third-party server will use. Go to http://www.iana.org/assignments/gssapi-service-names for IANA's list of standard Kerberos service names.

The instructions are as follows:

1 On your Open Directory server, open the Terminal application.

2 Run `kadmin.local` with root privileges.

This puts you into a `kadmin` shell with `kadmin.local:` as your prompt:

```
server17:~ ladmin$ sudo kadmin.local

Authenticating as principal root/admin@SERVER17.PRETENDCO.COM with password.
```

3   Use the `add_principal` command to create a Kerberos principal for the NFS service for a1.pretendco.com in the default Kerberos realm. Use the `-randkey` option to create a random encryption key for this principal (the alternative is for you to interactively specify a password):

`kadmin.local: add_principal -randkey nfs/a1.pretendco.com`

`WARNING: no policy specified for nfs/a1.pretendco.com@SERVER17.PRETENDCO.COM;`
`defaulting to no policy`

You can ignore the policy warnings, as it not a problem to have principals without a policy. Because you did not specify any encryption types, `kadmin.local` used the three default encryption types. You may need to check the documentation for the third-party service to determine if it requires you to use specific encryption types. See the `man` page entry for `kadmin` for details on specifying encryption types when creating principals.

4   Use the `get_principal` command of `kadmin.local` to inspect the details of the principal that you just created. Note that there are three keys associated with the principal, one for each of the three default encryption types:

`kadmin.local: get_principl nfs/a1.pretendco.com`

`Principal: nfs/a1.pretendco.com@SERVER17.PRETENDCO.COM`

`Expiration date: [never]`

`Last password change: Wed May 28 17:20:51 CDT 2008`

`Password expiration date: [none]`

`Maximum ticket life: 0 days 10:00:00`

`Maximum renewable life: 7 days 00:00:00`

`Last modified: Wed May 28 17:20:51 CDT 2008 (root/admin@SERVER17.PRETENDCO.COM)`

`Last successful authentication: [never]`

`Last failed authentication: [never]`

`Failed password attempts: 0`

```
Number of keys: 3

Key: vno 2, Triple DES cbc mode with HMAC/sha1, no salt

Key: vno 2, ArcFour with HMAC/md5, no salt

Key: vno 2, DES cbc mode with CRC-32, no salt

Attributes:

Policy: [none]
```

5   Export the keytab with the `ktadd` command of `kadmin.local`. Specify a keytab name with the `-k` option, and then specify the principal to export. You will see output for each of the three encryption types:

```
kadmin.local: ktadd -k /Volumes/thumb/nfs.keytab nfs/a1.pretendco.com

Entry for principal nfs/a1.pretendco.com with kvno 3, encryption type Triple DES cbc
mode with HMAC/sha1 added to keytab WRFILE:/Volumes/thumb/nfs.keytab.

Entry for principal nfs/a1.pretendco.com with kvno 3, encryption type ArcFour with
HMAC/md5 added to keytab WRFILE:/Volumes/thumb/nfs.keytab.

Entry for principal nfs/a1.pretendco.com with kvno 3, encryption type DES cbc mode
with CRC-32 added to keytab WRFILE:/Volumes/thumb/nfs.keytab.
```

6   Quit the `kadmin.local` interactive shell:

```
kadmin.local: quit
```

You need to use documentation for the third-party server to perform the next sequence of tasks, which are outside the scope of this reference guide:

1.   Copy the keytab to the third-party server.

2.   Import the keytabs into the third-party server.

3.   Configure the system-wide Kerberos configuration on the third-party server.

4.   Configure the services on the third-party server.

What You've Learned

▶   You can bind Mac OS X to a third-party directory service that provides user identification and authentication services; and you can also bind it to an Open Directory shared domain that provides managed preferences and other services. This is sometimes referred to as the Magic Triangle.

▶   You can promote Mac OS X Server to an Open Directory server, then bind it to a third-party directory service, so that Mac OS X Server can provide managed preferences and other services to Mac OS X computers that bind to both domains.

▶   You can use Workgroup Manager to drag users from a third-party directory service into Open Directory groups, then apply managed preferences to the Open Directory groups.

▶   Even though using the Active Directory plug-in to bind Mac OS X Server to Active Directory automatically sets up Kerberos principals and populates your Mac OS X Server keytab, you need to take an extra step to configure your Mac OS X Server services to use the Active Directory Kerberos realm. You can either use the Join Kerberos button in Server Admin or you can issue the `dsconfigad -ssoutil` command with root privileges.

▶   You can use Server Preferences or Workgroup Manager to create an augmented user record, which you can use to add information about Mac OS X Server services to a user from a different directory node. You cannot use the augment to replace any information in the original user record.

▶   You can use the `kadmin.local` command to read in keytabs created on a third-party Kerberos server, read in existing keytabs from /etc/krb5.keytab, and write the combined list back out to /etc/krb5.keytab.

▶   You can use `kadmin.local` to generate principals and keytabs for arbitrary services on third-party servers, and then export the keytab to a file.

▶   You may need to manually edit the systemwide Kerberos configuration file /Library/Preferences/edu.mit.Kerberos if you integrate with a third-party Kerberos realm that is not Active Directory.

▶   You may need to manually configure Mac OS X Server services to use a third-party Kerberos realm. You can use `PlistBuddy`, `defaults`, or a text editor to view and modify the configuration files, whose locations in the file system vary.

References

Documentation

▶ Mac OS X Server Command-Line Administration for Version 10.5 Leopard
  http://images.apple.com/server/macosx/docs/Command_Line_Admin_v10.5.pdf

▶ Mac OS X Server Open Directory Administration for Version 10.5 Leopard,
  Second Edition
  http://images.apple.com/server/macosx/docs/Open_Directory_Admin_v10.5.pdf

Apple Knowledge Base Documents

▶ Mac OS X Server 10.5: Bind Server to Active Directory After Completing Server Assistant
  http://docs.info.apple.com/article.html?artnum=306529

▶ Mac OS X Server version 10.5: iChat Client Does Not Authenticate with Active
  Directory Credentials
  http://docs.info.apple.com/article.html?artnum=306749

▶ Mac OS X Server version 10.5: Enabling Wiki Access for Active Directory Users
  http://docs.info.apple.com/article.html?artnum=306750

Books

▶ Garman, Jason. *Kerberos The Definitive Guide* (O'Reilly & Associates, Inc., 2003).

Websites

▶ Apple Server Admin Tools Downloads
  http://www.apple.com/support/downloads/serveradmintools105.html

▶ Record Augmentation, Part 1: The Cylinder of Destiny
  http://www.afp548.com/article.php?story=20071210105328355

▶ Active Directory Plug-in Tips
  http://www.afp548.com/article.php?story=20070525232923771

▶ Cycling the AD Machine Account
  http://www.afp548.com/article.php?story=20061217110502523

▶ Respecting AD Account Workstation Restrictions
  http://www.afp548.com/article.php?story=20061128094058598

▶   Using Microsoft's Services for UNIX to Serve NFS Home Directories
     http://www.afp548.com/article.php?story=20050323055442233

▶   Generic Security Service Application Program Interface (GSSAPI)/Kerberos/Simple
     Authentication and Security Layer (SASL) Service Names
     http://www.iana.org/assignments/gssapi-service-names

▶   Kerberos, Part 3: Kerberos on Member Servers
     http://www.afp548.com/article.php?story=20060724104018616

Review Quiz

1.   If you first bind a standalone Mac OS X Server computer to Active Directory, then pro-
     mote it to an Open Directory master, what service does not get created in the process?

2.   How can you use Workgroup Manager to add users from a third-party directory node
     to the list members of an Open Directory group?

3.   What tools can you use to create an augmented user record?

4.   What kind of information can you augment with an augmented user record?

5.   What command-line tool can you use to configure Mac OS X Server services to use
     the Active Directory Kerberos realm if the Join Kerberos button is not available in
     Server Admin?

6.   What command in `kadmin` or `kadmin.local` can you use to create a service principal for
     a service hosted by a third-party server?

7.   What file controls which Kerberos realm the Apple Filing Protocol (AFP) service par-
     ticipates in?

8.   How can you extract principals from an Open Directory server KDC to prepare to
     copy them to a third-party server?

Answers

1.   If Mac OS X Server is bound to Active Directory when you promote it to Open Directory
     master, `slapconfig` recognizes that it is already associated with a Kerberos realm and does
     not create a new Kerberos realm. This is noted in /Library/Logs/slapconfig.log.

2. Use Workgroup Manager on a Mac OS X computer that is bound to both the third-party directory service node and the Open Directory node. Choose an Open Directory group; click the Add (+) button to add users to the group; click the Globe icon in the Users and Groups drawer to change the directory node; and then drag users from the third-party node into the list of members for the Open Directory group.

3. You can create an augmented user record with Server Preferences if your server is in Workgroup configuration, or Workgroup Manager if your server is in Advanced configuration.

4. You can augment a user record with information about specific Mac OS X Server services, such as iCal, iChat, and Mail services.

5. `sudo dsconfigad -enableSSO`

6. `kadmin.local -q "add_principal -randkey service/servername"` where `service` is the standard Kerberos abbreviation for the service, and `servername` is the host name of the server hosting the service.

7. /Library/Preferences/com.apple.AppleFileServer.plist

8. You can use the `ktadd` command of `kadmin` or `kadmin.local` to add a principal to a keytab, then copy the keytab to the third-party server.

Appendix A

Extending Your Novell eDirectory Schema

If the majority of your users are already defined in a Novell eDirectory node, you may decide to extend your eDirectory schema to provide support for attributes and object classes specifically for Apple objects.

MacEnterprise.org (http://www.macenterprise.org/) hosts detailed instructions, LDAP Data Interchange Format (LDIF) files specifically tailored for eDirectory, and a plist file for custom mappings in Directory Utility. Download the files and import the LDIFs using Novell tools. If you restrict access to objects and attributes, whether you use an LDAP proxy user or the [Public] user, grant read address to the new object classes and attributes for the appropriate user. Use Directory Utility to set up your Mac OS X computers to use the newly extended eDirectory node.

Confirm That You Need to Extend Your Schema

Before you go to the trouble of extending your eDirectory schema, determine that extending the schema is an appropriate solution for your problems.

Deciding Not to Extend Your Schema

The LDIF file that MacEnterprise.org provides is an update to the LDIF file that has been used for years—Apple does not support it, however.

If you already have an Open Directory system and administrators in place, and you do not want to allow the administrators who maintain your Mac OS X systems to edit objects in your eDirectory, you may choose to use a dual-directory solution rather than to extend your eDirectory schema.

If you can meet your needs with local static and dynamic mappings, you may not need to extend your eDirectory schema. You can employ "unused" attributes in eDirectory—but that isn't a very sustainable method because the "unused" attributes might be used at some later date. In addition, you will have directory data in attributes that are not labeled appropriately, which adds complication for anyone trying to understand your directory.

One reason for extending your schema is to provide something to map to for dsAttrTypeStandard:HomeDirectory. Two other reasons for extending your schema are to provide mount records and to use managed preferences, each of which are discussed in the following sections.

Providing Mount Records

Unlike the Active Directory plug-in, the LDAPv3 plug-in that you use to integrate with eDirectory does not automatically create mount records; you must create them manually.

You can use Workgroup Manager to connect to a Mac OS X Server computer that hosts an Apple Filing Protocol (AFP) share point for home folders, and then create a mount record for that share point in the eDirectory node.

If you want to manually create a mount record with eDirectory tools or `dscl`, see "Providing Records for Automount" in Chapter 3 for the required attributes. Once you create a mount record, be sure to map the mount record with Directory Utility so that the Mac OS X client can use it.

Using Managed Preferences

There are a few options for providing managed preferences.

If you use an auxiliary Open Directory server, you can:

▶ Bind your Mac OS X computer to both eDirectory and Open Directory nodes.

▶ Use Apple tools such as Workgroup Manager, `dscl`, and `dseditgroup` to add eDirectory users to Open Directory groups.

▶ Configure managed preferences to Open Directory groups and computers.

If you have specific needs for one particular user, you can create an Open Directory group for that user and apply managed preferences for that group. You do not need to extend the schema in order to do this, but you do need to ensure that you have an Open Directory server available for your Mac OS X computers.

If your organization has several physical locations connected by slow links, you might find that extending your eDirectory schema is a smaller project than placing Open Directory replicas at each physical location.

If you extend the eDirectory schema you can use Apple tools such as Workgroup Manager and `dscl` to assign managed preferences directly to individual users, and you do not need an Open Directory server for managed preferences.

Extend Your eDirectory Schema

Although you could use Novell tools such as iManager to create and update individual attributes and object classes, this method is labor-intensive and leaves a lot of room for making mistakes. Instead it is recommended that you extend your schema using LDIF files (see Chapter 2), so your changes are documented and there is less opportunity for error. You can use Novell tools such as ConsoleOne or `ldapmodify` to import LDIF files.

See MacEnterprise.org to obtain the leopard-attributes.ldif and leopard-objectclasses.ldif files and accompanying instructions.

This is the basic procedure for extending your eDirectory schema, but the downloadable instructions provide more detail:

1   Upload the LDIF files to your Novell server.

2   Use the ConsoleOne Wizard NDS Import/Export to import the leopard-attributes.ldif file, first testing the import, then importing the file.

3   Use the ConsoleOne Wizard NDS Import/Export to import the leopard-objectclasses. ldif file, first testing the import, then importing the file.

4   Optionally, create an Apple organizational unit (OU) to house the Apple objects, and then create OUs for Computers, ComputerLists, and Mounts inside that OU.

5   Modify the LDAP permissions for [Public] or for the user that you will use for the LDAP bind from Mac OS X, to allow Mac OS X to read the newly added object classes and attributes.

6   At a Mac OS X computer, copy the custom mappings file eDirectoryv5.plist to /Library/ Application Support/Directory Access/Templates. Use Directory Utility to create a new LDAPv3 service for the eDirectory service, use the custom template, and specify the eDirectory search base (see the section "Mapping Records and Attributes" in Chapter 3).

7   At a Mac OS X computer, install the Server Admin tools, bind to eDirectory, and use Workgroup Manager to create mount records and edit managed preferences information (see "Using Workgroup Manager to Edit eDirectory Objects," below).

After you extend your eDirectory schema, the basic interfaces for your eDirectory tools such as iManager do not change to reflect the new schema extensions, and you may have to modify your workflow for creating new users so that their attributes for Mac OS X are appropriately populated. For instance, Novell eDirectory users do not normally have an integer uniqueID, but this is mandatory for Mac OS X users.

Using Workgroup Manager to Edit eDirectory Objects

With Workgroup Manager you can create your mount records and edit your managed preferences. Follow these steps:

1   Use Directory Utility or command-line tools to bind Mac OS X to your eDirectory domain.

2   Install the Mac OS X Server Administration Tools from Mac OS X Server installation media or with a downloadable package from Apple. If there are any updates available for the Server Administration Tools, install them (you can use Software Update, which is available from the Apple menu).

3   Open Workgroup Manager. From the Server menu, choose View Directories. Click OK if you get the warning "You are working in the local configuration database, which is not visible to the network."

4   Confirm that the globe in the upper-left corner of Workgroup Manager indicates you are viewing the eDirectory domain; otherwise click the globe and change the directory.

5   Click the lock in the upper-right corner or Workgroup Manager to authenticate as a directory administrator for eDirectory.

6   Use Workgroup Manager to edit eDirectory objects, such as managed preferences for individual users or mount records for the node.

Understanding the Authentication Challenge with eDirectory

You use the LDAPv3 plug-in to bind to eDirectory. eDirectory users do not have anything you can map to for `dsAttrTypeStandard:AuthenticationAuthority`, so authentication for eDirectory users happens via an LDAP bind (see "Understanding How a User Authenticates at the Login Window" in Chapter 3).

You don't want the LDAP bind to happen in the clear, so you could protect LDAP with TLS/SSL. By default, however, the LDAP client in Mac OS X v10.5 is configured to not trust any TLS/SSL certificate until you take specific steps (outlined in Chapter 5, in "Configuring LDAP Client to Accept a TLS Certificate").

If your eDirectory is hosted by a SuSE Linux Enterprise Server (SLES), as opposed to Netware 6.5, you could use its Kerberos realm, as it is an MIT Kerberos 5–compatible system.

Appendix B
Extending Your Active Directory Schema

If the majority of your users are already defined in an Active Directory node, you may decide to extend your Active Directory schema to provide support for attributes and object classes specifically for Apple objects.

Administrators have been reluctant to extend the Active Directory schema because it was impossible to reverse a change in versions of Windows Server prior to Windows Server 2003. If your Active Directory Domain Controllers are running Windows Server 2003 or later, however, this is no longer as much of an issue, because you can make schema changes inactive. Nevertheless, a change to the Active Directory schema affects all the Domain Controllers in your forest, and you should carefully consider your changes and test them before extending your schema.

Confirm That You Need to Extend Your Schema

Before you go to the trouble of extending your Active Directory schema, determine that extending the schema is an appropriate solution for your problems.

Deciding Not to Extend Your Schema

The LDAP Data Interchange Format (LDIF) files that you can obtain to extend your Active Directory schema are well tested and have been used for several years, and the process is automated to prevent typos and other mistakes. However, Apple does not support these files.

If you already have an Open Directory system and administrators in place, and you do not want to allow the administrators who maintain your Mac OS X systems to have access to edit objects in your Active Directory, you may choose to use a dual-directory solution rather than to extend your Active Directory schema.

If you can meet your needs with local static and dynamic mappings, you may not need to extend your Active Directory schema. You can employ "unused" attributes in Active Directory—but that isn't a very sustainable method because the "unused" attributes might be used at some later date. In addition, you will have directory data in attributes that are not labeled appropriately, which adds complication for anyone trying to understand your directory.

The two main reasons for extending your schema are to provide mount records and to use managed preferences, each of which are discussed in the following sections.

Providing Mount Records

If you use the option "Use UNC path from Active Directory to derive network home location," the Active Directory plug-in creates a mount record for your Mac OS X workstation to support the Windows share point. When the "Use UNC path" option is disabled, there are no mount records in the search path; once you enable the "Use UNC path," the Active Directory plug-in dynamically creates a mount record. Follow these instructions to see how the process works:

1   On a Mac OS X computer that is bound to Active Directory, run the following commands to disable the option "Use UNC path from Active Directory to derive network home location":

```
client17:~ cadmin$ sudo dsconfigad -useuncpath disable

Settings changed successfully

client17:~ cadmin$ sudo killall DirectoryService
```

2   Use `dscl` to search for mount records in the search path.

There should be no mount records listed from Active Directory.

```
client17:~ cadmin$ dscl /Search list /Mounts
```

3   Use `dsconfigad` to enable the option "Use UNC path from Active Directory to derive network home location":

```
client17:~ cadmin$ sudo dsconfigad -useuncpath enable

Settings changed successfully
```

4   Use `echo` to display the value of a user's home directory.

`echo` causes `DirectoryService` to look up the value, but it doesn't attempt to *move* to that directory, which you might not have authorization to do:

```
client17:~ cadmin$ echo ~aduser1

/Network/Servers/dc1.pretendco.com/winhomes/aduser1
```

5   Repeat the `dscl` command from step 2 to search for mount records. The mount record to support the user's home holder is listed; `DirectoryService` and the Active Directory plug-in automatically created it.

```
client17:~ cadmin$ dscl /Search list /Mounts

dc1.pretendco.com:/winhomes
```

6   Inspect the mount record with `dscl`; use the backslash to escape the colon in the special character in the mount record name. Note the warning in the Comment field that this record is dynamically generated:

```
client17:~ cadmin$ dscl /Search list /Mounts

dc1.pretendco.com:/winhomes
```

```
client17:~ cadmin$ dscl /Search read /Mounts/dc1.pretendco.com\:/winhomes

AppleMetaNodeLocation:

 /Active Directory/pretendco.com

Comment:

 Dynamically generated - DO NOT ATTEMPT TO MODIFY

Keywords:

 Synthesized Data

RecordName: dc1.pretendco.com:/winhomes

VFSLinkDir: /Network/Servers

VFSOpts: net url==smb://dc1.pretendco.com/winhomes

VFSType: url
```

Using Managed Preferences

There are a few options for using managed preferences.

If you use an auxiliary Open Directory server, you can:

▶ Bind your Mac OS X computer to both Active Directory and Open Directory nodes.

▶ Use Apple tools such as Workgroup Manager, dscl, and dseditgroup to add Active Directory users to Open Directory groups.

▶ Configure managed preferences to Open Directory groups and computers.

If you have specific needs for one particular user, you can create an Open Directory group for that user and apply managed preferences for that group. You do not need to extend the schema in order to do this, but you do need to ensure that you have an Open Directory server available for your Mac OS X computers.

If your organization has several physical locations connected by slow links, you might find that extending your Active Directory schema is a smaller project than placing Open Directory replicas at each physical location.

If you extend the Active Directory schema you can use Apple tools such as Workgroup Manager and `dscl` to assign managed preferences directly to individual users, and you do not need an Open Directory server for managed preferences.

Extend Your Active Directory Schema

Although you could use the Active Directory schema plug-in for the Microsoft Management Console to manually create and update attributes and object classes, this method is labor intensive and leaves a lot of room for making mistakes. It is instead recommended that you extend your schema using LDIF files (see Chapter 2) so your changes are documented and there is less opportunity for error. Microsoft offers the command-line tool `ldifde` (LDIF Directory Exchange) to import LDIF files.

See the Integrating Mac OS X and Active Directory webpage at http://images.apple.com/itpro/articles/adintegration for more information about obtaining and using a set of files to extend your Active Directory schema.

The basic procedure contained is as follows:

1. Determine which Domain Controller is assigned to the Flexible Single Master Operations (FSMO) role of schema master; you must perform the commands to extend the schema on this server.

2. Enable schema changes on the schema master FSMO.

3. Determine your Active Directory search base.

4. Use `ldifde` commands to import the LDIF files. First create the attributes, then create the object classes that use the new attributes.

5. Disable schema changes on the schema master FSMO.

After you extend your Active Directory schema, your Active Directory tools such as Active Directory Users and Computers will not change to reflect the new schema extensions. You can use Microsoft tools such as `ldifde` or Microsoft Management Console to create and edit Apple-specific objects in Active Directory. You can use Apple tools such as Workgroup Manager or `dscl` to edit objects in Active Directory, but you cannot use Apple tools to create Active Directory users.

To use the Apple tools, perform the following steps on a computer running Mac OS X that is bound to Active Directory:

1   Use Directory Utility or command-line tools to bind Mac OS X to your Active Directory domain.

2   Install the Mac OS X Server Administration Tools from Mac OS X Server installation media or via a downloadable package from Apple. If there are any updates available for the Server Administration Tools, install them; you can use Software Update, which is available from the Apple menu.

3   Open Workgroup Manager. From the Server menu, choose View Directories. Click OK if you get the warning "You are working in the local configuration database, which is not visible to the network."

4   Confirm that the globe in the upper-left corner of Workgroup Manager indicates you are viewing the Active Directory domain; if it does not, click the Globe icon and change the directory.

5   Click the Lock icon in the upper-right corner of Workgroup Manager to authenticate as a directory administrator for Active Directory.

6   Use Workgroup Manager to edit Active Directory objects.

> **NOTE** ▶ As of Mac OS X Server v10.5.3, Workgroup Manager allows you to enable calendaring to specify a Calendar Host. This change does not get saved, however, if your set of LDIFs does not address the *dsAttrTypeStandard:ServicesLocator* attribute. This is a concern only if you are already using Mac OS X Server to host calendaring services, in which case you should use augmented user records to store information about such Mac OS X Server services as calendaring services. See Chapter 8 for details.

Appendix C

Understanding the Local KDC

The local Key Distribution Center (LKDC) feature, new to Mac OS X v10.5 and Mac OS X Server v10.5, facilitates single sign-on for Apple Filing Protocol (AFP) file sharing and screen sharing. Because the LKDC shows up when you look at various configuration files, you may want to understand how it fits in with the other authentication services. The bottom line is that once your computer running Mac OS X or Mac OS X Server joins a Kerberos realm, its services no longer use the LKDC, and it shouldn't interfere with authentication.

Every computer running Mac OS X v10.5 and Mac OS X Server v10.5 has its own LKDC that facilitates access to the Kerberized services running locally.

Follow the instructions below to demonstrate that you can obtain a Kerberos ticket-granting ticket (TGT) from another computer's LKDC by browsing for services and authenticating. The other computer must not be part of another Kerberos realm, otherwise its services will not be configured for its LKDC.

The steps are as follows:

1   On a remote Mac OS X computer that is not joined to a Kerberos realm (in this example, client16), open the Accounts pane in System Preferences and authenticate as a local administrator if necessary.

2   On the remote Mac OS X computer, select Guest Account from the accounts list, and select the "Allow guests to connect to shared folders" checkbox.

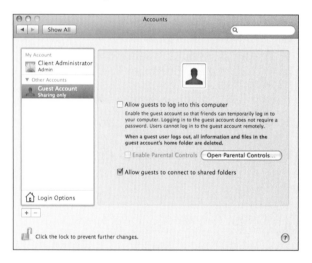

3   On the remote Mac OS X computer, open the Sharing pane in System Preferences, select the File Sharing checkbox, click Options, and then select "Share files and folders using AFP."

4   On the remote Mac OS X computer, enable Screen Sharing.

5   On your Mac OS X computer, use the Finder to browse for file services. Open a new Finder window, and click the icon for the other Mac OS X computer (client16) in the SHARED section of the Finder sidebar.

Your computer attempts to connect as Guest for AFP file sharing. In the figure below, you have connected from one Mac OS X computer (client17) to another (client16). Client16 has allowed AFP guest access. Note the text below the toolbar in Finder: "Connected as: Guest." Note also the two buttons in the upper-right corner: Share Screen for Virtual Network Computing (VNC) for screen sharing and Connect As for file sharing.

6   On your Mac OS X computer, click Connect As to authenticate as a user rather than a Guest. Authenticate as a local user on the remote Mac OS X computer.

7   On your Mac OS X computer, open the Kerberos application, in /System/Library/ CoreServices.

Note that you have a TGT (krbtgt) and and an AFP service ticket (afpserver) from the remote Mac OS X computer's LKDC. This is somewhat amazing, as you did not configure your local Mac OS X computer to be part of the remote computer's LKDC realm, and all you had to do was select a service and authenticate. Do not close the Kerberos application or window; you will use it later.

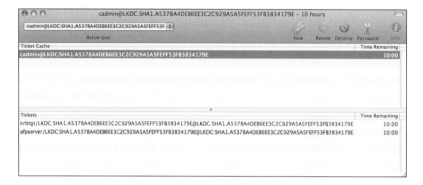

8   On your Mac OS X computer, in the Finder window, note that the status under the toolbar is "Connected as: cadmin," and the two buttons in the upper-right corner are Share Screen and Disconnect.

Now that you have a TGT for the remote computer's LKDC on your Mac OS X computer, you can click Share Screen and automatically obtain a service ticket for the VNC screen sharing service.

9   Click Share Screen.

The Screen Sharing application should automatically open with a session for the remote computer, without you having to provide authentication again. Mac OS X automatically obtains the necessary service ticket on your behalf.

10 On your Mac OS X computer, quit the Screen Sharing application.

11 On your Mac OS X computer, note that the Kerberos application window now shows that you have a new service ticket for VNC.

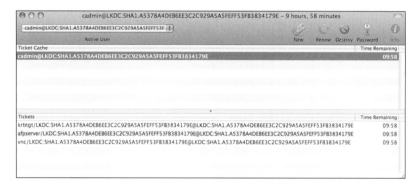

12 On your Mac OS X computer, quit the Kerberos application and click Disconnect in the Finder window.

13 On the remote Mac OS X computer, disable file sharing and screen sharing.

The Apple Knowledge Base article at http://support.apple.com/kb/TS1245 addresses the situation in which you image multiple computers from the same image after the LKDC has been generated. The article is also applicable if you erase your /etc/krb5.keytab or /var/db/krb5kdc/principal, perhaps while troubleshooting or experimenting. The article contains the steps necessary to regenerate your principal database and keytab. However, you will then need to regenerate your local user principals. One way to do this is to use the passwd command of the dscl command with the following syntax for each local user:

```
dscl -u root -P rootpassword . -passwd /Users/username userpassword
```

where -P *rootpassword* specifies the root password, and *userpssword* is the user's password. You need to know the local user's password in order to create a user principal in the LKDC, because the user's password is the key associated with the principal.

Index

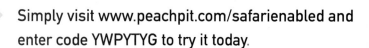